AUTODESK® 3DS MAX® 2013

ESSENTIALS

Randi L. Derakhshani
Dariush Derakhshani

WILEY

John Wiley & Sons, Inc.

Acquisitions Editor: Mariann Barsolo
Development Editor: Lisa Bishop
Technical Editor: RC Torres
Production Editor: Liz Britten
Copy Editor: Kathy Grider-Carlyle
Editorial Manager: Pete Gaughan
Production Manager: Tim Tate
Vice President and Executive Group Publisher: Richard Swadley
Vice President and Publisher: Neil Edde
Book Designer and Compositor: Jeff Lytle and Kate Kaminski; Happenstance Type-O-Rama
Proofreader: Nancy Bell
Indexer: Ted Laux
Project Coordinator, Cover: Katherine Crocker
Cover Designer: Ryan Sneed
Cover Image: Randi L. Derakhshani and Dariush Derakhshani

Dear Reader,

Thank you for choosing *Autodesk® 3ds Max® 2013 Essentials.* This book is part of a family of premium-quality Sybex books, all of which are written by outstanding authors who combine practical experience with a gift for teaching.

Sybex was founded in 1976. More than 30 years later, we're still committed to producing consistently exceptional books. With each of our titles, we're working hard to set a new standard for the industry. From the paper we print on, to the authors we work with, our goal is to bring you the best books available.

I hope you see all that reflected in these pages. I'd be very interested to hear your comments and get your feedback on how we're doing. Feel free to let me know what you think about this or any other Sybex book by sending me an email at nedde@wiley.com. If you think you've found a technical error in this book, please visit http://sybex.custhelp.com. Customer feedback is critical to our efforts at Sybex.

Best regards,

NEIL EDDE
Vice President and Publisher
Sybex, an Imprint of Wiley

To Max Henry

ACKNOWLEDGMENTS

We are thrilled to be a part of *Autodesk® 3ds Max® 2013 Essentials*, a complete update and style change to our previous *Introducing Autodesk® 3ds Max®* series. Education is an all-important goal in life and should always be approached with eagerness and earnestness. We would like to show appreciation to the teachers who inspired us; you can always remember the teachers who touched your life, and to them we say thanks. We would also like to thank all of our students, who taught us a lot during the course of our many combined academic years.

Having a good computer system is important with this type of work, so a special thank you goes to HP for keeping us on the cutting edge of workstation hardware. Special thanks go to Mariann Barsolo, Lisa Bishop, Liz Britten, and Kathy Grider-Carlyle, our editors at Sybex who have been professional, courteous, and ever patient. Our appreciation also goes to technical editor RC Torres, who worked hard to make sure this book is of the utmost quality. We could not have done this revision without their help.

In addition, thanks to Dariush's mother and brother for their love and support, not to mention the life-saving babysitting services.

Writing on the HP Elitebook

We would like to thank HP for providing us with a fully decked-out Elitebook 8760w, which we primarily used to write this book. What struck us about the laptop was that it was not only portable, making it easy for a writing team to collaborate, but it was powerful enough to run truly demanding tasks. It takes a special machine to run graphics intensive applications, such as Autodesk 3ds Max, and we were thrilled to write this book on the HP Elitebook.

Running an Intel i7 CPU alongside 16GB of RAM and an Nvidia Quadro 5010M (with a whopping 6GB of memory) gave us the muscle we needed to run multiple applications alongside 3ds Max splendidly. Dual 320GB hard drives was plenty of space for Windows 7 Professional and its applications, and still left lots of room for renders. We opted out of the RAID option to mirror the drives (you can also stripe them for performance), but that doesn't mean we neglected our backup duties with this machine!

The 8760w was easily integrated into a gigabit network in the home office, and on fast Wifi everywhere else, so we had constant access to the home network and the hundreds upon hundreds of files necessary to write this book (and all their backups!).

And since we are so very image conscious (as in the screen!), we wondered if the images we created and captured for this book would be done justice on "just a laptop screen." The Elitebook has a stunning 17″ 30bit IPS display panel that put those questions to rest real quick! The HP's screen is no less than professionally accurate and calibrated for optimum image clarity and correct color. Barely a handful of high-end mobile workstations could even come close to meeting the demands image professionals put on their gear. But this notebook HP DreamColor display is remarkable, there's just no other way to put it, going as far as besting any of our desktop screens in color and vibrancy.

With performance at such a high level, and in a nice portable form factor, we were easily convinced to perform all of our intensive work for this book on the Elitebook. Going back to a desk-bound tower quickly became not an option anymore. Thanks HP!

ABOUT THE AUTHORS

Randi L. Derakhshani is a staff instructor with The Art Institute of California–Los Angeles. She began working with computer graphics in 1992 and was hired by her instructor to work at Sony Pictures Imageworks, where she developed her skills with the Autodesk® 3ds Max® program and Nuke, among many other programs. A teacher since 1999, Randi enjoys sharing her wisdom with young talent and watching them develop at The Art Institute. Currently, she teaches a wide range of classes, from Autodesk® 3ds Max®, Maya, and ZBrush to compositing with The Foundry's Nuke. Juggling her teaching activities with caring for a little boy makes Randi a pretty busy lady.

Dariush Derakhshani is a visual effects supervisor and Supervisor of Games at Zoic Studios in Culver City, California, and a writer and educator in Los Angeles, California, as well as Randi's husband. Dariush used Autodesk® AutoCAD® software in his architectural days and migrated to using 3D programs when his firm's principal architects needed to visualize architectural designs in 3D on the computer. Dariush started using Alias PowerAnimator version 6 when he enrolled in USC Film School's Animation program, and he has been using Alias/Autodesk animation software for the past 14 years. He received an M.F.A. in Film, Video, and Computer Animation from the USC Film School in 1997. He also holds a B.A. in Architecture and Theater from Lehigh University in Pennsylvania. He worked at a New Jersey architectural firm before moving to Los Angeles for film school. He has worked on feature films, music videos, and countless commercials as a 3D animator, as a CG/VFX supervisor, and sometimes as a compositor. Dariush also serves as an editor and is on the advisory board of *HDRI 3D*, a professional computer graphics (CG) magazine from DMG Publishing.

CONTENTS AT A GLANCE

CONTENTS

INTRODUCTION

Welcome to Autodesk® 3ds Max® 2013 Essentials. The world of computer-generated imagery (CG) is fun and ever-changing. Whether you are new to CG in general or are a CG veteran new to 3ds Max designing, you'll find this book the perfect primer. It introduces you to Autodesk 3ds Max and shows how you can work with the program to create your art, whether it is animated or static in design.

This book exposes you to all facets of 3ds Max software by introducing and plainly explaining its tools and functions to help you understand how the program operates—but it does not stop there. This book also explains the use of the tools and the ever-critical concepts behind the tools. You'll find hands-on examples and tutorials that give you firsthand experience with the toolsets. Working through them will develop your skills and the conceptual knowledge that will carry you to further study with confidence. These tutorials expose you to various ways to accomplish tasks with this intricate and comprehensive artistic tool. These chapters should give you the confidence you need to venture deeper into 3ds Max software's feature set, either on your own or by using any of the software's other learning tools and books as a guide.

Learning to use a powerful tool can be frustrating. You need to remember to pace yourself. The major complaints CG book readers have are that the pace is too fast and that the steps are too complicated or overwhelming. Addressing those complaints is a tough nut to crack, to be sure. No two readers are the same. However, this book offers the opportunity to run things at your own pace. The exercises and steps may seem confusing at times, but keep in mind that the more you try and the more you fail at some attempts, the more you will learn how to operate the 3ds Max engine. Experience is king when learning the workflow necessary for *any* software program, and with experience come failure and aggravation. But try and try again. You will find that further attempts will always be easier and more fruitful.

Above all, however, this book aims to inspire you to use the 3ds Max program as a creative tool to achieve and explore your own artistic vision.

Who Should Read This Book

Anyone who is interested in learning to use the 3ds Max tools should start with this book.

If you are an educator, you will find a solid foundation on which to build a new course. You can also treat the book as a source of raw materials that you can

adapt to fit an existing curriculum. Written in an open-ended style, Autodesk®
3ds Max® 2013 Essentials contains several self-help tutorials for home study, as
well as plenty of material to fit into any class.

What You Will Learn

You will learn how to work in CG with Autodesk® 3ds Max 2013. The important
thing to keep in mind, however, is that this book is merely the beginning of your
CG education. With the confidence you will gain from the exercises in this book,
and the peace of mind you can have by using this book as a reference, you can
go on to create your own increasingly complex CG projects.

What You Need

Hardware changes constantly and evolves faster than publications can keep up.
Having a good solid machine is important to a production, although simple home
computers will be able to run the 3ds Max software quite well. Any laptop (with
discrete graphics; not a netbook) or desktop PC running Windows XP Professional,
Windows Vista, or Windows 7 (32- or 64-bit) with at least 2GB of RAM and an
Intel Pentium Core 2 Duo/Quad or AMD Phenom or higher processor will work. Of
course, having a good video card will help; you can use any hardware-accelerated
OpenGL or Direct3D video card. Your computer system should have at least a
2.4GHz Core 2 or i5/i7 processor with 2GB of RAM, a few GBs of hard drive space
available, and a GeForce FX or ATI Radeon video card. Professionals may want
to opt for workstation graphics cards, such as the ATI FirePro or the Quadro FX
series of cards. The following systems would be good ones to use:

- ▶ Intel i7, 4GB RAM, Quadro FX 2000, 400GB 7200 RPM hard disk

- ▶ AMD Phenom II, 4GB RAM, ATI FirePro V5700, 400GB hard disk

You can check the list of system requirements at the following website: www
.autodesk.com/3dsmax.

What Is Covered in This Book

Autodesk® 3ds Max® 2013 Essentials is organized to provide you with a quick
and essential experience with 3ds Max software to allow you to begin a fruitful
education in the world of computer graphics.

Chapter 1, "The 3ds Max Interface," begins with an introduction to the
interface for 3ds Max® 2013 to get you up and running quickly.

Chapter 2, "Your First 3ds Max Project," is an introduction to modeling concepts and workflows in general. It shows you how to model using 3ds Max tools with polygonal meshes and modifiers to create a bedroom dresser.

Chapter 3, "Modeling in 3ds Max: Architectural Model Part I," takes your modeling lesson from Chapter 2 a step further by showing you how to use some of the Architectural, Engineering and Construction (AEC) tools to build an interior space using a room from an image.

Chapter 4, "Modeling in 3ds Max: Architectural Model Part II," continues with the interior space from Chapter 3 by adding some furniture. The main focus of this chapter is the Graphite Modeling ribbon and its many tools.

Chapter 5, "Animating a Bouncing Ball," teaches you the basics of 3ds Max animation techniques and workflow by animating a bouncing ball. You will also learn how to use the Track View–Curve Editor to time, edit, and finesse your animation.

Chapter 6, "Animating a Thrown Knife," rounds out your animation experience by showing the animation concepts of weight, follow-through, and anticipation when you animate a knife thrown at a target.

Chapter 7, "Character Poly Modeling: Part I," introduces you to the first of three chapters on creating a low-polygon mesh character model of a soldier. In this chapter, you begin by blocking out the primary parts of the body.

Chapter 8, "Character Poly Modeling: Part II," continues the soldier model, focusing on using the Editable Poly toolset. You will finish the body and add hands and boots.

Chapter 9, "Character Poly Modeling: Part III," finishes the model of the special operations soldier started in Chapter 7. You will create the head and merge in elements such as goggles and a face mask and integrate them into the scene.

Chapter 10, "Introduction to Materials: Interiors and Furniture," shows you how to assign textures and materials to your models. You will learn to texture the couch, chair, and window from Chapter 4, as you learn the basics of working with 3ds Max materials and UVW mapping.

Chapter 11, "Textures and UV Workflow: The Soldier," furthers your understanding of materials and textures and introduces UV workflows in preparing and texturing the soldier.

Chapter 12, "Character Studio: Rigging," covers the basics of Character Studio in creating a biped system and associating the biped rig to the soldier model.

Chapter 13, "Character Studio: Animation," expands on Chapter 12 to show you how to use Character Studio to create and edit a walk cycle using the soldier model.

Chapter 14, "Introduction to Lighting: Interior Lighting," begins by showing you how to light a 3D scene with the three-point lighting system. It then shows you how to use the tools to create and edit 3ds Max lights for illumination, shadows, and special lighting effects. You will light the furniture to which you added materials in Chapter 10.

Chapter 15, "3ds Max Rendering," explains how to create image files from your 3ds Max scene and how to achieve the best look for your animation by using proper cameras and rendering settings when you render the Interior scene.

Chapter 16, "mental ray and HDRI," shows you how to render with mental ray. Using Final Gather, you will learn how to use indirect lighting as well as get a brief intro to HDRI lighting.

As a bonus we include this chapter on Particles to be found on the companion web page:

Chapter 17, "Particles," introduces you to 3ds Max's particle systems and space warps when you create a firing machine gun.

The companion web page to this book at www.sybex.com/go/ 3dsmax2013essentials provides all the sample images, movies, and files that you will need to work through the projects in *Autodesk® 3ds Max® 2013 Essentials*.

 NOTE This book is a great primer for Autodesk 3ds Max. If you're interested in taking the Autodesk Certification exams for 3ds Max go to www.autodesk.com/certification **for information and resources.**

The Essentials Series

The *Essentials* series from Sybex provides outstanding instruction for readers who are just beginning to develop their professional skills. Every *Essentials* book includes these features:

► Skill-based instruction with chapters organized around projects rather than abstract concepts or subjects

► Suggestions for additional exercises at the end of each chapter, where you can practice and extend your skills

► Digital files (via download) so you can work through the project tutorials yourself. Please check the book's web page at www.sybex.com/go/3dsmax2013essentials for these companion downloads.

 NOTE You can contact the authors through Wiley or on Facebook at http://www.facebook.com/3dsMaxEssentials.

CHAPTER 1

The 3ds Max Interface

This chapter explains the Autodesk® 3ds Max® software interface and its basic operation. You can use this chapter as a reference as you work through the rest of this book, although the following chapters and their exercises will orient you to the 3ds Max user interface (UI) quickly. It's important to be in front of your computer when you read this chapter, so you can try out the techniques as we discuss.

Topics in this chapter include the following:

▶ **The workspace**

▶ **Transforming objects using gizmos**

▶ **Graphite Modeling Tools ribbon**

▶ **Command panel**

▶ **Time slider and track bar**

▶ **File management**

The Workspace

This section presents a brief rundown of what you need to know about the UI and how to navigate the 3ds Max 3D workspace.

User Interface Elements

Figure 1.1 shows the 3ds Max UI. At the very top left of the application window is a large button (⟳) called Application; clicking it opens the Application menu, which provides access to many file operations. Also running along the top is the Quick Access toolbar, which provides access to common commands, and the InfoCenter, which offers support for various

Autodesk applications. Some of the most important commands in the Quick Access toolbar are file management commands such as Save File and Open File. If you do something and then wish you hadn't, you can click the Undo Scene Operation icon ( ) or press Ctrl+Z. To redo a command or action that you just undid, click the Redo Scene Operation button ( ) or press Ctrl+Y.

Quick Access Toolbar
Provides some of the most commonly used file-management commands, as well as Undo and Redo.

Menu Bar
The title of each menu indicates the purpose of the commands on the menu.

Command Panel Tabs
The Command panel is where all the editing of parameters occurs. Many functions and creation options are accessed here. The Command panel is divided into tabs that access different panels such as the Creation panel, Modify panel, etc.

InfoCenter
The InfoCenter gives you access to information about the 3ds Max program and other Autodesk products.

Application Button
Opens application menu that appears when clicked and provides file-management commands.

Main Toolbar
Provides quick access to tools and dialogs for many of the most common tasks.

Graphite Modeling Tools
This UI element (also called the Graphite Modeling ribbon) gives you access to many editing tools for your scene, as well as many other tools for creating and selecting.

Time Slider
Shows the current frame and allows for changing the current frame by moving (or scrubbing) the time bar.

Track Bar
The track bar provides a timeline showing the frame numbers. Select an object to view its animation keys on the track bar.

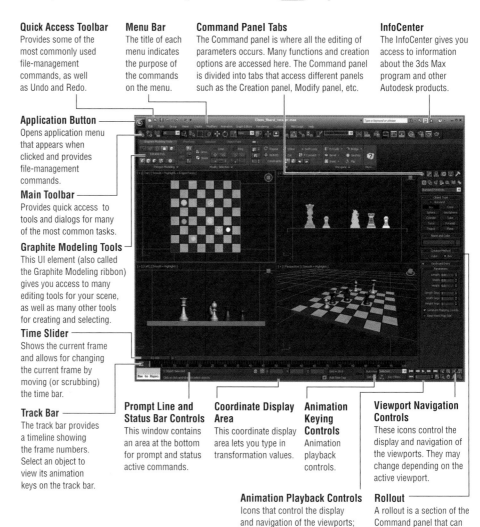

Prompt Line and Status Bar Controls
This window contains an area at the bottom for prompt and status active commands.

Coordinate Display Area
This coordinate display area lets you type in transformation values.

Animation Keying Controls
Animation playback controls.

Viewport Navigation Controls
These icons control the display and navigation of the viewports. They may change depending on the active viewport.

Animation Playback Controls
Icons that control the display and navigation of the viewports; icons may change depending on the active viewport.

Rollout
A rollout is a section of the Command panel that can expand to show a listing of parameters or contract to just its heading name.

FIGURE 1.1   The 3DS Max interface elements

TABLE 1.1 The 3ds Max Interface Elements

	Element	Function
1	Application button	Opens Application menu that provides file management commands.
2	Main toolbar	Provides quick access to tools and dialog boxes for many of the most common tasks.
3	Graphite Modeling Tools ribbon	Provides access to a wide range of tools to make building and editing models in the 3ds Max software fast and easy. In Figure 1.1, the ribbon is oriented in a horizontal position; later in the chapter you will learn how to customize the ribbon.
4	Quick Access toolbar	Provides some of the most commonly used file management commands, as well as Undo and Redo.
5	Menu bar	Provides access to commands grouped by category.
6	InfoCenter	Provides access to information about 3ds Max software and other Autodesk products.
7	Command panel tabs	Where all the editing of parameters occurs; provides access to many functions and creation options; divided into tabs that access different panels, such as the Creation panel, Modify panel, etc.
8	Rollout	A section of the Command panel that can expand to show a listing of parameters or collapse to just its heading name.

TABLE 1.1 *(Continued)*

	Element	Function
9	Viewports	You can choose different views to display in these four viewports, as well as different layouts from the Viewport Label menus.
10	Time slider	Shows the current frame and allows you to change the current frame by moving (or scrubbing) the time bar.
11	Track bar	Provides a timeline showing the frame numbers; select an object to view its animation keys on the track bar.
12	Prompt line and status bar controls	Prompt and status information about your scene and the active command.
13	Coordinate display area	Allows you to enter transformation values.
14	Animation keying controls	Animation playback controls.
15	Viewport navigation controls	Icons that control the display and navigation of the viewports; icons may change depending on the active viewport.

Just below the Quick Access toolbar is the menu bar, which runs across the top of the UI. The menus give you access to a ton of commands—from basic scene operations, such as Undo under the Edit menu, to advanced tools such as those found under the Modifiers menu. Immediately below the menu bar is the main toolbar. It contains several icons for functions such as the three Transform tools: Move, Rotate, and Scale (⊹ ○ ▱).

When you first open the 3ds Max program, the workspace has many UI elements. Each is designed to help you work with your models, access tools, and edit object parameters.

Viewports

You'll be doing most of your work in the viewports. These windows represent three-dimensional space using a system based on Cartesian coordinates. That is a fancy way of saying "space on X-, Y-, and Z-axes."

You can visualize X as left–right, Z as up–down, and Y as in–out (into and out of the screen from the Top viewport). The coordinates are expressed as a set of three numbers such as (0, 3, –7). These coordinates represent a point that is at 0 on the X-axis, 3 units up on the Y-axis, and 7 units back on the Z-axis.

Four-Viewport Layout

The 3ds Max viewports are the windows into your scene. By default, there are four main views: front, top, left, and perspective. The first three—front, top, and left—are called orthographic (2D) views. They are also referred to as *modeling windows*. These windows are good for expressing exact dimensions and size relationships, so they are good tools for sizing up your scene objects and fine-tuning their layout. The General Viewport Label menu (■) in the upper-left corner of each viewport provides options for overall viewport display or activation, as shown in Figure 1.2. It also gives you access to the Viewport Configuration dialog box.

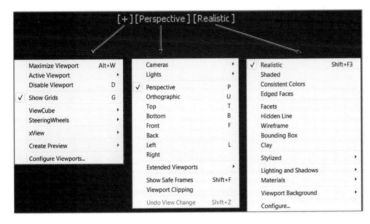

FIGURE 1.2 The Viewport Label menu

The Perspective viewport displays objects in 3D space using perspective. Notice in Figure 1.1 how the distant objects seem to get smaller in the Perspective viewport. In actuality, they are the same size, as you can see in the orthographic viewports. The Perspective viewport gives you the best representation of what your output will be.

To select a viewport, click in a blank part of the viewport (not on an object). If you do have something selected, it will be deselected when you click in the blank space. You can also right-click anywhere in an inactive viewport to activate it without selecting or deselecting anything. When active, the view will have a mustard-yellow highlight around it. If you right-click in an already active viewport, you will get a pop-up context menu called the Quad menu. You can use the Quad menu to access some basic commands for a faster workflow. We will cover this topic in the "Quad Menus" section later in this chapter.

ViewCube

The ViewCube navigation control, shown in Figure 1.3, provides visual feedback of the current orientation of a viewport, lets you adjust the view orientation, and allows you to switch between standard and isometric views.

Home Button: Resets
viewport to Home View

Compass indicates the
north direction for the scene.
You can toggle the compass
display below the ViewCube
and specify its orientation with
the Compass settings.

Using the left mouse button,
you can switch to one of the
available preset views, or rotate
the current view.

FIGURE 1.3 The ViewCube navigation tool

The ViewCube is displayed by default in the upper-right corner of the active viewport, superimposed over the scene in an inactive state to show the orientation of the scene. It does not appear in camera or light views. When you position your cursor over the ViewCube, it becomes active. Using the left mouse button, you can switch to one of the available preset views, rotate the current view, or change to the home view of the model. Right-clicking opens a context menu with additional options.

Mouse Buttons

Each of the three buttons on your mouse plays a slightly different role when manipulating viewports in the workspace. When used with modifiers such as the Alt key, they are used to navigate your scene, as shown in Figure 1.4.

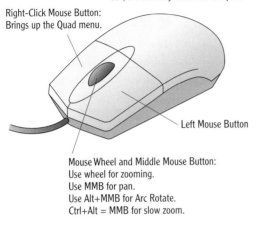

Specialized Quad menus become available
when you press any combination of Shift,
Ctrl, or Alt in any standard viewport.

Right-Click Mouse Button:
Brings up the Quad menu.

Left Mouse Button

Mouse Wheel and Middle Mouse Button:
Use wheel for zooming.
Use MMB for pan.
Use Alt+MMB for Arc Rotate.
Ctrl+Alt = MMB for slow zoom.

FIGURE 1.4 **Breakdown of the three computer
mouse buttons**

Quad Menus

When you click the right mouse button (right-click) anywhere in an active viewport, except on the viewport label, a Quad menu is displayed at the location of
the mouse cursor (see Figure 1.5). The Quad menu can display up to four quadrant areas with various commands without making you switch back and forth
between the viewport and rollouts on the Command panel (the area of the UI to
the right—more on this later in the "Command Panel" section).

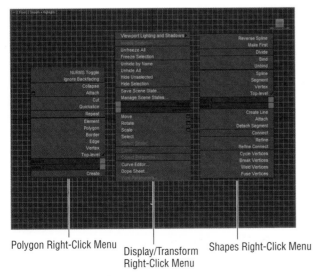

Polygon Right-Click Menu   Shapes Right-Click Menu

Display/Transform
Right-Click Menu

FIGURE 1.5 **Quad menus**

The two right quadrants of the default Quad menu display generic commands, which are shared between all objects. The two left quadrants contain context-specific commands, such as Mesh tools and Light commands. You can also repeat your last Quad menu command by clicking the title of the quadrant.

The Quad menu contents depend on what is selected. The menus are set up to display only the commands that are available for the current selection; therefore, selecting different types of objects displays different commands in the quadrants. Consequently, if no object is selected, all of the object-specific commands will be hidden. If all of the commands for one quadrant are hidden, the quadrant will not be displayed.

Cascading menus display submenus in the same manner as a right-click menu. The menu item that contains submenus is highlighted when expanded. The submenus are highlighted when you move the mouse cursor over them.

Some of the selections in the Quad menu have a small icon next to them. Clicking this icon opens a dialog box where you can set parameters for the command.

To close the menu, right-click anywhere on the screen or move the mouse cursor away from the menu and click the left mouse button. To reselect the last selected command, click in the title of the quadrant of the last menu item. The last menu item selected is highlighted when the quadrant is displayed.

The Caddy Interface

Like the Quad menu, the new caddy interface is designed to keep your eyes in the viewports while providing context-sensitive tools. The caddies replace the Settings dialog boxes available in previous 3ds Max versions. Depending on the tool, clicking the Settings button (identified as a small arrow below the name of the tool) displays the tool-specific caddy directly over the selected objects or sub-objects. Figure 1.6 shows the Extrude Polygons caddy. Each tool's caddy is slightly different and may include more than one parameter.

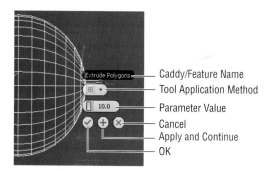

FIGURE 1.6 The Extrude Polygons caddy

Pausing your cursor over any of the highlighted features changes the caddy title to reflect the name of that feature. Clicking a feature with a down arrow opens a drop-down menu where you can choose an option. There are three methods for executing the changes in a caddy: OK, Apply And Continue, and Cancel. Clicking OK applies the parameter values set and then closes the caddy. Clicking Apply And Continue applies the parameter values but keeps the caddy open. Clicking Cancel terminates the command.

Displaying Objects in a Viewport

Viewports can display your scene objects in a few ways. If you click the viewport's name, you can switch that panel to any other viewport angle or point of view. If you click the Viewport display mode, a menu appears to allow you to change the display mode. The display mode names differ depending on the graphics drive mode you selected when starting the 3ds Max program. This book uses the default display mode Nitrous.

The most common view modes are Wireframe mode and Realistic mode. Wireframe mode displays the edges of the object, shown in Figure 1.7 (left). It is the fastest mode to use because it requires less computation on your video card. The Realistic mode is a shaded view where the objects in the scene appear solid; it shows realistic textures with shading and lighting, shown in Figure 1.7 (middle). Edged faces displays the edged faces over the shaded object, shown in Figure 1.7 (right).

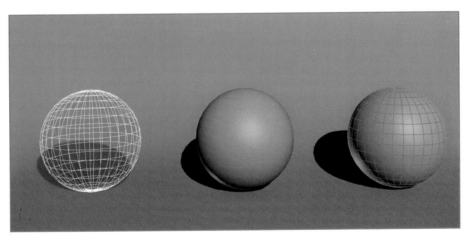

FIGURE 1.7 Viewport rendering options with the default Nitrous driver modes

Each viewport displays a ground-plane grid (as shown in the Perspective viewport), called the *home grid*. This is the basic 3D-space reference system where the X-axis is red, the Y-axis is green, and the Z-axis is blue. It's defined by three fixed planes on the coordinate axes (X, Y, Z). The center of all three axes is called the *origin,* where the coordinates are (0, 0, 0). The home grid is visible in the 3ds Max default settings when you start the software, but it can be turned off in the right-click Viewport menu or by pressing the G key.

Selecting Objects in a Viewport

Click an object to select it in a viewport. If the object is displayed in Wireframe mode, its wireframe turns white while it is selected. If the object is displayed in a Shaded mode, a white bracket appears around the object.

To select multiple objects, hold down the Ctrl key as you click additional objects to add to your selection. If you Alt+click an active object, you will deselect it. You can clear all your active selections by clicking in an empty area of the viewport.

Changing/Maximizing the Viewports

To change the view in any given viewport—for example, to go from a perspective view to a front view—click the current viewport's name. From the menu, select the view you want to have in the selected viewport. You can also use keyboard shortcuts. To switch from one view to another, press the appropriate key on the keyboard, as shown in Table 1.2.

TABLE 1.2   Viewport Shortcuts

Viewport	Keyboard shortcut
Top view	T
Bottom view	B
Front view	F
Left view	L
Camera view	C
Orthographic view	U
Perspective view	P

If you want to have a larger view of the active viewport than is provided by the default four-viewport layout, click the Maximize Viewport Toggle icon (▣) in the lower-right corner of the 3ds Max window. You can also use the Alt+W keyboard shortcut to toggle between the maximized and four-viewport views.

Viewport Navigation

The 3ds Max program allows you to move around its viewports either by using key/mouse combinations, which are highly preferable, or by using the viewport controls found in the lower-right corner of the 3ds Max UI. An example of navigation icons is shown for the Top viewport in Figure 1.8, though it's best to become familiar with the key/mouse combinations.

FIGURE 1.8
Viewport navigation controls are handy, but the mouse keyboard combinations are much faster to use for navigation in viewports.

Open a new, empty 3ds Max scene. Experiment with the following controls to get a feel for moving around in 3D space. If you are new to 3D, using these controls may seem odd at first, but it will become easier as you gain experience and should become second nature in no time.

Pan   Panning a viewport slides the view around the screen. Using the middle mouse button (MMB), click in the viewport and drag the mouse pointer to pan the view.

Zoom   Zooming moves your view closer to or farther away from your objects. To zoom, press Ctrl+Alt and MMB+click in your viewport, and then drag the mouse up or down to zoom in or out, respectively. You may also use the scroll wheel to zoom.

Orbit   Orbit will rotate your view around your objects. To orbit, press Alt and MMB+click and drag in the viewport. By default, Max will rotate about the center of the viewport.

Transforming Objects Using Gizmos

Using gizmos is a fast and effective way to transform (move, rotate, and/or scale) your objects with interactive feedback. When you select a Transform tool such as Move, a gizmo appears on the selected object. Gizmos let you manipulate objects in your viewports interactively to transform them. Coordinate display boxes at the bottom of the screen display coordinate, angular, or percentage information on the position, rotation, and scale of your object as you transform it. The gizmos appear in the viewport on the selected object at their pivot point as soon as you invoke one of the Transform tools, as shown in Figure 1.9.

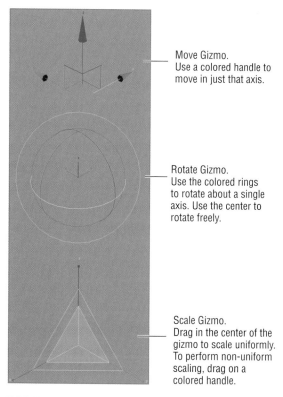

Move Gizmo.
Use a colored handle to move in just that axis.

Rotate Gizmo.
Use the colored rings to rotate about a single axis. Use the center to rotate freely.

Scale Gizmo.
Drag in the center of the gizmo to scale uniformly. To perform non-uniform scaling, drag on a colored handle.

FIGURE 1.9   Gizmos for the Transform tools

You can select the Transform tools by clicking the icons in the main toolbar's Transform toolset ( ) or by invoking shortcut keys: W for Move, E for

Rotate, and R for Scale. In a new scene, create a sphere by choosing Create ➤ Standard Primitives ➤ Sphere. In a viewport, click and drag to create the Sphere object. Follow along as the Transform tools are explained next.

Move

Invoke the Move tool by pressing W (or accessing it through the main toolbar), and your gizmo should look like the top image in Figure 1.9. Dragging the X, Y, or Z axis handle moves an object on that specific axis. You can also click on the plane handle, the box between two axes, to move the object in that two-axis plane.

Rotate

Invoke the Rotate tool by pressing E, and your gizmo will turn into three circles, as shown in the middle image in Figure 1.9. You can click on one of the colored circles to rotate the object on the axis only, or you can click anywhere between the circles to freely rotate the selected object in all three axes.

Scale

Invoke the Scale tool by pressing the R key, and your gizmo will turn into a triangle, as shown in the bottom of Figure 1.9. Clicking and dragging anywhere inside the yellow triangle will scale the object uniformly on all three axes. By selecting the red, green, or blue handles for the appropriate axis, you can scale along one axis only. You can also scale an object on a plane between two axes by selecting the side of the yellow triangle between two axes.

Graphite Modeling Tools Ribbon

The Graphite Modeling tools (also called the Graphite Modeling Tools ribbon) is a section of the UI directly under the main toolbar (as you saw earlier in Figure 1.1). The Graphite Modeling Tools ribbon provides you with a wide range of tools to make building and editing 3ds Max models fast and easy. All the available tools are divided into tabs that are organized by function and then further divided into panels. For example, the Graphite Modeling Tools tab contains the tools you use most often for polygon modeling and editing, organized into separate panels for easy, convenient access. In the following chapters, you will make copious use of the Graphite Modeling tools (see Figure 1.10).

FIGURE 1.10   The Graphite Modeling Tools ribbon

The panels found in the Polygon: Edit tab are

- ▶ The Edit Polygons panel

- ▶ The Selection panel

- ▶ The Favorites panel

- ▶ The Geometry (All) panel

- ▶ The sub-object panel (refers to when working with component types: Vertex, Edge, Border, Polygon, Element)

- ▶ The Loops panel

- ▶ The Additional panels

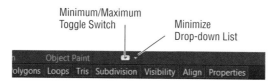

FIGURE 1.11   The default position of the Graphite Modeling Tools ribbon

One easy way to customize the ribbon is by using the Minimum/Maximum Toggle switch as shown in Figure 1.11. By clicking on the button, you cycle through the minimum/maximum options; when you maximize the ribbon, you are able to view most of the controls.

Command Panel

Everything you need to create, manipulate, and animate objects can be found in the Command panel running vertically on the right side of the UI (Figure 1.1). The Command panel is divided into tabs according to function. The function or toolset you need to access will determine which tab you need to click. When you encounter a panel that is longer than your screen, a thin vertical scroll bar is displayed on the right side. Your cursor also turns into a hand that lets you click and drag the panel up and down.

You will be exposed to more panels as you progress through this book. Table 1.3 is a rundown of the Command panel functions and what they do.

TABLE 1.3 Command Panel Functions

Icon	Name	Function
✳	Create panel	Lets you create objects, lights, cameras, etc.
◢	Modify panel	Lets you apply and edit modifiers to objects
🔧	Hierarchy panel	Lets you adjust the hierarchy for objects and adjust their pivot points
◎	Motion panel	Lets you access animation tools and functions
▢	Display panel	Lets you access display options for scene objects
⟋	Utilities panel	Lets you access several 3ds Max functions, such as motion capture utilities and the Asset browser

Object Parameters and Values

The Command panel and all its tabs give you access to an object's parameters. Parameters are the values that define a specific attribute of or for that object. For example, when an object is selected in a viewport, its parameters are shown in the Modify panel, where you can adjust them. When you create an object, that object's creation parameters are shown (and editable) in the Create panel.

Modifier Stack

In the Modify panel, you'll find the modifier stack (Figure 1.12). This UI element lists all the modifiers that are active on any selected object. Modifiers are actions applied to an object that change it somehow, such as bending or warping. When creating an object, you can stack modifiers on top of each other and then go back and edit any of the modifiers in the stack (for the most part) to adjust the object at any point in its creation. You will see this in practice in the following chapters.

FIGURE 1.12 The modifier stack in the Modify panel

Objects and Sub-objects

An object or *mesh* is composed of polygons that define the surface. For example, the facets or small rectangles on a sphere are *polygons,* all connected at common edges at the correct angles and in the proper arrangement to make a sphere. The points that generate a polygon are called *vertices.* The lines that connect the points are called *edges.* Polygons, vertices, and edges are examples of sub-objects and are all editable so that you can fashion any sort of surface or mesh shape you wish.

To edit these sub-objects, you have to convert the object to an editable polygon, which you will learn how to do in the following chapters.

Time Slider and Track Bar

Running across the bottom of the 3ds Max UI are the Time slider and the track bar, as shown earlier in Figure 1.1. The Time slider allows you to move through any frame in your scene by *scrubbing* (moving the slider back and forth). You can move through your animation one frame at a time by clicking on the arrows on either side of the Time slider or by pressing the < and > keys.

You can also use the Time slider to animate objects by setting keyframes. With an object selected, right-click on the Time slider to open the Create Key dialog box, which allows you to create transform keyframes for the selected object.

The track bar is directly below the Time slider. The track bar is the timeline that displays the timeline format for your scene. More often than not, the track bar is displayed in frames, with the gap between each tick mark representing frames. On the track bar, you can move and edit your animation properties for the selected object. When a keyframe is present, right-click it to open a context menu where you can delete keyframes, edit individual transform values, and filter the track bar display.

The Animation Playback controls in the lower right of the 3ds Max UI (⋈ ⫷ ▷ ⫸ ⋈) are similar to the ones you would find on a VCR (remember those?) or DVD player.

File Management

The 3ds Max program provides several subfolders automatically grouped into projects for you. Different kinds of files are saved in categorized folders under the project folder. For example, scene files are saved in a Scenes folder and rendered images are saved in a Render Output folder within the project folder. The projects are set up according to what types of files you are working on, so everything is neat and organized from the get-go. The 3ds Max software automatically creates this folder structure for you once you create a new project, and its default settings keep the files organized in that manner.

The conventions followed in this book and on the accompanying web page (www.sybex.com/go/3dsmax2013essentials) follow this project-based system so that you can grow accustomed to it and make it a part of your own workflow. It pays to stay organized.

Setting a Project

The exercises in this book are organized into specific projects such as Dresser, the one you will tackle in the next chapter. The Dresser project will be on your hard drive, and the folders for your scene files and rendered images will be in that project layout. Once you copy the appropriate projects to your hard drive, you can designate which project to work on by choosing Application ➢ Manage ➢ Set Project Folder. Doing so will send the current project to that project folder. For example, when you save your scene, you will automatically be taken to the Scenes folder of the current project.

Designating a specific place on your PC or server for all your project files is important, as is having an established naming convention for its files and folder.

For example, if you are working on a project about a castle, begin by setting a new project called Castle. Choose Application ➢ Manage ➢ Set Project Folder, as shown in Figure 1.13. In the dialog box, click Make New Folder to create a folder named Castle on your hard drive. The 3ds Max program will automatically create the project and its folders.

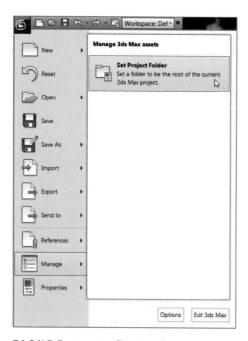

FIGURE 1.13   Choosing Set Project Folder

Once you save a scene, one of your scene filenames should look like this: Castle_GateModel_v05.max. This tells you right away it's a scene from your Castle project and that it is a model of the gate. The version number tells you that it's the fifth iteration of the model and possibly the most recent version. Following a naming convention will save you oodles of time and aggravation.

Version Up!

After you've spent a significant amount of time working on your scene, you will want to *version up*. This means you save your file using the same name, but you increase the version number by 1. Saving often and using version numbers are useful for keeping track of your progress and protecting yourself from mistakes and from losing your work.

To version up, you can save by selecting Application ➤ Save As and manually changing the version number appended to the end of the filename. The 3ds Max program also lets you do this automatically by using an increment feature in the Save As dialog box. Name your scene file and click the Increment button (the + icon) to the right of the filename text. Clicking the Increment button appends the filename with 01, then 02, then 03, and so on as you keep saving your work using Save As and the Increment button.

THE ESSENTIALS AND BEYOND

In this chapter you learned about the interface and how to navigate 3D space using the 3ds Max program. As you continue with the following chapters, you will gain experience and confidence with the UI, and many of the features that seem daunting to you now will become second nature.

ADDITIONAL EXERCISES

▶ From the Create panel, choose Standard Primitives and create each one of the primitives. Pay attention to each object's parameters to become familiar with each object's capabilities.

▶ Explore the viewport labels for rendering types and changing viewports.

▶ Convert each primitive to an editable polygon and, using the selection tools, practice selecting and deselecting vertices, edges, and polygons.

CHAPTER 2

Your First 3ds Max Project

Modeling in 3D programs is like sculpting or carpentry; you create objects out of shapes and forms. Even a complex model is just an amalgam of simpler parts or shapes/volumes. The successful modeler can dissect a form down to its components and translate them into surfaces and meshes.

The Autodesk® 3ds Max® modeling tools are incredibly strong for polygonal modeling, so the focus of the modeling in this book is on polygonal modeling. In addition to mechanical models, you will model an organic low-polygon-count model—a soldier fit for a game—and use that model to animate a character with Character Studio.

In this chapter, you will learn modeling concepts and how to use 3ds Max modeling toolsets. You will also tackle a model to get a sense of a workflow using 3ds Max software.

Topics in this chapter include the following:

▶ **Starting to model a chest of drawers**

▶ **Modeling the top**

▶ **I can see your drawers**

▶ **Modeling the bottom**

▶ **Creating the knobs**

Starting to Model a Chest of Drawers

Begin by modeling a chest of drawers (or dresser) to develop your modeling muscles. This exercise introduces you to primitives and polygons. You will be modeling by editing the polygon component, called *editable-poly* modeling. Why buy a chest of drawers when you can just make one using 3ds Max tools? Be sure you make it large enough for all your socks.

Ready, Set, Reference!

You're so close to modeling something! You'll want to get some sort of reference for what you're modeling. Study the photo in Figure 2.1 for a look at the desired result.

FIGURE 2.1 Model this chest of drawers.

There are plenty of reference photos to help you build different parts of the chest. You may want to flip through the pictures on the following pages to get a better idea of what you will be modeling.

Of course, if this were your chest of drawers, you could have captured tons of pictures already, right?

Ready, Set, Model!

Download the Dresser project, `Dresser.zip`, from the book's web page at `www.sybex.com/go/3dsmax2013essentials`. Place the files on your hard drive. Open the 3ds Max 2013 program and set a 3ds Max project, and then choose the `Dresser` folder from your hard drive.

Modeling the Top

To begin modeling the chest of drawers, follow these steps:

1. Begin with a new scene (choose Application ➢ New ➢ New All, and then click OK in the New Scene dialog box).

2. Select the Perspective viewport, which is set to Realistic display mode by default. Enable Edged Faces mode in the viewport by moving the cursor to Viewport Labels in the upper left and clicking Realistic. This opens a drop-down menu. Choose Edged Faces. This shows the wireframe edges of the object. (You can also use the keyboard short-cut F4 to toggle Edged Faces on or off.)

3. In the Command panel, choose the Create tab (■), click the Geometry icon, and make sure Standard Primitives is selected. In the Object Type rollout, click Box. You are going to create a box using the Keyboard Entry rollout shown in Figure 2.2. These options allow you to specify the exact size and location to create an object in your scene.

FIGURE 2.2
The Keyboard Entry rollout

4. Leave the X, Y, and Z values at 0, but enter these values: Length of **15**, Width of **30**, and Height of **40**. Click Create to create a box aligned in the center of the scene with the specified dimensions.

5. With the box still selected, go to the Modify tab (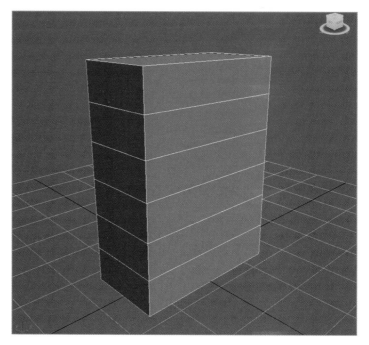). You can see the box's parameters here. You will need to add more height segments, so change the Height Segs parameter to **6**. Your box should look like the one in Figure 2.3.

FIGURE 2.3 The box from which a beautiful chest of drawers will emerge

6. To start the process of using the Graphite modeling tools, you will convert the box to an editable poly. Below the main toolbar and in the Graphite Modeling Tools ribbon, click the Polygon Modeling tab. This expands and you see the Convert To Poly button. Click it, as shown in Figure 2.4.

7. Also in the top of the Polygon Modeling tab, you see a line of icons as shown at the top of Figure 2.5. These are the components, or sub-objects, of your object. Click the Polygon icon (■) or use the keyboard shortcut by pressing 4 to enter the Polygon sub-object mode. Now select the polygon on the top of the box. As you can see in the viewport, the polygon is shaded red when it's selected.

All the editable polygons have specific keyboard shortcuts that allow the user to quickly navigate through the sub-object levels. Vertex level is 1, Edge is 2, Border is 3, Polygon is 4, Element is 5, and Ctrl+B returns to object level, which takes you out of the sub-object level and allows you to edit the object as a whole.

▶

FIGURE 2.4 Convert the box to an editable poly.

FIGURE 2.5 The Bevel caddy controls

8. In the Polygons tab in the Graphite Modeling Tools ribbon, click the Extrude settings box to the right of the Bevel button, which opens the Bevel caddy controls, as shown in Figure 2.5. In the following steps, you are going to bevel several times to create the lip on the crown of the dresser shown in Figure 2.6.

9. In the text boxes of the Bevel caddy, enter the following parameters: Height: **0.5** and Outline: **1.3**. Keep Bevel Type (the top button in the caddy) set to Group. Click Apply and Continue ( ); the 3ds Max program applies the specified settings, without closing the caddy, to give you results that should be similar to Figure 2.7.

10. In the still open Bevel caddy, input these parameters: Height: **0.3** and Outline: **0**, as shown in Figure 2.8. Click Apply and Continue.

11. For the last bevel, input the following values: Height: **0.1** and Outline: **−0.3**. Click OK ( ). Your dresser's top should resemble Figure 2.9.

FIGURE 2.6 The lip of the real dresser

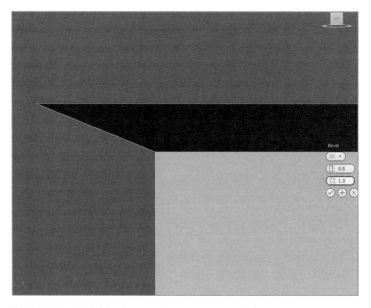

FIGURE 2.7 The first bevel for the crown of the dresser

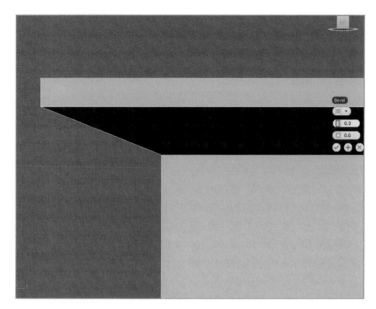

FIGURE 2.8 The second bevel

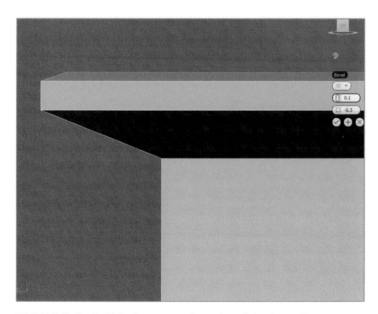

FIGURE 2.9 This shows a rough version of the dresser's crown.

12. Click the Edge icon (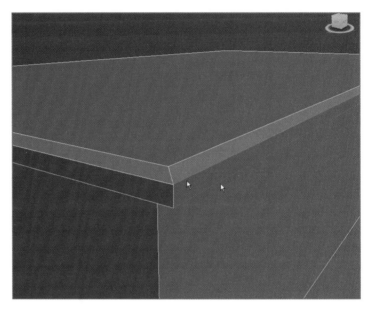) in the Polygon Modeling tab on the Graphite Modeling ribbon or press 2 on your keyboard to enter the Edge sub-object mode. Select the two new edges that were created with the bevel, as shown in red in Figure 2.10.

FIGURE 2.10 Select these two edges.

13. Go to the Graphite Modeling Tools ribbon, and in the Selection tab, select the Loop Selection tool. The keyboard shortcut is Alt+L. This selects an edge loop based on your current sub-object selection. An *edge loop* is essentially edges that loop all the way around an object, making it much easier to adjust models.

14. Now with the edges selected (looped) all around the top of the dresser, go to the Edges tab in the Graphite Modeling Tools ribbon. Choose the Chamfer tool and be sure to select the Chamfer Settings box, as shown in Figure 2.11, to bring up the Chamfer caddy.

15. In the Chamfer caddy, enter the following parameters: Edge Chamfer Amount: **0.1** and Connect Edge Segments: **2**; then click OK. Figure 2.12 shows the result.

FIGURE 2.11 The Edges tab

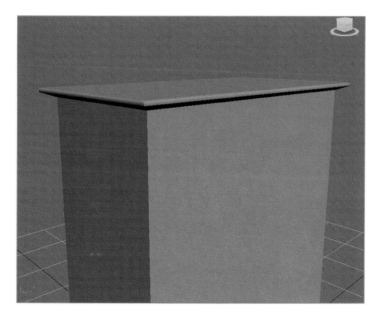

FIGURE 2.12 The top of the dresser is ready.

These values are not necessarily set in stone. You can play around with the settings to get as close to the image as you can or to add your own design flair. Set your project to the Dresser and load the Dresser01.max scene file from the Scenes folder in the Dresser project from the companion web page.

I Can See Your Drawers

In the beginning of this exercise, you created a box with six segments for its height. You can use those segments to create the drawers. This entails thinking ahead and planning your model before you start working on an object; using another tool to add segments for the drawers after the box is made is much more laborious.

For simplicity's sake, in this exercise you will not create drawers that can open and shut. If this dresser were to be used in an animation in which the drawers would be opened, you would make them differently. Figure 2.13 shows the drawers and an important detail you need to consider.

Gap between drawers and dresser main body

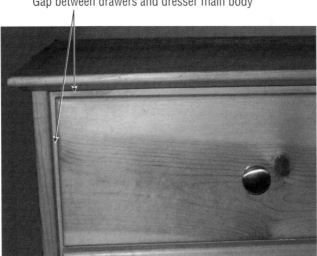

FIGURE 2.13 Notice the small gap around the edge of the box. This gap represents the space between the drawer and the main body of the dresser.

To model the drawers, begin with these steps:

1. Go to Polygon mode (press 4), and select the six polygons on the front of the box that represent the drawers. Hold the Ctrl key while selecting the additional polygons to allow you to make multiple polygon selections. You can toggle between shaded and wireframe selected by pressing F2.

2. In the Graphite Modeling Tools ribbon, go to the Polygons tab and click the Inset Settings button to bring up the Inset caddy. Set the Inset Amount to −0.6, as shown in Figure 2.14, and keep the top button's Inset Type set to Group. Click OK.

FIGURE 2.14
The Inset Settings
caddy controls

You can load the Dresser02.max scene file from the Scenes folder in the Dresser project from the companion web page to check your work or to continue.

3. Keep those newly inset polygons selected (or select them) and go back to the Polygons tab to select the Bevel Settings button to bring up the caddy. Change the Height to –0.5, keep Type set to Group, and click Apply and Continue. The polygons now extrude inward a little bit, as shown in Figure 2.15 (left). Next, set the Height Amount to **0** and the Inset Amount to **–0.6**, as shown in Figure 2.15 (right), and click OK in the Bevel Setting dialog box.

4. In the original reference picture (refer to Figure 2.1), the top drawer of the dresser is split into two, so you need to create an edge vertically in that top-drawer polygon to create two drawers. Go to Edge mode and select the top and bottom horizontal edges on the top drawer, as shown in red in Figure 2.16.

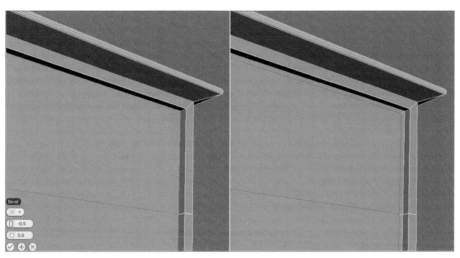

FIGURE 2.15 This shows Bevel performing an extrude (left) and then another inset (right).

FIGURE 2.16 Select the upper and lower edges of the top drawer.

5. Go to the Graphite Modeling Tools ribbon and in the Loops tab, click the Connect Settings button to bring up the caddy (Figure 2.17). Set Segments to 1, Pinch to 0, and Slide to 0 (Figure 2.18), and then click OK.

6. Select the two polygons in the newly created top drawers. Go back to the Polygons tab and click Inset Settings, set Amount to 0.25. This time you are going to change Inset Type from Group to By Polygon, as shown in Figure 2.19.

FIGURE 2.17 The Loops tab with an arrow pointing to the Connect tool

FIGURE 2.18
The Connect Edges
caddy

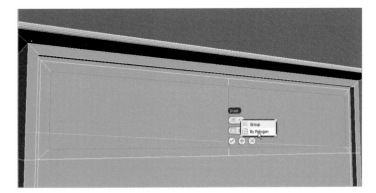

FIGURE 2.19 The Inset caddy with settings for the top drawers

This setting insets each polygon individually instead of performing this operation on multiple, contiguous polygons (which is what the Group option does). Click OK to commit the Inset operation and close the caddy. Your polygons should resemble the ones in Figure 2.20.

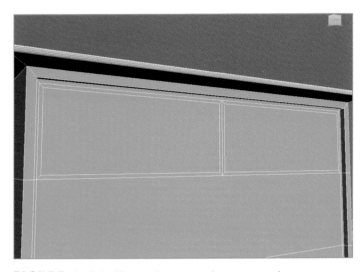

FIGURE 2.20 The top drawers are inset separately.

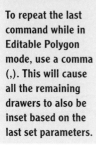

To repeat the last command while in Editable Polygon mode, use a comma (,). This will cause all the remaining drawers to also be inset based on the last set parameters.

7. Perform the same inset operation on the remaining drawer polygons on the front of the box. Set the Amount to .25, and set Inset Type to By Polygon. This will inset the five lower, wide drawers, as shown in Figure 2.21.

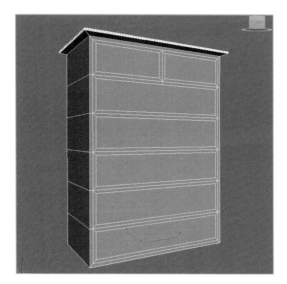

FIGURE 2.21 The remaining drawers are inset.

8. Select all of the drawer polygons. Go to the Polygons tab and click Extrude Settings. Set Height to **0.7**. You don't need it to extrude very much; you just want the drawers to extrude a bit more than the body of the dresser (Figure 2.22).

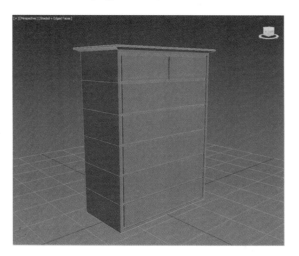

FIGURE 2.22 The drawers are extruded.

You can load the Dresser03.max scene file from the Scenes folder in the Dresser project from the companion web page to check your work or to skip to this part in the exercise.

Modeling the Bottom

Now it is time to create the bottom of the dresser. This dresser doesn't have legs, but nonetheless has a nice detail at the bottom, as you can see in Figure 2.23. To create this detail, you need to extrude a polygon.

FIGURE 2.23 An angle view of the dresser's bottom corner

1. Enter Polygon mode (press 4). You may already be in Polygon sub-object mode if you are continuing with your own file. Select the polygon on the bottom of the dresser, as shown in red in Figure 2.24.

2. In the Graphite Modeling Tools ribbon, go to the Polygons tab and click the Extrude Settings button to bring up the caddy. Change Height to **2.5**, as shown in Figure 2.25, and click OK. This will extrude a polygon out from the bottom of the dresser, essentially adding a segment to the box, as shown in Figure 2.26.

FIGURE 2.24 Select the polygon at the bottom
of the dresser.

FIGURE 2.25
The Extrude Polygons
caddy

FIGURE 2.26 Extrude the bottom of the dresser.

3. The polygon will still be selected, so click the Inset Settings button to bring up its caddy. Change Amount to **0.6**, and click OK. This creates an inset polygon, as shown in Figure 2.27.

4. The polygon should still be selected, so click the Extrude Settings button to bring up the caddy, enter a height of –2.0, and click OK. Figure 2.28 shows how the bottom of the dresser has moved up into itself slightly.

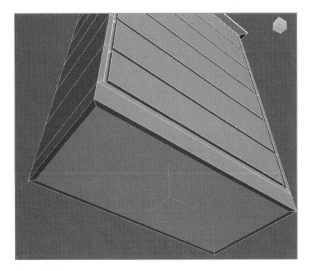

FIGURE 2.27 The inset polygon

FIGURE 2.28 The dresser's bottom lip

To create the detail on the bottom, you need to cut into the newly extruded polygons to create the "legs" in the corners of the dresser that you saw in Figure 2.23. To do this, you will use the ProBoolean tool. This method uses two or more objects to create a new object by performing a Boolean operation.

You need another object to flesh out the shape to cut from the bottom of the dresser. You are going to create this object in the shape of the cutout at the bottom of the dresser (refer to Figure 2.23). It is a very specific shape starting with a simple rectangle.

5. In the Command panel, click the Create tab (⬤), click the Shapes icon (🔲), and click the Rectangle tool, as shown in Figure 2.29.

FIGURE 2.29
Select the Rectangle tool.

6. In a front view, create a rectangle with Length of 3.0 and Width of 26.0, as shown in the top of Figure 2.30. Press W or click the Select And Move Tool (✛), select the rectangle shape, and move it so it is sitting in front of the dresser, as shown in Figure 2.30.

7. In the Command panel, select the Modify tab (▦); and in the modifier stack, right-click the Rectangle entry. From the context menu, choose Editable Spline, as shown in Figure 2.31. In the Editable Spline parameters, open the Selection rollout and click the Vertex icon (◨) to enter Vertex sub-object mode. An editable spline provides controls for manipulating an object as a spline object and at three sub-object levels: Vertex, Segment, and Spline.

8. In the Front viewport, select the two top vertices by clicking and dragging a selection box around them. In the Geometry rollout, click the Fillet tool, as shown in Figure 2.32.

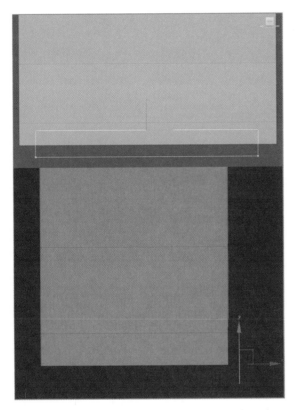

FIGURE 2.30 Move the rectangle into place. The top image shows the Front viewport; the bottom image shows the Left viewport.

FIGURE 2.31 Converting a shape into an editable spline

FIGURE 2.32
The Fillet tool

9. Click and drag one of the two selected vertices to create a rounded corner. Because both vertices are selected, they will both get the fillet, as shown in Figure 2.33. The amount of the fillet is 0.9. You can watch the value of the fillet in the Geometry rollout.

10. With the rectangle shape selected, select the Modify tab. Above the modifier stack is a drop-down menu. From the modifier list, choose Extrude, which will then appear in the modifier stack above the existing editable spline object. Use an amount of 30.0 and then move the extrusion so that it penetrates both sides of the dresser.

11. Do the same to the side of the dresser:

    a. Create another rectangle, but make it smaller to fit the side of the dresser.

    b. Convert to an editable spline as in step 7.

    c. Select the two top vertices and fillet them.

    d. Add an Extrude modifier and change Amount to 40.0.

    e. Place that object penetrating through both sides of the dresser, as shown in Figure 2.34.

Now for the ProBoolean operation itself. Don't get this confused with the regular Boolean operation, however.

1. To begin, select the object you want to keep—in this case, the Dresser object.

2. In the Create panel, select the Geometry rollout; choose Compound Objects from the drop-down menu, and at the bottom of the Object Type rollout, click the ProBoolean button.

3. In the Pick Boolean rollout, click the Start Picking button (Figure 2.35).

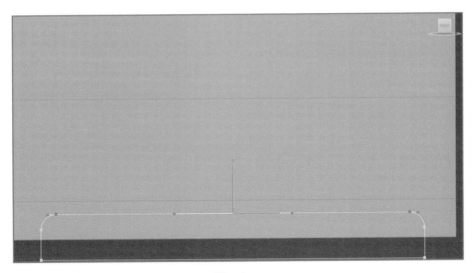

FIGURE 2.33 The two vertices are filleted.

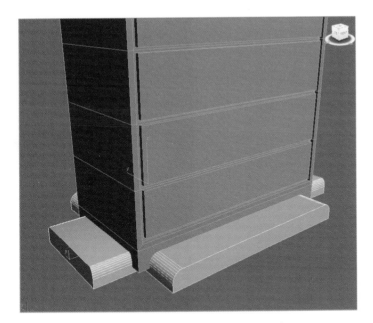

FIGURE 2.34 Objects placed for Boolean operation

FIGURE 2.35
Click the Start Picking
button.

4. Click both extruded rectangles placed at the bottom of the dresser. By default, ProBoolean is always set to Subtraction, so the object's shape will be subtracted from the dresser, as shown in Figure 2.36.

5. In the Name text box (shown in the Command panel's Modify tab to the far right of Figure 2.37), change the name of the object to **Dresser**, and pick a nice light color. Go grab yourself a frosty beverage!

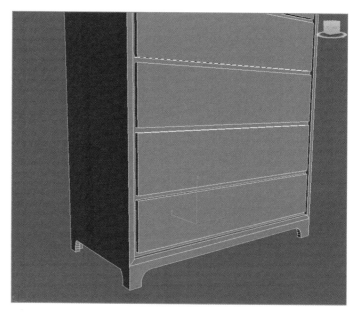

FIGURE 2.36 The finished dresser bottom

The finished dresser body should look like the dresser in Figure 2.1. Remember to save this version of your file. You can load the Dresser04.max scene file from the Scenes folder in the Dresser project on the companion web page to check your work or to skip to this point in the exercise.

FIGURE 2.37 Assigning a name and a color to the finished dresser body

Creating the Knobs

Now that the body of the dresser is done, it's time to add the knobs. We will use splines and a few surface creation tools new to your workflow. Goosebumps, anyone? Take a look at the reference for the knobs in Figure 2.38. You are going to create a profile of the knob and then rotate the profile around its axis to form a surface. This technique is known as *lathe*, not to be mistaken for *latte*, which is a whole different deal and not covered in this book.

A *spline* is a group of vertices and connecting segments that form a line or curve. To create the knob profile, you are going to use the line spline, shaped in the outline of—you guessed it—a knob. The Line tool allows you to create a freeform spline.

FIGURE 2.38 A drawer knob

You can use your last file from the Dresser exercise, or you can load Dresser04.max from the Scenes folder of the Dresser project from the companion web page. To build the knobs, follow these steps:

1. Make sure you are in the Left viewport so you can see which side of the dresser the drawers are on, as shown in Figure 2.39. You are going to create a profile of half the knob, as shown in Figure 2.40. Don't worry about creating all the detail in the knob, because detail won't be seen; a simple outline will be fine.

2. Select Create ➢ Shapes ➢ Line. Use the current default values in the Creation Method rollout.

> **Click once to create a corner vertex for a line, but click and drag to create a Bézier vertex if you want to put a curve into the line.**

3. In the Left viewport, click once to lay down a vertex for this line, starting at the bottom of the profile for the knob (Figure 2.41). This is the starting point for the curve. When you are creating a line, every click lays down the next vertex for the line. If you want to create a curve in the line, click once and drag the mouse in any direction to give the vertex a curvature of sorts. This curve vertex creates a curve in that part of the line. You need to follow the rough outline of

a knob, so click and drag where there is curvature in the line. Once you have laid down your first vertex, continue to click and drag more vertices for the line clockwise until you create the half-profile knob shape shown earlier in Figure 2.40.

FIGURE 2.39 Left view of the dresser

FIGURE 2.40 The intended profile curve for the knob

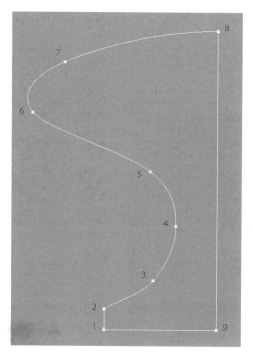

FIGURE 2.41 The vertices of the knob's profile line are numbered according to the order in which they were created.

Figure 2.41 shows the profile line with the vertices numbered according to their creation order.

4. Once you lay down your last vertex at the bottom, finish the spline by either right-clicking to release the Line tool or clicking the first vertex you created to close the spline. For this example, it doesn't matter which method you choose. Either an open or closed spline will work; a closed spline is shown in Figure 2.41. Drawing splines entails a bit of a learning curve, so it might be helpful to delete the one you did first and try again for the practice. Once you get something resembling the spline in Figure 2.41, you can edit it. Don't drive yourself crazy; just get the spline as close as you can.

5. With the spline selected, in the Modify panel's modifier stack, choose Line. Click the plus sign (+) to expand the list of sub-objects, as shown in Figure 2.42.

> **To create a straight orthogonal line segment between two vertices, press and hold Shift to keep the next vertex orthogonal to the last vertex, either horizontally or vertically.**

FIGURE 2.42 Line
sub-object modes

VERTEX TYPES

When working on splines, you may want to change the vertex type; the easiest way to do this is to right-click over a vertex and choose the type you want.

Smooth creates a smooth continuous curve without tangent handles to edit.

Corner creates a sharp corner without tangent handles to edit.

Bezier has adjustable tangent handles that are locked.

Bezier Corner has adjustable tangent handles that are unlocked or broken and can create sharp corners.

Editing the Profile

A line's sub-objects are similar to the Editable Spline sub-object modes. A spline is made up of three sub-objects: a vertex, a segment, and a spline. A *vertex* is a point in space. A *segment* is the line that connects two vertices. To continue with the project, follow these steps:

1. Choose the vertex sub-object for the line. Make sure you are still working in the Left viewport. Use the Move tool to click one of the vertices. Use the Move tool to edit the shape to better fit the outline of the knob.

   To catch up to this point and have the profile already created for you, load the Dresser05.max file from the companion web page.

2. The profile line is ready to turn into a 3D object. This is where the modifiers are used. Get out of sub-object mode for your line. Choose Modifiers ➤ Patch/Spline Editing ➤ Lathe. When you first put the

Lathe modifier on your spline, it probably won't look anything like the knob (see Figure 2.43)—but don't panic; right now the object is turned inside out! Select Y and Max and adjust the parameters to match Figure 2.44.

FIGURE 2.43 Eek! That isn't a knob at all.

FIGURE 2.44 The titillating parameters for the Lathe modifier

3. Adjust the Perspective viewport so you can see the top of the knob. You may notice a strange artifact. To correct this, check the Weld Core box under the Parameters rollout for the lathe.

That's it! Check out Figure 2.45 for a look at the lathed knob. By using splines and the Lathe procedure, you can create all sorts of surfaces for your models. In the next section, you will resize the knob, position it, and copy it to fit on the drawers.

FIGURE 2.45 The lathe completes the knob.

Now that you have a knob, you may need to adjust it and make it the right size. If you still want to futz with the knob, go back down the stack to the Line to edit your spline. For example, you may want to scale the knob a bit to better fit the drawer (refer to the reference photo in Figure 2.38). Select the Scale tool, and click and drag until the original line is about the right size in your scene. The Lathe modifier will re-create the surface to fit the new size. You can also delete the knob and restart with another line for more practice.

Copying the Knob

In the following steps, you will copy and position the knob for the drawers.

1. Position and rotate the knob to fit on to the front of a top drawer. Change its default color (if you want) and change its name to **Knob**.

2. You'll need a few copies of the original knob, one for each drawer. Choose Edit ➢ Clone to open the Clone Options dialog box (Figure 2.46). You are going to use the Instance option. Click OK to create an instance.

There are several ways to clone a 3D object. The previously discussed method is one way; my preferred way is to use the Shift+Transform technique. This is when you use Shift+Move/Rotate/ Scale to create a clone of the object. For the Dresser knobs, select the knob, hold Shift and move the knob to the desired location. When you let go of the mouse, the Clone dialog box appears.

Certification
Objective

THE CLONE DIALOG BOX

Making a *copy* creates a completely separate clone from the original. An *instance* is a copy, but it is still connected to the original. If you edit the original or an instance, all of the instances change (including the original). A *reference* is dependent on the original, and the connection only goes one way; change the original and the reference will change, but change the reference and only it will be affected.

3. Position the instanced knob in the middle of the other top drawer.

4. Using additional instances of the original knob, place knobs in the middle of all the remaining drawers of your dresser, as shown in Figure 2.47.

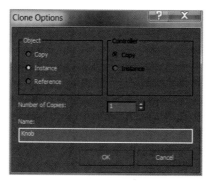

FIGURE 2.46 Using an instance to copy the knob

FIGURE 2.47 The dresser, knobs and all

As you saw with this exercise, there are plenty of tools for the Editable Poly object. Your model doesn't have to be all of the same type of modeling, either. In this example, you created the dresser with *box modeling* techniques, where you begin with a single box and extrude your way into a model, and with surface-creation techniques using splines.

You can compare your work to the scene file `Dresser06.max` from the `Scenes` folder of the Dresser project from the companion web page.

THE ESSENTIALS AND BEYOND

In this chapter, you learned how to model with 3ds Max software. By exploring the modeling toolsets and creating a dresser, you saw firsthand how the primary 3ds Max modeling tools operate.

You learned how to create a primitive box, and from that you learned to use editable polygons and the Graphite modeling tools, ProBoolean, shapes, editable splines, and the Lathe tool to make a simple dresser.

ADDITIONAL EXERCISES

▶ Select the edges around the dresser drawers and use Chamfer to add a bit of roundness to the dresser.

▶ Model one of the drawers so that you can animate it, opening and closing. You can do this by selecting the polygons for one of the drawers and deleting them. Then create a primitive box the size of a drawer.

▶ Play around with the knobs and create different styles. You can find examples at www.sybex.com/go/3dsmax2013essentials.

▶ Create a similar piece of furniture such as a nightstand to match the style of the dresser.

CHAPTER 3

Modeling in 3ds Max: Architectural Model Part I

Building models in 3D is as simple as building them out of clay, wood, stone, or metal. Using Autodesk® 3ds Max® to model something may not be as tactile as physically building it, but the same concepts apply: you have to identify how the model is shaped and figure out how to break it down into manageable parts that you can piece together into the final form.

Instead of using traditional tools to hammer or chisel or weld a shape into form, you will use the vertices of the geometry to shape the computer-generated (CG) model. As you have seen, the 3ds Max polygon toolset is quite robust.

In this chapter, you will explore the many 3ds Max architectural modeling tools by building components such as walls, doors, windows. These objects are called Architecture Engineering and Construction (AEC) tools, and they are parametric to give them an advantage over imported geometry from CAD programs. There are many ways you can build an interior space—simply put, a couple of boxes and you're done—but to really create a refined and realistic interior, you will need to take time to add details.

Topics in this chapter include the following:

▶ **Units setup**

▶ **Importing a CAD drawing**

▶ **Creating the walls**

▶ **Creating the doors**

▶ **Creating the windows**

▶ **Adding a floor and ceiling**

FIGURE 3.1 Images of the room to be created

Figure 3.1 shows the room that you will create in this chapter. There are a few changes from the original room. The opening that leads to the hallway is going to become a door.

Units Setup

When you open the 3ds Max program, a system of measurement is set up to measure geometry in your scene. By default your file is set to Generic Units, where one unit is defined as 1.000 inch. You can change the Generic Units to equal any system of measurement you prefer; you can use Standard English units (feet and inches) or metric. You should choose your measure of units before you begin creating your scene and not during the modeling process. You can do so with the following steps:

    1. Go to the Customize menu and choose Units Setup, as shown in Figure 3.2.

FIGURE 3.2 The Units Setup dialog box

2. Change the Units from the default Generic Units to US Standard.

3. From the drop-down menu, choose Feet w/Decimal Inches.

Importing a CAD Drawing

Using reference materials will help you efficiently create your 3D model and achieve a good likeness in your end result. The temptation to just wing it and start building the objects is strong, especially when time is short and you're raring to go. This temptation should always be suppressed in deference to a well-thought-out approach to the task. Sketches, photographs, and drawings can all be used as resources for the modeling process. Not only are references useful for giving you a clear direction in which to head, but you can also use references directly in the 3ds Max software to help you model. Photos, especially those taken from different sides of the intended model, can be added to a scene as background images to help you shape your model.

For this chapter, you will be using an AutoCAD drawing as the reference and as a template to build the walls, doors, and windows. For this book, you will be supplied with a CAD drawing that will make it much easier to follow the reference. In the future, if you don't have a drawing using detailed measurements of the room in question, you can create your own layout or blueprints because proper measurements and scale are vital when you're creating a convincing interior space.

To import the AutoCAD drawing:

1. Select Application ➢ Manage ➢ Set Project Folder and choose the ArchModel project, downloaded from the book's web page at www .sybex.com/go/3dsmax2013essentials.

2. Click the Application button (⑤) and choose Import ➢ Import. Because you have already set your project to the ArchModel project, you will be taken straight to the *import* folder for that project. Select the Room.dwg file. This is an AutoCAD drawing file that contains no 3D objects; it contains a drawing using 2D vector lines.

3. The AutoCAD DWG/DFX Import Options dialog box will open, as shown in Figure 3.3. In the Derive AutoCAD Primitive By drop-down menu, choose One Object and then click OK.

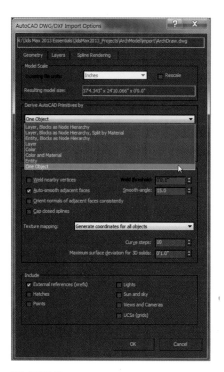

FIGURE 3.3 The AutoCAD DWG/DGX
Import Options dialog box

The viewport should show a 2D collection of lines making up the layout of a room. This is a CAD drawing of the living room and dining room of a typical house, which was created for this book by Nastasia Jorgenson, an interior design student from the Art Institute of California – Los Angeles. The drawing has three basic parts: the walls, windows, and doors, as shown in Figure 3.4. The figure has some colors associated with the walls, doors, and windows. These colors will not be reflected in the imported drawing.

Creating the Walls

The Wall objects you will create are a part of the AEC Extended objects and are designed for use in the architectural, engineering, and construction fields. To begin, follow these steps:

1. Select and maximize the Top viewport (Alt+W).

2. In the main toolbar, right-click the Snaps button (³n) to bring up the Grid and Snap Settings dialog box. Uncheck Grid and check Vertex, as shown in Figure 3.5. Close the dialog box, and then click the Snaps

button (or press the S key). This will make it possible to snap from the vertex in the AutoCAD drawing.

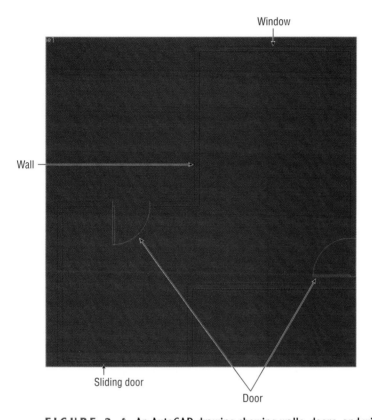

FIGURE 3.4 An AutoCAD drawing showing walls, doors, and windows

FIGURE 3.5 The Snaps dialog box

3. Go to the Create panel and from the Standard Primitive drop-down menu, choose AEC Extended and click the Wall button.

4. You should see the wall parameters. Change the Width to **0′5.0″**; this will define the thickness of the wall. Change the Height to **8′0.0″**; this will define the height of the wall. Change the Justification to **Left**, as shown in Figure 3.6.

FIGURE 3.6 The Wall Parameter dialog box

5. In the top viewport, click and release on an outside corner of the AutoCAD drawing, and then move to a connected corner and click to set the position of that corner. This will create a wall 0′5″ thick and 8′0″ tall between the two corners you clicked. Continue around the room clicking on the wall corners, making sure you snap to the vertex of the lines at each corner. Disregard the doors and windows in the drawing and put your walls right over them. When you have made it all the way around the room, click on the same corner where you started. A pop-up warning will ask if you want to Weld Point. Click Yes and right-click to release the wall primitive. The finished wall is shown in Figure 3.7.

With the wall selected, go to the Modify panel and look at the parameters. In the modifier stack, click on the black box with the plus sign. The wall has three components: Vertex, Segment, and Profile. You can edit a wall primitive in a way similar to how you edit splines. If you want to edit the walls, say to straighten out a wall or extend a wall to make a space bigger, select the Vertex component in the Modify panel. At the corners of the room, you should see small plus signs; select one of these plus signs and move it to adjust that wall.

You can also adjust the wall primitive by changing the height or depth of the wall in the Modify panel by clicking the Segment component. Then click on a wall in your scene. Go to the wall parameters; at the bottom of the rollout, you will see the parameter for changing those settings, as shown in Figure 3.8.

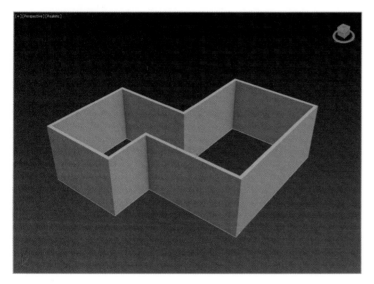

FIGURE 3.7 The finished wall shown in the Perspective viewport

FIGURE 3.8 Wall
parameters for a segment

Now that the walls are laid out, we'll move on to the doors.

Creating the Doors

The 3ds Max AEC door models that are available allow you to control the look of the door—not just size but the frame and glass inserts as well. They also let you determine whether the door is open or closed. The types of door include: Pivot, which is the most common type of door, Bifold, and Sliding. To perform this exercise, you can use your last file from the ArchModel exercise, or you can load

ArchModel01.max from the Scenes folder of the Arch Model project from the book's companion web page at www.sybex.com/go/3dsmax2013essentials.

1. Select the walls if they aren't already selected. Turn on See Through mode in your viewport by clicking Alt+X. The walls will appear slightly transparent with a gray cast, but you will be able to see the AutoCAD drawing underneath.

2. Go to the Create panel. From the Standard Primitive drop-down menu, choose Doors. Choose Pivot under Object Type.

3. Unmaximize the Top viewport, but make sure the Top viewport is active and zoom in to the horizontal door in the AutoCAD drawing.

4. 3D Snaps should still be active. If Snaps are not active go to the main toolbar and select the Snaps toggle ⊞.

5. From the right side of one of the door openings, click and drag to the left side of the opening in the AutoCAD drawing underneath, until it snaps. Then move the cursor and click again to set the door thickness. After that, click and drag the cursor toward the top of the viewport to adjust the door height. You won't be able to see the adjustment in the Top viewport, so you should look in another viewport as you drag to set the height. Click again to set any height; you will set the correct height in the next step.

6. Go to the Modify panel and enter the correct height parameter for the door: **6′8″**, and check Flip Hinge, as shown in Figure 3.9. This will make the door swing into the room.

FIGURE 3.9 The Door object parameters

7. In the main toolbar, select the Link tool () and click from the door to the wall, as shown in Figure 3.10. This will make a doorway opening in the wall.

FIGURE 3.10 Use the Link tool to create an opening in the wall for the door.

The next type of door to be added is the sliding glass door, as shown in Figure 3.1 (right image). In the AutoCAD drawing, the sliding door is the opening labeled as such at the bottom of the image, as shown in Figure 3.4.

8. In the Top viewport, zoom into the sliding door in the AutoCAD drawing.

9. Go to the Create panel. From the Standard Primitive drop-down menu choose Doors. Choose Sliding under Object Type.

10. Start by clicking from the right outside of the door's drawing and then dragging to the left outside of the door's drawing, making sure to snap to the door line in the drawing. This will establish the width of the sliding door. Then move your cursor to the inside of the door drawing and click when your cursor snaps to the line. Next, drag the cursor to set any height. Click to finish, don't worry if you can't get the height correct, just type **6′8″** in the Parameters type-in area, as you did for the first door. Because of the Snap tool, the width and depth of the door will already be correct.

11. Switch to the Perspective viewport and check to see if the sliding door looks correct.

12. Again use the Link tool (🔗) and click from the door to the wall to create the opening in the wall.

13. The finished sliding door is shown in Figure 3.11.

Add the remaining vertical door using the previous steps. This is a good time to save your file. You will create the window in the room in the next exercise.

Creating the Window

AEC Window objects work in a way that is similar to the way the Wall and Door objects work. There are six window types; you will be using the fixed window for this section. You can use your last file from the ArchModel exercise, or you can load ArchModel02.max from the Scenes folder of the ArchModel project from the companion web page to continue.

1. Go to the Create panel. From the Standard Primitive drop-down menu, choose Windows. Choose Fixed under Object Type.

2. Make sure your Snap tool is still active; if it has been turned off, use the keyboard shortcut (S) to toggle it back on.

3. Create the Window object as you did the Door objects. Use the snaps to click and drag from left to right following along the drawing; then click and drag to create the depth and then the height.

4. Use the Link tool and click from the window to the wall to create the opening in the wall, just as with the doors.

5. Press S to turn off Snaps.

6. Switch to a Perspective viewport so you can see the newly created window; then select and move the window up so it is centered on the wall, as shown in Figure 3.12.

7. Select the wall and press Alt+X to turn off See-Through mode. The model to this point is shown in Figure 3.13.

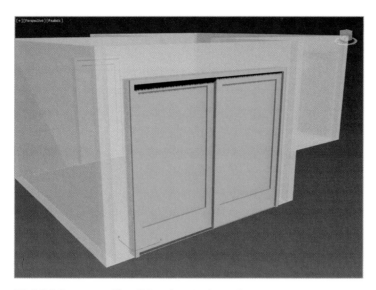

FIGURE 3.11 The sliding door in the wall

FIGURE 3.12 The window is centered on the wall.

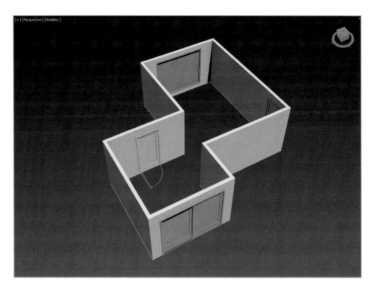

FIGURE 3.13 Walls with doors and a window

Adding a Floor and Ceiling

You can use your last file from the ArchModel exercise, or you can load ArchMode103.max from the Scenes folder of the ArchModel project from the companion web page. What's a room without a floor or ceiling? Not any room we want to walk into. To create the floor and ceiling for your room, you will use the Line tool to create a shape:

1. Go to the Create panel and click the Shapes button (); then click on the Line tool, as shown in Figure 3.14.

FIGURE 3.14 Select the Line tool.

2. Press S on your keyboard to turn on the Snaps tool.

3. In the Top viewport, click a corner of the room, then click the other corners around the room in either direction, and then click again on the corner where you started. The Close Spline pop-up will appear. Click Yes. This closes the line to form a closed shape.

4. Select the line you just created.

5. Go to the Modify panel (![icon]). From the Modify List drop-down menu, choose Extrude, as shown in Figure 3.15.

FIGURE 3.15 From the Modify List drop-down menu, choose Extrude.

6. Now look at the Extrude parameters, change the amount to **0'0.1"**. You just need a small amount of thickness to give to the floor's shape.

7. Switch to the Front viewport and move the new Floor object down so the top of the floor lines up with the bottom of the walls.

8. Name the new object **Floor**.

9. To create the ceiling, you are going to make a clone of the floor. Select the floor, and while holding the Shift key, move the Floor object up toward the top of the wall. When you let go of the mouse, a Clone Options dialog box will appear, as shown in Figure 3.16. Choose Copy from the Object section, rename the object to **Ceiling**, and click OK.

For now, you don't need to have the Ceiling object visible; you will be using it in a later chapter when you light this scene. For now, you can hide the Ceiling object. Center your cursor over the Ceiling object and right-click. From the Quad menu, select Hide Selection, as shown in Figure 3.17. When you are ready to have the ceiling back in your scene you can right-click anywhere in your scene and select Unhide All. You can also choose Unhide By Name to bring up a dialog box with which you can choose a specific item from a list to unhide.

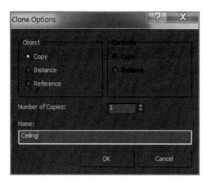

FIGURE 3.16 The Clone Options dialog box

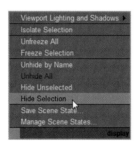

FIGURE 3.17 Use the right-click menu to access the Quad menu and choose Hide Selection from the display section.

Creating Baseboard Moldings

In architectural terminology, a *baseboard* is a board covering the area where the wall meets the floor. Baseboards are used to cover the gap between the wall and the floor, as well as add a sense of style to a room. In this space, there are two types of baseboard molding: one called *quarter round,* a convex molding that has a cross section in the form of an ellipse; and a second one that is a standard shape that is taller and not so round, as shown in Figure 3.18.

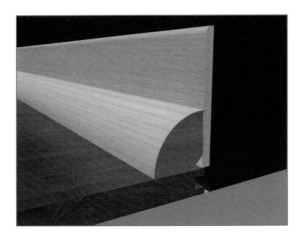

FIGURE 3.18 A cross section of the quarter round
(front) and standard baseboard molding (behind)

This room does not have a baseboard, so it would be a great way to add some
pizzazz to the room. Also, you can add *crown molding* where the top of the wall
meets the ceiling.

Creating the Corner Round Baseboard

You can use your last file from the ArchModel exercise, or you can load
`ArchModel04.max` from the Scenes folder of the ArchModel project from the
book's companion web page at `www.sybex.com/go/3dsmax2013essentials`. To
begin creating the baseboard, you will use the Line tool to create a path that will
show the length of the baseboard in relation to the walls. The baseboard goes all
around the room but stops at the doors.

1. Select and maximize the Top viewport (Alt+W), and then switch to
   render type Wireframe (press F3).

2. Go to the Create panel and click the Shapes button (◨), and then
   click the Line tool.

3. Select the Line tool. Look at the bottom of the interface; the X, Y, Z
   Transform type-in area shows the coordinate location of the tool as
   you move. To start the line in an exact location, watch the coordinates change in the Transform type-in and click on the area at the
   desired coordinate value, as shown in Figure 3.19. The coordinates for
   the first point are X: **−2′5.612″**, Y: **−11′1.981″**, Z: **0′0‴**. Be sure to click
   and release the mouse button to create a corner point. To keep the
   line straight, hold down the Shift key while moving to the next location in the next step.

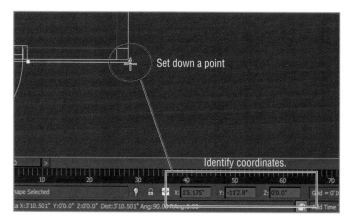

FIGURE 3.19 Set down a point for the line in an exact coordinate location. Watch the Transform type-in area at the bottom of the interface.

4. The next point will be at the coordinates X: **1'5.193"**, Y: **−11'1.981"**, Z: **0'0"**. Continue holding the Shift key and move to the next coordinate location X: **1'5.193"**, Y: **0'9.193"**, Z: **0'0"**. Then move to the next coordinate location, X: **13'2.791"**, Y: **0'9.69"**, Z **0'0"**.

5. The last points coordinates are X: **13'2.791"**, Y: **−13'2.741"**, Z: **0'0"**. Right-click to exit from the Line tool. This should create a line, as shown in red in Figure 3.20.

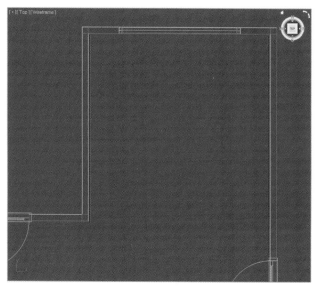

FIGURE 3.20 The red line is the path that will be used for the baseboard.

In the previous section, specific coordinates were given for the line; don't worry if you don't follow these coordinates exactly. You may need to make changes to fit your scene. Most likely it will need to be adjusted, but that will be easier to do after the molding has been created. Now, to create the shape of the molding, start with the corner round, as shown on the left of Figure 3.21 in the following steps.

6. Switch from the Top viewport to the Front viewport (press F).

7. Go to the Create panel and click the Shapes button (▣), and then click on the Circle tool.

8. Create a circle with a radius of 1″. Locate the circle so it is on the ground somewhere to the right of the window; its location is not important as long as you can find it easily.

9. Go to the Modify panel and right-click on the Circle entry in the modifier stack and choose Editable Spline from the list, as shown in Figure 3.22. This will allow you to edit the circle's vertices to reshape.

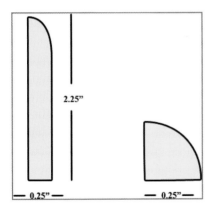

FIGURE 3.21 Profile of the standard (right) and corner round (left) baseboard molding

10. Select Vertex from the Selection rollout. Select the vertex at the bottom of the circle and delete it by pressing the Delete key on your keyboard. Then move the vertex on the left of the circle so it is aligned with the vertex at the top of the circle. Then right-click over that same vertex and choose from the Quad menu ➢ Tools1 ➢ Corner. This will change the vertex from a Bézier with tangent handles to linear lines to create a sharp corner.

11. Select the vertex at the top and right side of the circle, right-click over one of them, and choose from the Quad menu ➢ Tools 1 ➢ Bézier Corner. This will break the handles and allow you to move them independently.

FIGURE 3.22 Convert the circle shape into an editable spline to continue editing its shape.

12. Select the top vertex and adjust the tangent handle so the left side is straight down. Repeat with vertex on the right of the circle. Refer to the right image in Figure 3.21 as a reference for what the shape should look like.

13. Exit Vertex mode by clicking on the Vertex icon in the Selection rollout.

Now you've created the profile shape for the quarter-round molding, next will be the standard shape molding.

Creating the Standard Moldings

Now let's start the standard baseboard shape; it is shown in Figure 3.20 on the right side. The shape is very similar to the corner round but taller and flatter. This time you will start with a different shape.

1. Go to the Create panel and click the Shapes button (![icon]); then click on the Rectangle tool. Right next to the corner-round shape in the Front viewport, create a rectangle with these parameters: Length: **2.25"** and Width: **0.25"**.

2. Go to the Modify panel, and right-click on the Rectangle in the modify stack and choose Editable Spline from the list. Select Vertex from the Selection rollout.

3. Select and move the vertex at the top right of the rectangle down a bit, and then adjust the left tangent so it is pointing up. This should give a nice curve to that side of the rectangle. You should have the two profile shapes looking as shown in Figure 3.23.

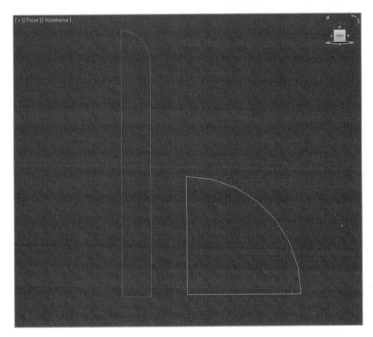

FIGURE 3.23 Standard and corner round shapes

4. Minimize your viewport so you can have the four views back (Alt+W).

5. Move the two profile shapes so you can see them, as well as the start of the baseboard line you created around the walls earlier in preceding section.

6. Select the baseboard line that goes around the walls. Go to the Create menu ➢ Compound Object ➢ Loft, and in the parameters, under the Creation Method rollout, click the Get Shape button.

7. Click on the corner round's profile shape. An extruded geometry will be created out from the corner-round profile shape. This is a loft object, as shown in Figure 3.24.

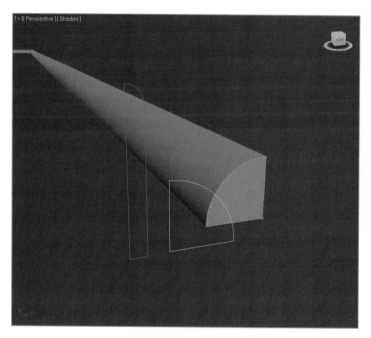

FIGURE 3.24 The corner-round baseboard loft object

8. Select the baseboard line again and repeat steps 6 and 7, making sure to select the standard profile shape this time, to create the standard baseboard geometry.

These loft objects will need to be moved into their proper places. This cannot be done by just selecting and moving them. The separate segments of the loft need to be adjusted to the wall. The first thing is to edit the shapes on the loft objects.

1. Select the standard baseboard loft object. Go to the Modify panel and in the modifier stack, click on the small black box with the plus sign and select Shape. Then on the loft object, select the profile shape at the end of the loft. When it is selected, the edges will turn red. This will allow you to edit the shape directly on the loft object.

2. Move the loft shape so its back side is up against the wall and the bottom is against the floor. Use whichever viewports you need to do this and don't worry if the Corner-Round Baseboard object is in the way; hide it if necessary. It will be moved next. When it looks correct, click again on Loft in the modify stack to exit that loft/shape.

3. Rename the loft to **Molding Standard**.

4. Repeat steps 1 and 2 on the Corner-Round object to place it correctly up against the standard molding. When finished, rename to **Molding Corner Round**. The color is set to a neutral gray for now; the final moldings are shown in Figure 3.25.

FIGURE 3.25 The finished baseboard molding

You can continue with the steps in this section to create baseboard moldings for the entire room. Now that you have built the room from the AutoCAD drawing, you will fill the room with furniture to create an interior design visualization of the room in the following chapter.

THE ESSENTIALS AND BEYOND

In this chapter, you learned how to use some of the 3ds Max architectural tools. You started by importing an AutoCAD drawing and using it to create the walls, doors, and windows of a room. You explored some previously used tools and used some new ones, such as loft to create baseboards to flesh out the design of the room.

ADDITIONAL EXERCISES

▶ Try importing different AutoCAD drawings and creating your own space. You can find free AutoCAD drawing on many websites.

▶ Complete the room by adding the baseboard molding all around the room.

▶ Try creating a different profile for the molding. Go to websites that show molding profiles or just make up your own.

▶ Create crown molding; this type of molding sits at the top of the wall and rests on the ceiling.

▶ Use some of the other AEC primitives; add a different type of window or door.

CHAPTER 4

Modeling in 3ds Max: Architectural Model Part II

In this chapter, you will continue working with the interior space from the previous chapter by modeling and adding some furniture—specifically, a couch and chair.

Topics in this chapter include:

▶ **Modeling the couch**

▶ **Modeling the chair**

Modeling the Couch

When you are starting a modeling project, make sure you have plenty of measurements, as shown in Figure 4.1's photo of the couch you'll model in this chapter. Always remember: reference, reference, reference. Modeling this couch is a very straightforward process. If you break it down into separate components, it is just 16 different sized boxes. The boxes are soft and cushy; they have various details, but nonetheless they are still just boxes. With the exception of the lounge end of the couch, the top cushion is the only piece on the couch that isn't a box shape.

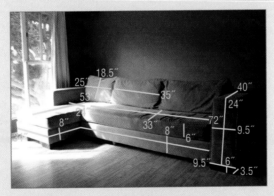

FIGURE 4.1 Couch with measurements

Blocking Out the Couch Model

Blocking out the model means creating a simpler version of the model starting with whatever primitives fit the bill—in this case, boxes. Using the measurements shown in Figure 4.1, you will create a series of boxes and then orient them to mimic the couch. The first piece you'll create is the bottom (the part between the seat cushions and the feet). Its measurements are 8-inches high by 72-inches wide by 31.5-inches deep. In the previous chapter, you used standard units of measurement (feet and inches); but for this chapter, you will use the default Generic units. If your Units are still set to feet and inches, refer to Chapter 3, "Modeling in 3ds Max: Architectural Model Part I," under "Units Setup" at the beginning of the chapter, to review how to change it to Generic Units.

1. In a new 3ds Max® file, select the Perspective viewport, and then go to the Command panel and choose Create ➢ Geometry, and click on Box. In the Keyboard Entry rollout, enter Length: 33, Width: 72, and Height: 8, but don't change the XYZ type-ins. Then click on the Create button. The box should be in the center of the scene.

2. Next, create the cushion above this box. Select the box with the Move tool, and then hold Shift and move the box up in the Z-axis to create a new box so that it is on top of the old box. This is a quick method you can use to clone an object. The Clone Options dialog box will appear, as shown in Figure 4.2.

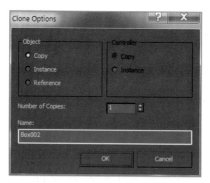

FIGURE 4.2 In the Clone Option dialog box, select Copy and click OK.

3. In the Clone Options dialog, select Copy and click OK. Go to the Modify panel and change the Height of the new cushion box to 6.0.

4. As in step 1, create another box, but change the parameters to Length: 40, Width: 9.5, and Height: 24. This becomes the Side Armrest object. Move the box so it sits on the right side of the two stacked boxes. Create a clone for the left side of the couch using the same Move and Shift technique in the steps 2 through 3.

Now for the back piece, this is the part the back cushions sit on. We don't see it in the picture in Figure 4.1, but it is there.

5. Create a box with the measurements Length: 6, Width: 96, and Height: 27, and then move it behind the seat-cushion boxes to form the backrest, as shown in Figure 4.3 (left). Don't worry if the boxes don't fit together like a puzzle; just get them close.

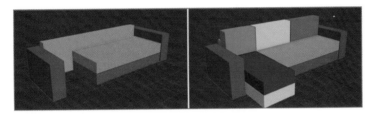

FIGURE 4.3 The first few pieces to start the couch (left); The blocked-out couch (right)

Creating the chaise part of the couch is a bit more challenging. You'll create a box now, and later you can alter it with the wing on the side.

6. Select the Perspective viewport. In the Keyboard Entry rollout, input the measurements Length: 53, Width: 24, and Height: 8, and click the Create button. Move the new box to the left of the seat cushions. Hold Shift and move the new box up so it is sitting on the old box, and choose Copy from the dialog window. In a similar fashion, use Move and the Shift key to make a copy of the couch's side armrest box and move it to the left side of the couch.

7. Create another box with the measurements Length: 8, Width: 35, and Height: 18.5. Click the Create button to create a box for the back pillows. Move the box so that it is sitting on the top of the seat cushions and against the right armrest. Make a clone of this box and move it to the left, so it is next to the other pillow. Make one more clone, and move it to the left so it sits on top of the chaise seat cushions. This box is too big. With the box selected, go to the Modify panel and change the Width to 24.0. The completed blocked-out couch is shown in Figure 4.3 (right).

This process is getting a bit tedious, but you still need to create the backrest cushions. Refer to Figure 4. 1 for the measurements you'll need. There should be three backrest cushions (two the same size and one that is smaller). Move them into place on the couch to finish blocking out of the couch, as shown in Figure 4.3. As you are creating the couch pieces, name them. Use descriptive names to help you keep the project organized.

Once you begin adding more detail to the couch pieces, you'll have to make some adjustments to them by resizing and repositioning them.

Using NURMS to Add Softness

Non-Uniform Rational Mesh Smooth (NURMS) is a subdivision surface technique that allows you to take a low-poly model and smooth the surface into a high-poly model. This isn't a lighting trick; you are actually changing the geometry of the model. When you apply NURMS to your model, you will see a control cage in the shape of the low-poly model; this is the mesh you actually model. Subdivision increases the poly count of your model; every level of subdivision increases the number of polygons by a factor of four. At a subdivision level (or iteration) of 1, one polygon in the control cage will become four polygons in the subdivided model. At an iteration level of 2, that one polygon becomes 16 polygons, and so on. When you're working on a model with NURMS, it is best to work with a lower iteration level and then render with a higher level of iterations. Be cautious; poly counts rise very quickly and an iteration count needlessly high can slow you down.

Polygons are flat between the vertices, but when NURMS is turned on, a flat polygon starts to curve and smooth out as it subdivides. When you use NURMS smoothing, the more distance there is between the edges on a mesh, the smoother the result will be. When you want sharp corners, just place the edges close together. When you turning on NURMS, those close edges will retain their sharpness better. If you want a smoother, more rounded surface, then place the edges farther apart.

The best way to model with smooth surfaces is to use quad polygons in a grid formation; two splines will cross each vertex—and because each spline flows from vertex to vertex uninterrupted, the splines will continue and the 3d form will be smoothed predictably. If you have a vertex with more or less than four edges coming out of it, the splines will end and the mesh may not smooth the way you expect it to. If you want to fully understand the concept of splines flowing and ending across a 3D surface as a result of subdivision leads, spend some time studying topology, which is key to creating good 3D models that subdivide well when animated.

Many of the couch cushions will receive the same treatment, so let's go over the next technique using only the side armrest of the couch and the chaise lounge section. After you're finished with that, you can practice the techniques on the remaining couch boxes yourself. Continue with the project from the previous exercise or open the Couch_01.max file from the Scenes folder of the Arch Model project from the companion web page.

1. Select the Right Armrest object. Right-click on it, and from the Quad menu, select Isolate Selection. This turns off the view of the other objects in the scene to allow you to focus on this one piece. Set the rendering type to Edge Faces (F4).

2. In the Graphite Modeling Tools ribbon, select Polygon Modeling ➤ Convert to Poly. Then choose the Edit tab and click on Use NURMS (◨). You will see a box that looks like the air was let out of it, as shown in Figure 4.4.

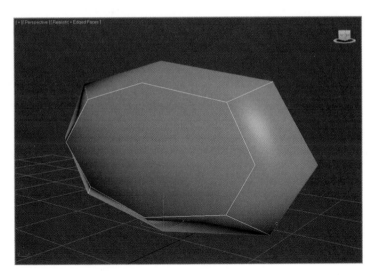

FIGURE 4.4 Couch side arm with NURMS applied

If you refer to the picture of the arm of the couch from Figure 4.1, you'll see that the arm is much more structured and closer to the shape of a box than this deflated balloon. You still need to sharpen the corners by adding more edges to the base model.

3. Back in the Graphite Modeling Tools ribbon, select the Edit tab and click the Use NURMS button again to turn it off. Editing the box is easier at this stage while it is still in box form.

4. In the Edit tab, click on the SwiftLoop tool and hover your cursor over the box to reveal a loop of edges on the box. Place one of the lines shown in Figure 4.5 by clicking where you want the loop to be added on the box. Place the other three loops shown in Figure 4.5.

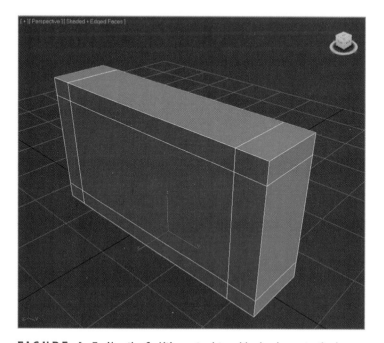

FIGURE 4.5 Use the SwiftLoop tool to add edge loops to the box.

5. Turn on NURMS again to see the difference with the SwiftLoop. If you refer to the reference picture of the arm in Figure 4.1, you can see that the couch arm is even more squared off than the current mesh. In the next section, you will how to add more detail.

Adding Details to the Couch

The next step in the process of creating the couch is to add the *piping,* which is the round decorative trim along the seam of the pillows, as shown in Figure 4.6.

1. In the Graphite Modeling Tools ribbon, select Polygon Modeling and click on Edge mode. Select the edges on the box that are identified in Figure 4.7.

2. Go to the Edges tab, and open the Chamfer Settings caddy. Change Edge Chamfer Amount to **0.15** and click OK.

FIGURE 4.6 Decorative piping runs along the seams of the couch.

Select these edges on both sides of the box.

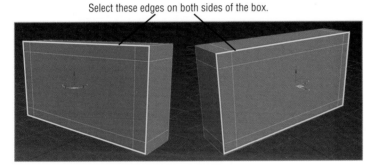

FIGURE 4.7 Select the highlighted edges.

3. Switch to Polygon mode and select the polygons that were created with the Chamfer.

4. In the Graphite Modeling Tools ribbon, go to the Polygons tab and choose Extrude.

5. Change the Extrusion type to Local Normal, as shown in Figure 4.8.

FIGURE 4.8 Set the Extrusion Type to Local Normal.

6. Set the Extrusion Height to –0.2 and select Apply and Continue
   (⊕). This will keep the caddy open and allow you to perform
   another Extrude.

7. Change the Extrusion Height to 0.3.

8. Go to the Edit tab and select Use NURMS (▦).

The couch looks pretty good, but if you look closely you can see that it is
still very choppy around the corners. The NURMS iterations need to be turned
up. When you turn on Use NURMS, a Use NURMS tab appears in the Graphite
Modeling Tools ribbon (sometimes a floating window will appear instead). In the
Use NURMS tab, turn the Iterations up to 2. The finished product looks pretty
good, as shown in Figure 4.9.

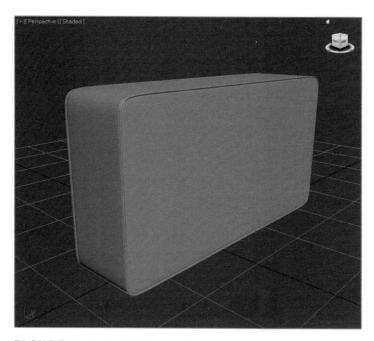

FIGURE 4.9 The finished couch arm

Now it is time to perform the same piping detail on all the remaining couch
pieces except the chaise pieces. The seat cushion and three back cushions need
to have piping just like the couch arm, so you need to repeat steps 1 through 8
for the cushions. The seat base and couch back don't have any piping so they just
need to be smoothed using NURMS. Make sure to add edge loops at the corners to

create the right amount of smoothing and detail. Play around with the settings to match the reference model as much as possible. Finally, you can select vertices and polygons and move them around to give the surfaces a more random and organic or "lived-in" appearance. In Figure 4.10, everything but the chaise lounge part of the couch was finished using NURMS with an iteration level of 2.

FIGURE 4.10 Finished pieces of the couch

The Chaise Lounge

The chaise lounge isn't that much different from the rest of the couch. It just has a wing section that comes out from the side, as shown in Figure 4.11. Continue with your own couch file or load Couch_02.max from the Scenes folder of the Arch Model project from the companion web page at www.sybex.com/go/3dsmax2013essentials.

1. Select the chaise cushion box (the one on top). In the Graphite Modeling Tools ribbon, select Polygon Modeling ➢ Convert to Poly.

2. In the Edit tab, select SwiftLoop and place a new edge loop on the box, as shown in Figure 4.12.

FIGURE 4.11 The chaise lounge section of the couch

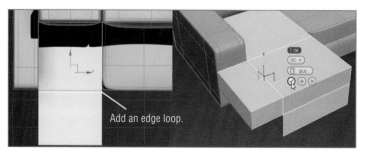

FIGURE 4.12 Use SwiftLoop to add an edge loop in the area shown in this top view of the chase cushion box.

3. Swing your view around to see the left side of the couch. Enter Poly mode and select the polygon on the left side where you placed the edge loop, and from the Polygons tab, select Extrude settings, set the Extrude amount to **10.0**, and click OK, as shown in Figure 4.12.

4. Repeat steps 1 through 3 for the base of the chaise section of the couch.

Now that you have completed the chaise lounge section of the couch, you just have to add the finishing touches. Repeat the same steps you performed to smooth out the meshes using NURMS, add the piping detail at the edges, and move some vertices around to give the cushion a lived-in look.

Creating the Couch Feet

The final pieces you need to create for the couch are the feet. The feet are all the same, so you just need to create one foot and copy it for the other three. In Figure 4.13, look at the feet and note that they are a box shape that is thinner on the bottom. Continue with your own couch file or load the Couch_03.max from the Scenes folder of the Arch Model project from the companion web page.

1. Go to the Command panel's Create panel, and select Geometry and click on Box. Click and drag in the Perspective viewport to create a box that will be the first foot.

2. Then go to the Command panel's Modify panel, and enter Length: 4.0, Width: 9.5, and Height: 3.0 parameters. In the Modify panel, click on the modify list to expand an alphabetical list of modifiers. From that list, choose Taper.

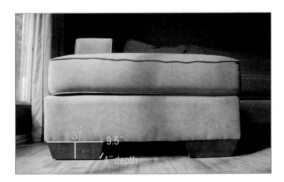

FIGURE 4.13 The couch feet with measurements

A *modifier* changes the geometric structure of a model and a Taper modifier will move the vertices near the end closer together. Using a Taper modifier is an easy way to make simple changes to your model.

3. When the Taper is applied, nothing will happen to your model until you change the Taper parameters. Change the Amount to 0.15, as shown in Figure 4.14.

4. Now move the couch foot into place under one of the corners of the couch. Use the clone operation (hold down the Shift key while you move the foot) to make duplicates of the foot and place them around the bottom of the couch at the remaining corners.

5. Take the time to select each couch foot box and rename it; use a simple naming convention such as Couch Feet01, 02, 03, etc.

FIGURE 4.14
The Taper parameters

Now that the couch is finished, as shown in Figure 4.15, it should resemble the original couch, but perhaps without the lived-in look and feel the real couch has. You can create some of that look by moving vertices and polygons around so that it does not look quite so perfect.

FIGURE 4.15 The final couch

Modeling the Chair

To model the chair, you'll be taking a different approach. You'll use a spline technique that the 3ds Max software is particularly good at. If you are used to Maya CV curves, the Bezier will seem a bit awkward; but if you are used to Photoshop's Pen tool, then the 3ds Max Line tools way of making lines should be pretty easy. It isn't just the way you make the lines that makes the 3ds Max tools so nice; it's also the tools you use to make the lines into 3D objects.

Figure 4.16 shows the chair that will be modeled in this section. After saving the previous exercise's file, click on the Applications button and choose Reset from the list that appears. This will set your interface and file back to a startup state. Start a new 3ds Max file.

FIGURE 4.16 The chair for the spline modeling exercise

Adding a Viewport Background Image

Placing an image into the viewport's background allows you to use that image as a modeling reference. Figure 4.17 show the chair with the measurements.

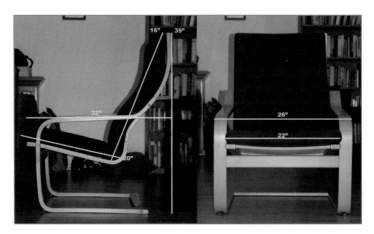

FIGURE 4.17 The chair with its measurements

1. Click once in the Left viewport to select it. Select Alt+B to open the Viewport Configuration dialog box already set to the Background tab, and choose the Use Files option.

2. Under Setup, check Lock Zoom/Pan to link the image you'll import to the viewport zoom.

3. In Aspect Ratio, select Match Bitmap to prevent the image from being distorted.

4. Click the Files button and navigate to the ScenesAssets/Images folder of the Arch Model project that you can download from the companion web page. Select SplineChair_SideView.tif and click OK in the dialog box.

   The image will appear in the viewport, but you won't be able to move it around or see it in any other views. Before you go any further, you need to consider the scale of the image because it will affect the scale of chair. It makes sense to build the chair to a human scale.

5. Zoom out in the Left viewport until the image fits into the viewport.

6. Then enter the Viewport Background dialog box again (Alt+X) and check the Lock Zoom/Pan to turn it off. Click OK, as shown in Figure 4.18.

7. Zoom out again in the Left viewport. The image stays put while the home grid moves. Each grid square equals 10 inches, and the chair has a 39-inch height and 32-inch width. As such, zoom out from the grid until the height of the chair has about four grid squares and the width should take care of itself.

Repeat the same steps for the Front viewport, so that you have a front-view image in the Front viewport, and instead use the SplineChair_FrontView.tif image file in the ScenesAssets/Images folder of the Arch Model project, as shown in Figure 4.19.

FIGURE 4.18 The Viewport Background dialog box

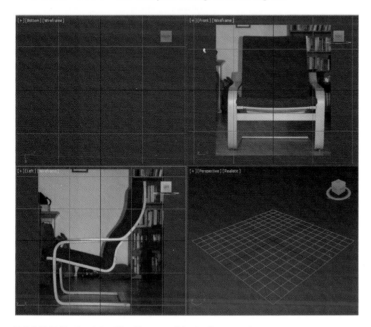

FIGURE 4.19 The Front and Left viewport images

Building the Splines for the Chair Frame

Now it's time to create the splines using the following steps:

1. Start by maximizing the Left viewport (Alt+W).

2. Click on the Command panel and select Create ➢ Shapes (⊞), and then select the Line tool. You will use the Line tool to create a spline that follows the side view of the chair.

3. Start the spline at the bottom of the image of the chair (at point 1 in Figure 4.20), click and let go of the mouse button to create a corner point. Move your mouse to the left, and click and let go to make another corner point at the part of the chair that curves up (2). Move up to the next curve in the frame and create another corner point (3). Continue right and make another point on the curve at the top of the arm rest (4), but this time click on the center of the curve and drag the mouse to create a nice curve in the spline. End the line at the top of the chair (5) by clicking and releasing the button, and then right-click to exit the Line tool.

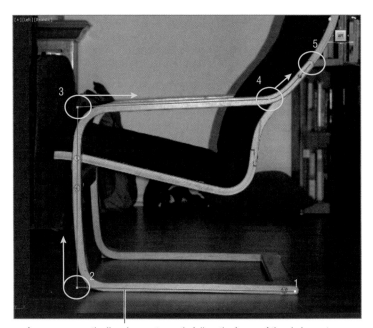

As you can see, the line does not exactly follow the frame of the chair—yet.

FIGURE 4.20 Create vertex points by following the numbers.

4. In the Modify panel, select Modifier Stack and enter Vertex mode.

5. Select the two vertices on the left, as shown in Figure 4.21.

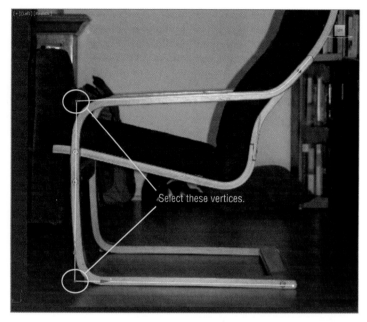

FIGURE 4.21 Select the two vertices on the left side of the chair frame.

6. In the Modify panel, in the Geometry rollout, locate the Fillet tool and use a Fillet value of 3.0 in the type-in box, as shown in Figure 4.22. This will take the single vertex and split it into two to curve the line between the new vertices.

FIGURE 4.22
Use the Fillet tool
to create a curve
between the new
vertices.

7. Switch to the Move tool (W) and select the spline. Then, in the Front viewport, move the spline so it lines up with one of the arms of the chair.

8. Make a clone by holding Shift+Move and aligning the spline to the other chair arm. When the Clone dialogs pops up, select Copy and then select OK.

Now, these two splines need to be attached to form a single spline. This will allow you to create the bridge piece that runs along the bottom of the frame.

9. With either spline selected, go to the Geometry rollout, click the Attach button, and then click on the other spline.

10. Enter Vertex mode if you are not already in it. In the Geometry rollout, click the Connect button.

11. In the Perspective view, rotate the viewport so you can see both splines. Click and drag from one vertex to the other, as shown in Figure 4.23.

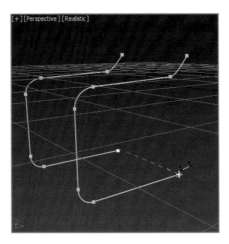

FIGURE 4.23 Use Connect to create a line between the two separate splines.

The 3ds Max software has a very cool function you can use to create a shape along a path. The splines you just created are the paths. In the parameters of the editable spline, there is a rollout called Rendering. The controls let you turn on and off the renderability of the spline and specify its thickness in a render of the scene. Once you enable the function, the mesh can be seen in the viewport and will show when rendered. The default 3d mesh that is enabled is a radial mesh, which would make a pipe of sorts, but there is also a rectangular mesh, and both shapes have parameters that can be edited.

12. With the splines selected, go to the Rendering rollout and check the boxes for Enable In Viewport and Enable In Renderer.

13. Select Rectangular and change the Length to **2.5** and the Width to **1.0**, as shown in Figure 4.24.

FIGURE 4.24
The Rendering parameters for the chair frame

Click on the Render button in the main toolbar (■) to see the results of the spline rendering, as shown in Figure 4.25.

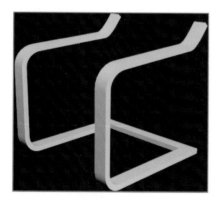

FIGURE 4.25 The rectangular mesh enabled

You can create the remaining parts of the frame, the seat and back, using the same technique. Using the viewport images, follow the same steps to create the rest of the chair frame. Continue with your chair file or load the SplineChair_ Start.max from the Scenes folder of the Arch Model project from the companion web page. This file has the completed seat/back frame, as shown in Figure 4.26.

FIGURE 4.26 The seat and back frame are attached and connected at the base and top.

Creating the Chair Cushion

For the chair cushion, you can't use the same spline technique you used on the frame. To create it, you have to return to the same technique you used for the couch: Create a simple box representation and then use NURMS to soften it up.

1. In a new 3ds Max file, go to the Command panel, select Create ➢ Geometry and click on Box. In the Box parameters, click on the Keyboard type-in rollout and enter Length: **3.0**, Width: **20.0**, and Height: **20.0**. Don't change the XYZ type-ins. Then click the Create button.

2. Select Alt+Q to enter Isolate Selection mode.

3. In the Graphite Modeling Tools ribbon, select Polygon Modeling ➢ Convert to Poly.

4. In the Edit tab, select SwiftLoop (⊕). Place an edge loop about three units from the bottom of the box, as shown in Figure 4.27.

5. Switch to Polygon mode (press 4); select the newly created polygon on the front face only.

6. In the Polygon tab, select the Extrude Settings box to bring up the caddy. Enter **20** units for the Height and click OK, as shown in Figure 4.28.

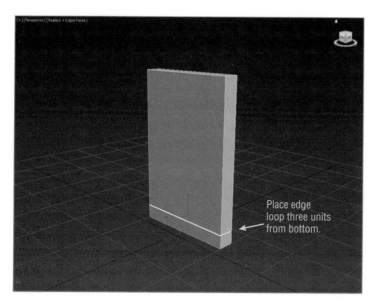

FIGURE 4.27 Using SwiftLoop, place an edge loop three units from the bottom of the box.

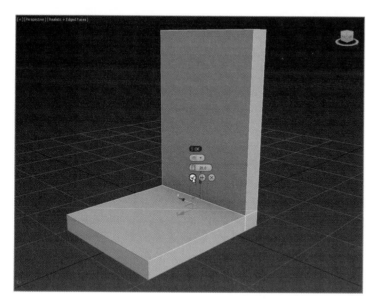

FIGURE 4.28 Extrude the poly 20 units in height.

7. In the Edit tab, select the SwiftLoop again, and place edge loops along the top and bottom edges, as well as along the left and right edges. This will keep the outer edges from curving in too much to keep its box shape.

8. Add two more edge loops at the top and bottom of the joint, as shown in Figure 4.29.

9. Go back to the Edit tab, and turn on Use NURMS.

10. Exit Isolate Selection mode (Alt+Q), and move and rotate the box to align it with the chair frame. It isn't going to match the frame until you edit the cushion a bit more.

11. In the Edit tab, select Use NURMS to turn it off.

12. Enter Edge mode (press 2) and select the edge above the joint. Hold Control and click (Ctrl+click) on a segment of the edge, and then hold Shift+click on another edge. This is a shortcut for selecting a loop of edges the long way (Graphite Modeling tool ➢ Selection tab ➢ Loop).

13. Once the edge is selected, move it up to where the lower curve is in the chair frame, and move it out to match the curve, as shown in Figure 4.30.

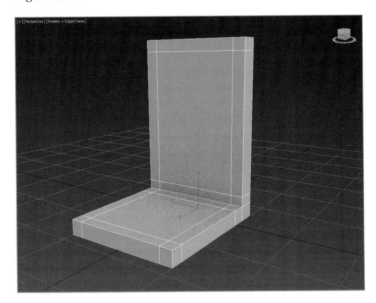

FIGURE 4.29 Seat cushion box with the SwiftLoops added

14. Add another SwiftLoop where the curve in the frame is toward the top, and then select and move that edge back to match the curvature in the frame.

15. Select and move the topmost edges; move and rotate them to match the frame. Turn on Use NURMS. Continue selecting, moving, and rotating edges until they are lined up with the chair frame.

FIGURE 4.30 Select the edge loop on the seat cushion box, and move up and out to match the curve in the chair frame.

To finish things off, add a few extra edges very close to the joint. Then on the back side, move those edges farther away from each other, but keep the edges on the front of the joint very close to each other, as shown in Figure 4.31. This creates a sort of crease because the edges are so close together.

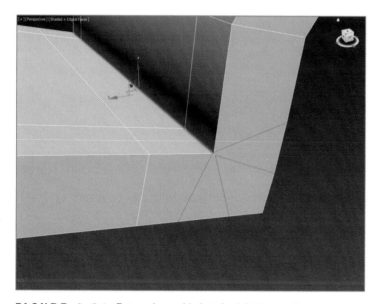

FIGURE 4.31 Extra edges added at the joint to create a crease.

Turn on Use NURMS, go to the Use NURMS tab and turn the Iterations up to 2. This will add more subdivisions and move the cushion. Finally, select the frame and change the color to brown, as shown in Figure 4.32. Take the time to select each object and name it accordingly: **Chair Cushion**, **Chair Frame Arms-Feet**, and **Chair Frame Seat-Back**.

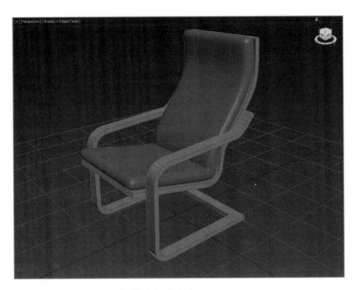

FIGURE 4.32 The finished chair

Bringing It All Together

Now that the furniture is built, it's time to furnish the room you built in the last chapter. You can do this by merging the furniture .max files into the room file. Merge allows you to load objects from one .max file into your current file. From the Scenes folder of the Arch Model project folder from the companion web page, open the ArchModel_Final.max file. This is the file that you completed in Chapter 3.

1. In the ArchModel_Final.max project file, click the Applications button (⊘) and select Import ➢ Merge.

2. When the Explore window opens, navigate to the Arch Model project folder, and find the spline chair and couch that were built earlier in this chapter. Select the Couch_03.max file and select Open.

3. The Merge dialog box will open, and you will see a list of objects available to merge from that file. At the bottom of the dialog box, select All, as shown in Figure 4.33, and click OK.

FIGURE 4.33 In the Merge dialog box, select All and click OK.

4. Merged objects come into a scene already selected. They always merge into a scene at the same X-, Y-, Z- coordinates they were at in their original file. If you click the Zoom Extends All Selected button located at the lower-right corner (▣), this will zoom in on the already selected couch objects.

5. Go to the Group menu and select Group. Name the Group **Couch** and click OK.

Grouping lets you combine objects into a group. A group uses something like an invisible carrying case, called a *dummy object,* to hold your objects. Select the group and move it around, and the objects will move along with it. A group has its own pivot point. You can transform and modify a group as if it were a single object. If you want to modify an individual object in the group, go to the Group menu and choose Open. A pink bracket will appear. The objects can be individually selected and modified inside the group. When you are finished and want to close the group, choose Group ➤ Close. Groups can also be nested, meaning you can have a group within a group. When you want to dissolve a group, just select the group and in the Group menu and choose Ungroup.

6. Move the couch to the right wall in the room. Check the images of the room for couch location (reference Figure 4.1 from the beginning of the chapter). Check the Front and Left viewports to make sure that the couch is level with the floor.

7. Repeat the steps 1 through 6 to merge in and place the spline chair using the file SplineChair_Final.max.

These two pieces of furniture look great, but they don't fill up the room very much. To help furnish your newly built room, you can merge some prebuilt items into the space to give it a more lived-in look. Repeat steps 1 through 6 for the extra furniture pieces, which can be found in the Chapter 04 Extra Furniture folder in the Scenes folder of the Arch Model project. The room will look better after you merge the objects, as shown in Figure 4.34. The next phase for you may be to create some of your own objects to populate the room.

FIGURE 4.34   The room with all the merged furniture

THE ESSENTIALS AND BEYOND

In this chapter, you took a closer look at many of the modeling tools you had already used in Chapter 2 when you made the dresser. The Graphite Modeling tool is a staple in the model-building arsenal. The two new main tools you looked at in this chapter were the NURMS tool and the Line tool. Both are very powerful tools that can give you a lot of flexibility when modeling complex pieces.

ADDITIONAL EXERCISES

▶ Create more furniture. To start, choose a piece that resembles the ones you've already created. Create another chair or table with a frame similar to the chair you completed in the chapter. Create some tables and chairs that feature chrome or stainless steel tube frames or create any style of cushy chair.

▶ Try to use some of the other Spline tools from previous chapters to create picture frames (Chapter 3, floor molding), lamps and vases (Chapter 2, dresser knobs), and maybe a side table or more chairs.

CHAPTER 5

Animating a Bouncing Ball

The best way to learn how to animate is to jump right in and start animating. By doing so, you'll take a good look at the 3ds Max® animation tools so you can start editing animation and developing your timing skills.

Topics in this chapter include the following:

▶ **Animating the ball**

▶ **Refining the animation**

A classic exercise for all animators is to create a bouncing ball. It is a straightforward exercise, but there is much you can do with a bouncing ball to show character. Animating a bouncing ball is a good exercise in physics as well as cartoon movement. You'll first create a rubber ball, and then you'll add cartoonish movement to accentuate some principles of the animation. Aspiring animators can use this exercise for years and always find something new to learn about bouncing a ball.

In preparation, download the Bouncing Ball project from the companion web page at www.sybex.com/go/3dsmax2013essentials to your hard drive. Set your current project by choosing Application ➢ Manage ➢ Set Project Folder and selecting the Bouncing Ball project that you downloaded.

Animating the Ball

Your first step is to keyframe the positions of the ball. As you learned in Chapter 1, "The 3ds Max Interface," *keyframing* is the process—borrowed from traditional animation—of setting positions and values at particular frames of the animation. The computer interpolates between these keyframes to fill in the other frames to complete a smooth animation.

Open the Animation_Ball_00.max scene file from the Scenes folder of the Bouncing Ball project you downloaded. If you receive a warning to Disable Gamma/LUT, click OK.

Start with the *gross animation,* or the overall movements. This is also called *blocking.* First, move the ball up and down to begin its choreography.

Follow these steps to animate the ball:

1. Move the pivot point for the ball from the center of the ball to the bottom of the ball. Select the ball, and then go to the Hierarchy panel (▦). Choose Pivot, and under the Adjust Pivot rollout, click the Affect Pivot Only button. Zoom in on the ball in the Front viewport and move the pivot so that it is at the bottom of the ball. Then click the Affect Pivot Only button again to deactivate—but you already knew that.

2. Move the Time slider to frame 10. The Time slider is at the bottom of the screen below the viewports, as shown in Figure 5.1. The Time slider is used to change your position in time, counted in *frames*.

FIGURE 5.1 The Time slider allows you to change your position in time and scrub your animation.

SCRUBBING THE TIME SLIDER

You can click and drag the horizontal Time slider bar to change the frame in your animation on the fly; this is called *scrubbing*. The bar displays the current frame/end frame. By default, your 3ds Max window may show a start frame of 0 and an end frame of 100.

3. Now, in the lower-right corner of the window, click the Auto Key button, as shown in Figure 5.2. Both the Auto Key button and the Time slider turn red. This means that any movement in the objects in your scene will be recorded as animation. How exciting!

FIGURE 5.2
The Auto Key
button records your
animations.

4. With the ball selected, move it along the Z-axis down to the ground plane, so it is 0 units in Z-axis when you release the mouse button in the Transform type-in box at the bottom of the interface. You can also just enter the value and press Enter.

This exercise has created two keyframes, one at frame 0 for the original position the ball was in, and one at frame 10 for the new position to which you just moved the ball.

Copying Keyframes

Now you want to move the ball up to the same position in the air as it was at frame 0. Instead of trying to estimate where that was, you can just copy the keyframe at frame 0 to frame 20.

You can see the keyframes you created in the timeline; they appear as red boxes. Red keys represent Position keyframes, green keys represent Rotation, and blue keys represent Scale. When a keyframe in the timeline is selected, it turns white. Now let's copy a keyframe:

1. Select the keyframe at frame 0; it should turn white when it is selected. Hold down the Shift key on the keyboard (this is a shortcut for the Clone tool), and click and drag the selected keyframe to copy it to frame 20. This will create a keyframe with the same animation parameters as the keyframe at frame 0, as shown in Figure 5.3.

FIGURE 5.3 Press Shift and move the keyframe to copy it to frame 20.

2. Click and drag the Time slider to scrub through the keyframes. Turn off Auto Key.

Once you copy keyframes if for any reason you want to change their parameters, you can access keyframe values in the timeline. Just right-click directly on the keyframe and a popup menu will appear. Choose from the menu what track you want to modify; you will get a type-in dialog to edit keyframe value.

Using the Track View–Curve Editor

Right now the ball is going down and then back up. To continue the animation for the length of the timeline, you could continue to copy and paste keyframes as you did earlier—but that would be very time-consuming, and you still need to do your other homework and clean your room. A better way is to loop, or *cycle*, through the keyframes you already have. An *animation cycle* is a segment of animation that is repeatable in a loop. The end state of the animation matches up to the beginning state, so there is no hiccup at the loop point.

In 3ds Max terminology, cycling animation is known as *parameter curve out-of-range types*. This is a fancy way to create loops and cycles with your animations and specify how your object will behave outside the range of the keys you have created. This will bring us to the Track View, which is an animator's best friend. You will learn the underlying concepts of the Curve Editor as well as its basic interface throughout this exercise.

The Track View is a function of two animation editors, the Curve Editor and the Dope Sheet. The Curve Editor allows you to work with animation depicted as curves on a graph that sets the value of a parameter against time. The Dope Sheet displays keyframes over time on a horizontal graph, without any curves. This graphical display simplifies the process of adjusting animation timing because you can see all the keys at once in a spreadsheet-like format. The Dope Sheet is similar to traditional animation exposure sheets, or X-sheets.

You will use the Track View – Curve Editor (or just the Curve Editor for short) to loop your animation in the following steps:

▶

Navigation inside the Track View – Curve Editor is pretty much the same as navigating in a viewport; the same keyboard/mouse combinations work for panning and zooming.

1. With the ball selected, in the menu bar choose Graph Editors ➢ Track View – Curve Editor. In Figure 5.4, the Curve Editor displays the animation curves of the ball so far.

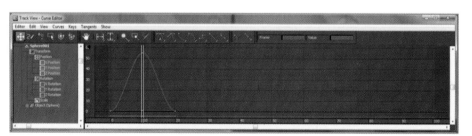

FIGURE 5.4 The Curve Editor shows the animation curves of the ball.

2. A menu bar runs across the top of the Curve Editor. In the Controller menu, select the Out-of-Range Types option, as shown in Figure 5.5.

FIGURE 5.5 Selecting Out-of-Range Types

3. Doing so opens the Param Curve Out-of-Range Types dialog box, shown in Figure 5.6. Select Loop in this dialog box by clicking its thumbnail. The two little boxes beneath it will highlight. Click OK.

4. Once you set the curve to Loop, the Curve Editor displays your animation, as shown in Figure 5.7. The out-of-range animation is shown as a dashed line. Scrub your animation in a viewport and see how the ball bounces up and down throughout the timeline range.

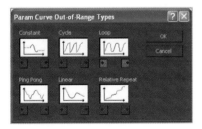

FIGURE 5.6 Choosing to loop your animation

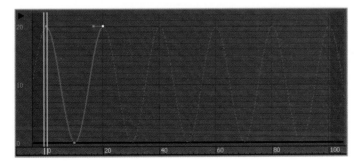

FIGURE 5.7 The Curve Editor now shows the looped animation curve.

Reading Animation Curves

As you can see, the Track View – Curve Editor (from here on called just the Curve Editor) gives you control over the animation in a graph setting. The Curve Editor's graph is a representation of an object's parameter, such as position (values shown vertically) over time (time shown horizontally). Curves allow you to visualize the interpolation of the motion. Once you are used to reading animation curves, you can judge an object's direction, speed, acceleration, and timing at a mere glance.

Here is a quick primer on how to read a curve in the Curve Editor.

In Figure 5.8, an object's Z Position parameter is being animated. At the beginning, the curve quickly begins to move positively (that is, to the right) on the Z-axis. The object shoots up and comes to an *ease-in*, where it decelerates to a stop, reaching its top height. The ease-in stop is signified by the curving beginning to flatten out at around frame 70.

In Figure 5.9, the object slowly accelerates in an *ease-out* in the positive Z direction until it hits frame 100, where it suddenly stops.

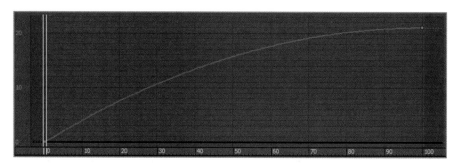

FIGURE 5.8 The object quickly accelerates to an ease-in stop.

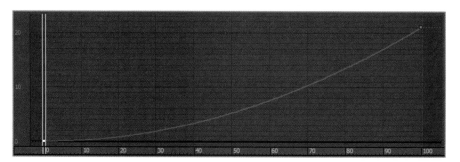

FIGURE 5.9 The object eases out to acceleration and suddenly stops at its fastest velocity.

In Figure 5.10, the object eases in and travels to an ease-out where it decelerates, starting at around frame 69, to where it slowly stops, at frame 100.

Finally, in Figure 5.11, to showcase another tangent type, step interpolation makes the object jump from its Z Position in frame 20 to its new position in frame 21.

Figure 5.12 shows the Curve Editor, with its major aspects called out for your information.

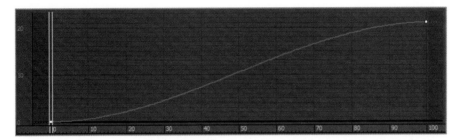

FIGURE 5.10 Ease-out and ease-in

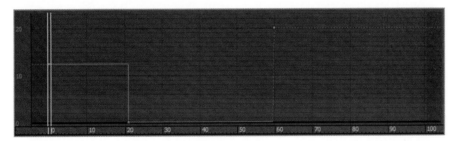

FIGURE 5.11 Step interpolation makes the object "jump" suddenly from one value to the next.

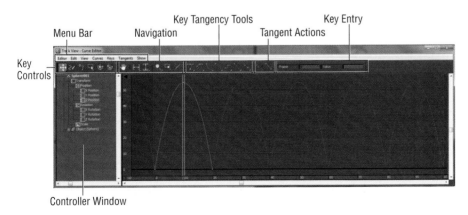

FIGURE 5.12 The Curve Editor

Refining the Animation

Let's play the animation now. In the bottom right of the interface, you will
see an animation player with the sideways triangle to signify Play. Select the
Camera01 viewport and click the Play button. The framework of the movement
is getting there. Notice how the speed of the ball is consistent. If this were a real
ball, it would be dealing with gravity; the ball would speed up as it got closer to
the ground and there would be "hang time" when the ball was in the air on its
way up as gravity took over to pull it back down.

This means you have to edit the movement that happens between the keyframes. This is done by adjusting *how* the keyframes shape the curve itself,
using tangents. When you select a keyframe, a handle will appear in the user
interface (UI), as shown in Figure 5.13.

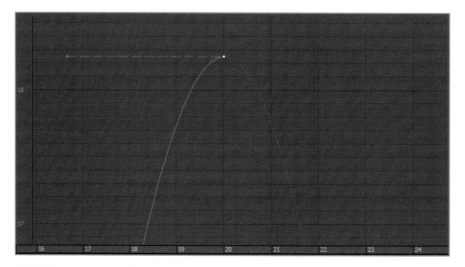

FIGURE 5.13 The keyframe's handle

This handle adjusts the tangency of the keyframe to change the curvature of
the animation curve, which in turn changes the animation. There are various
types of tangents, depending on how you want to edit the motion. By default the
Auto tangent is applied to all new keyframes. This is not what you want for the
ball, although it is a perfect default tangent type to have.

ANIMATION CONTROLLERS

Anything you animate is handled by a controller. Controllers store animation and they interpolate between values. The default controllers are

▶ **Position**: Position XYZ

▶ **Rotation**: Euler XYZ

▶ **Scale**: Bézier Scale

Editing Animation Curves

Let's edit some tangents to better suit your animation. The intent is to speed up the curve as it hits the floor and slow it down as it crests its apex. Instead of opening the Curve Editor through the menu bar, this time you are going to use the shortcut. Close the large Curve Editor dialog box, and then at the bottom-left corner of the interface, click the Open Mini Curve Editor button shown in Figure 5.14.

FIGURE 5.14
Click the Open Mini
Curve Editor button.

The Mini Curve Editor is almost exactly the same as the one you launch through the main menu. A few tools are not included in the Mini Curve Editor toolbar, but you can find them in the menu bar of the Mini Curve Editor.

To edit the curves, follow these steps:

1. Scroll down the Controller window on the left of the Mini Curve Editor by dragging the Pan tool (the hand cursor) to find the Ball object's position. Click on the Z Position track. This will bring only the curves that you want to edit to the Key Editing window.

2. The Z Position curve is blue, as is almost everything relating to the Z-axis. The little gray boxes on the curves are keyframes. Select the

keyframe at frame 10. You may need to scrub the Time slider out of the way if you are on frame 10. The key will turn white when selected. Remember, if you need to zoom or pan in the Curve Editor's Key Editing window, you can use the same shortcuts you would use to navigate in the viewports. You will change this key's tangency to make the ball fall faster as it hits and bounces off the ground.

3. In the Mini Curve Editor toolbar, change the tangent type for the selected keyframe from the Auto default to Fast by clicking the Set Tangents To Fast icon (). When you do this, you will see the animation curve change shape, as shown in Figure 5.15.

FIGURE 5.15 The effect of the new tangent type

4. Select the Camera viewport and play the animation. You can easily correlate how the animation works with the curve's shape as you see the Time slider travel through the Mini Curve Editor as the animation plays.

Finessing the Animation

Although the animation has improved, the ball has a distinct lack of weight. It still seems too simple and without any character. In situations such as this, animators can go wild and try several different things as they see fit. Here is where creativity helps hone your animation skills, whether you are new to animation or have been doing it for 50 years.

Animation shows change over time. Good animation conveys the *intent,* the motivation for that change between the frames.

Squash and Stretch

The concept of *squash and stretch* has been an animation staple for as long as there has been animation. It is a way to convey the weight of an object by deforming it to react (usually in an exaggerated way) to gravity, impact, and motion.

You can give your ball a lot of flair by adding squash and stretch to give the object some personality. Follow along with these steps:

1. Press the N key to activate Auto Key. In the Mini Curve Editor, drag the yellow double-line Time slider (called the track bar Time slider) to frame 10. Click and hold the Scale tool to access the flyout. Choose the Select And Squash tool (▣). Center the Scale cursor over the Z-axis of the Scale Transform gizmo in the Camera viewport. Click and drag down to squash down about 20 percent. Doing so will scale down on the Z-axis and scale up on the X- and Y-axes to compensate, as shown in Figure 5.16.

FIGURE 5.16 Use the Select And Squash tool to squash down the ball on impact.

2. Move to frame 0. Click and drag up to stretch the ball up about 20 percent (so that the ball's scale in *Z* is about 120). When you scrub through the animation, you will see that the ball stretched at frame 0; then the ball squashes and stays squashed for the rest of the time. You'll fix that in the next step.

   You need to copy the Scale key from frame 0 to frame 20 first, and then apply a loop for the Parameter Curve Out-of-Range Type. Because the Mini Curve Editor is open, it obstructs the timeline; therefore, you should copy the keys in the Mini Curve Editor. You can just as easily do so in the regular Curve Editor in the same way.

3. In the Mini Curve Editor, scroll in the Controller window until you find the Scale track for the ball. Highlight it to see the keyframes and animation curves. Click and hold the Move Keys tool in the Mini Curve Editor toolbar to roll out and access the Move Keys Horizontal tool (⬌)

4. Click and drag a selection marquee around the two keyframes at frame 0 in the Scale track to select them. Hold the Shift key and then click and drag the keyframes at frame 0 to frame 20.

5. In the Mini Curve Editor's menu bar, select Controller ➢ Out-of-Range Types. Choose Loop, and then click OK. Play the animation. The curves are shown in Figure 5.17.

FIGURE 5.17 The final curves

Setting the Timing

Well, you squashed and stretched the ball, but it still doesn't look right. That is because the ball should not squash before it hits the ground. It needs to return to 100 percent scale and stay there for a few frames. Immediately before the ball hits the ground, it can squash into the ground plane to heighten the sense of impact. The following steps are easier to perform in the regular Curve Editor rather than in the Mini Curve Editor. So close the Mini Curve Editor by clicking the Close button on the left side of its toolbar.

Open the Curve Editor to fix the timing, and follow these steps as if they were law:

1. Move the Time slider to frame 8; Auto Key should still be active. In the Curve Editor, in the Controller window select the ball's Scale track so that only the scale curves appear in the Editing window. In the Curve Editor's toolbar, click the Insert Keys icon (🔑). Your cursor will change to an arrow with a white circle at its lower right. Click on one of the Scale curves to add a keyframe on all the Scale curves at frame 8. Because scales *X* and *Y* are the same value, you will see only two curves instead of three.

2. Because they are selected, the keys will be white. In the Key Entry tools, you will find two text type-in boxes. The box on the left is the frame number, and the box on the right is the selected key's (or keys') value. Because more than one key with a different value is selected, there is no number in that type-in box. Enter **100** (for 100 percent scale) in the right type-in box, and a value of **100** for the scale in *X, Y,* and *Z* for the ball at frame 8, as shown in Figure 5.18.

FIGURE 5.18 Enter a value of 100.

3. Move the Time slider to frame 12, and do the same thing in the Curve Editor. These settings are bracketing the squash so that the squash happens only a couple frames before and a couple frames after the ball hits the ground. Press the N key to deactivate Auto Key. Save your work.

Once you play back the animation, the ball will begin to look a lot more like a nice cartoonish one, with a little character. Experiment by changing some of the scale amounts to have the ball squash a little more or less, or stretch it more or less to see how that affects the animation. See if it adds a different personality to the ball. If you can master a bouncing ball and evoke all sorts of emotions from your audience, you will be a great animator indeed.

Moving the Ball Forward

You can load the `Animation_Ball_01.max` scene file from the Bouncing Ball project on your hard drive (or from the companion web page) to catch up to this point or to check your work.

Now that you have worked out the bounce, it's time to add movement to the ball so that it moves across the screen as it bounces. Layering animation in this fashion, where you settle on one movement before moving on to another, is common. That's not to say you won't need to go back and forth and make adjustments through the whole process, but it's generally nicer to work out one layer of the animation before adding another. The following steps will show you how:

1. Move the Time slider to frame 0. Select the ball with the Select And Move tool, and move the ball in the Camera viewport to the left so it is still within the camera's view. That's about −30 units on the X-axis.

2. Move the Time slider to frame 100. Press the N key to activate Auto Key again. Move the ball to the right about 60 units so that the ball's X Position value is about 30.

3. Don't play the animation yet; it isn't going to look right. Go to the Curve Editor, scroll down in the Controller window, and select the X Position track for the ball, as shown in Figure 5.19.

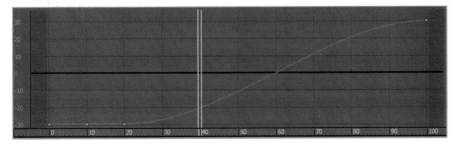

FIGURE 5.19 The X Position of the ball does not look right.

When you created the keyframes for the up and down movement of the ball (which was along the Z-axis), the 3ds Max software automatically created keyframes for the X and Y Position tracks, both with essentially no value. To fix it, keep following these steps.

4. Select the keyframes on the X Position track at frame 10 and frame 20, and delete them by pressing the Delete key on your keyboard.

5. Click the Parameter Curves Out-of-Range Types button, and select Constant. This removes the loop from the X Position track but won't affect the Z Position track for the ball's bounce. Press the N key to deactivate Auto Key. Play the animation. You can use the / (slash) button as a shortcut to play the animation.

6. There is still a little problem. Watch the horizontal movement. The ball is slow at the beginning, speeds up in the middle, and then slows again at the end. It eases out and eases in. This is caused by the default tangent, which automatically adds a slowdown as the object goes in and out of the keyframe. In the Curve Editor, select both keys for the X Position curve and click the Set Tangents To Linear icon (◥) to create a straight line of movement so there is no speed change in the ball's movement left to right.

Figure 5.20 shows the proper curve.

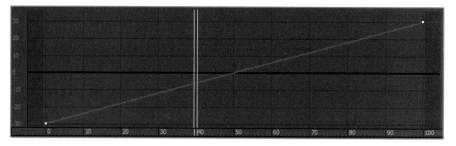

FIGURE 5.20 The X Position curve for the ball's movement now has no ease-out or ease-in.

Adding a Roll

You need to add some rotation, but there are several problems with this. One, you moved the pivot point to the bottom of the ball in the very first step of the exercise. You did that so the squashing would work correctly—that is, it would be at the point of contact with the ground. If you were to rotate the ball with the pivot at the bottom, it would look like Figure 5.21.

For the ball to rotate properly
the pivot needs to be in the center.

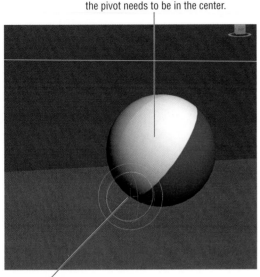

Pivot at the bottom makes the balls
rotate from the bottom.

FIGURE 5.21 The ball will not rotate properly
because the pivot is at the bottom.

Using the XForm Modifier

You need a pivot point at the center of the ball, but you can't just move the existing
pivot from the bottom to the middle—it would throw off all the squash and stretch
animation. Unfortunately, an object can have only one pivot point. To solve the
issue, you are going to use a modifier called *XForm*. This modifier has many uses.
You're going to use it to add another pivot to the ball in the following steps:

1. Select the ball. From the menu bar, select Modifiers ➤ Parametric
   Deformers ➤ XForm. You may also select this option from the modifier list in the Modify tab. XForm will be added to the ball in the modifier stack, and an orange bounding box will appear over the ball in
   the viewport. XForm has no parameters, but it does have sub-objects.

2. Expand the modifier stack by clicking the black box with the plus
   sign next to XForm. Then click Center. In the next step, you will use
   the Align tool to center the XForm's center point on the ball.

3. Click the Align tool, and then click on the ball. In the resulting dialog
   box, make sure the check boxes for X, Y, and Z Position are checked,
   which means those axes are active. Now click Center under Target
   Object, and then click OK. The XForm's center will move.

Now to be clear, this *isn't* a pivot point. This is the *center point* on the XForm modifier. If you go to the modifier stack and click on the sphere, the pivot point will still be at the bottom.

The XForm modifier allows the ball to rotate without its squashing and stretching getting in the way of the rotation. By separating the rotation animation for the ball's roll into the modifier, the animation on the Sphere object is preserved.

Animating the XForm Modifier

To add the ball's roll to the XForm modifier, follow along with these steps:

1. Turn on Auto Key and choose the Select And Rotate tool.

2. In the modifier stack, click on Gizmo for the sub-object of XForm. This is a very important step because it tells the modifier to use the XForm's center instead of using the pivot point of the ball.

3. In the Camera viewport, move the Time slider to frame 100 and rotate the ball 360 degrees on the Y-axis (you can use Angle Snap Toggle to make it easier to rotate exactly 360 degrees). Click on the XForm modifier to deactivate the sub-object mode. Play the animation.

THE BALL DOESN'T ROTATE 360 DEGREES!

If you rotate the ball in the third step 360 degrees but the ball does not animate, the 3ds Max software could potentially be interpreting 360 degrees to be 0 degrees in the Curve Editor, thereby creating a flat curve. If this is the case, you can try rotating the ball 359 degrees instead to force the animation to work. You could also manually change the value in the Curve Editor for the keyframe at frame 100 to a value of 360.

The ball should be a rubbery cartoon ball at this point in the animation. Just for practice, let's say you need to go back and edit the keyframes because you rotated in the wrong direction and the ball's rotation is going backward. Fixing this issue requires you to go back into the Curve Editor as follows.

1. Open the Curve Editor (mini or regular) and scroll down in the Controller window until you see the Ball tracks. Below the Ball's Transform track is a new track called Ball/Modified Object.

2. Expand the track by clicking on the plus sign in the circle next to the name. Go to the Gizmo track and select the Y Rotation track. You will see the Function curve in the Key Editing window.

3. You want the keyframe at frame 0 to have the value 0 and the keyframe at frame 100 to be a value of 360. Select both keyframes and change the tangents to Linear, as shown in Figure 5.22.

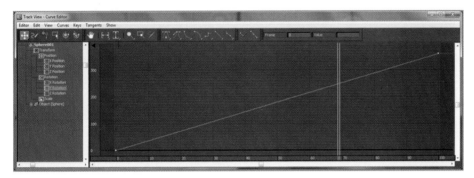

FIGURE 5.22 The XForm's gizmo selected in the Controller window with the rotation of the ball set to Linear Tangents

Close the Curve Editor and play the animation. Play the bounce ball.avi movie file located in the RenderOutput folder of the Bouncing Ball project to see a render of the animation. You can also load the Animation_Ball_02.max scene file from the Bouncing Ball project to check your work.

THE ESSENTIALS AND BEYOND

Working with the bouncing ball gave you quite a bit of experience with the 3ds Max animation toolset. There are several ways to animate a bouncing ball using the 3ds Max software. It is definitely a good idea to try this exercise a few times at first and then to come back to it later—after you have learned other 3ds Max techniques.

Animation can be a lot of fun, but it is also tedious and sometimes aggravating. A lot of time, patience, and practice are required to become good at animation. It all boils down to how the animation makes you think. Is there enough weight to the subjects in the animation? Do the movements make sense? How does nuance enhance the animation? These are all questions you will begin to discover for yourself. This chapter merely introduced you to how to make things move using the 3ds Max toolset. It gave you some basic animation techniques to help you develop your eye for motion. Don't stop here. Go back into the chapter and redo some of the exercises.

(Continues)

THE ESSENTIALS AND BEYOND   (Continued)

ADDITIONAL EXERCISES

Try different variations on the same themes, such as:

▶ Bounce the ball on the floor and then off a wall. Try bouncing the ball off a table, onto a chair, and then onto the floor.

▶ Animate three different types of balls bouncing next to one another, such as a bowling ball, a ping pong ball, and a tennis ball. Examples may be found at www.sybex.com/go/3dsmax2013essentials.

Most important, keep working at it!

CHAPTER 6

Animating a Thrown Knife

This chapter is a continuation of the animation work you began in
Chapter 5, "Animating a Bouncing Ball." It introduces you to some new
animation fundamentals—this time by animating a thrown knife.

Topics in this chapter include the following:

▶ **Anticipation and momentum in knife throwing**

Anticipation and Momentum in Knife Throwing

This exercise will give you more experience with 3ds Max® animation techniques. You will edit more in the Curve Editor (yeh!) and be introduced to the
concepts of anticipation, momentum, and secondary movement. First, download the Knife project from this book's companion web page (www.sybex.com/
go/3dsmax2013essentials). Set your 3ds Max project folder by choosing
Application ➢ Manage ➢ Set Project Folder and selecting the Knife project
that you downloaded.

Blocking Out the Animation

To begin this exercise, open the Animation_Knife_00.max file in the Knife
project and follow along here:

1. Move the Time slider to frame 30 and activate the Auto Key button.

2. Move the knife to the Target object, as shown in Figure 6.1.

FIGURE 6.1
Move the knife to the
target at frame 30.

3. Move the Time slider to frame 15, where the knife is halfway between its start and the target, and move the knife slightly up on the Z-axis so that the knife moves with a slight arc, as shown in Figure 6.2.

FIGURE 6.2 Move the knife up slightly
at frame 15.

4. Click the Time Configuration icon (▦) at the bottom of the UI next to the navigation controls. Figure 6.3 shows the Time Configuration dialog box. In the Animation section, change End Time to 30 from 100 and click OK. The Time slider will reflect this change immediately.

5. Play your animation, and you should see the knife move with a slight ease-out and ease-in toward the target, with a slight arc up in the middle. The animation of the knife needs to start at frame 0, so open the Curve Editor and scroll down in the Controller window until you see the X, Y, Z Position tracks for the knife. Hold the Ctrl key and select all three tracks to display their curves, as shown in Figure 6.4.

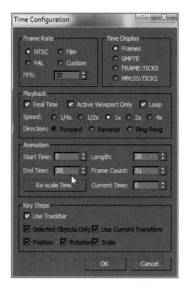

FIGURE 6.3 Change the frame range in the Time Configuration dialog box.

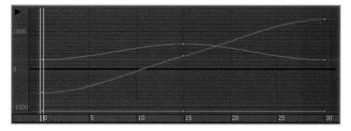

FIGURE 6.4 The initial curves for the knife

6. Drag a selection marquee around the three keys at frame 0. In the Key Controls toolbar, select and hold the Move Keys tool (⊞) to access the flyout icons, and select the Move Keys Horizontal tool in the flyout (⬌). Use this tool to move the keys to frame 10.

7. Doing so compacts the curve, so you need to move the keys at frame 15 to the new middle, frame 20. The finished curve is shown in Figure 6.5.

That's it for the gross animation (or *blocking*) of the shot. Did you have fun?

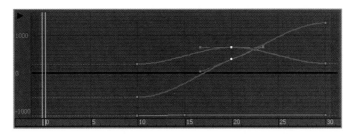

FIGURE 6.5 Finished curves with the position of the knife starting at frame 10

Trajectories

When it comes to animation, it is very helpful to be able to see an object's *trajectory* (the path the object is taking over time). Select the Knife object, go to the Command panel, click the Motion icon (image) to open the options shown in Figure 6.6, and then click Trajectories. Your viewports will display a red curve to show you the path of the knife's motion as it arcs toward the target, as shown in Figure 6.7.

FIGURE 6.6
Turning on Trajectories
for the knife

FIGURE 6.7 The curve shows the trajectory for the knife's motion.

The large, hollow, square points on the trajectory curve represent the keyframes set on the knife so far. Let's adjust the height of the arc using the trajectory curve. Select the Sub-Object button at the top of the Motion panel. Keys are your only sub-object choice in the pull-down menu to the right of the button. Select the middle keyframe and move it up or down to suit your tastes. Once you settle on a nice arc for the path of the knife, turn off Trajectories mode by clicking the Parameters button in the Motion panel.

As you can imagine, the Trajectories option can be useful in many situations. It not only gives you a view of your object's path, but it also allows you to edit that path easily and in a visual context, which can be very important.

Adding Rotation

Throwing knives is usually a bad idea, but you can throw something else at a target (the inanimate kind) to see how to animate your knife. You'll find that the object will rotate once or twice before it hits its target. To add rotation to your knife, follow these steps:

1. Move to frame 30, and press the E key for the Select And Rotate tool. Auto Key should still be active. In the Camera001 viewport, rotate on the Y-axis 443 degrees.

2. With the knife selected, go into the Curve Editor. Scroll down to find the X, Y, and Z Rotation tracks, and select them. Select the keys at frame 0, and then use the Move Keys Horizontal tool to shift the keyframes to frame 10. Press N to deactivate the Auto Key. Figure 6.8 shows the Curve Editor graph for the knife.

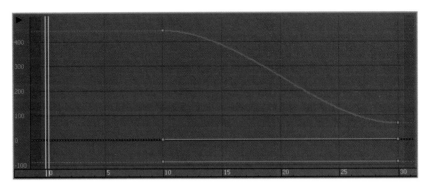

FIGURE 6.8 The Curve Editor graph for the knife

3. Play the animation, and you will see that the knife's position and rotation eases in and eases out. A real knife would not ease its rotations or movement. Its speed would be roughly consistent throughout the animation.

4. Go back to the Curve Editor; change Move Keys Horizontal back to Move Keys. Then select the X Position track, select all the keyframes, and switch the tangent to Linear. Now select the Z Position track; you'll need to finesse this one a bit more than you did the X Position track. You are going to use the handles on the tangents that appear when you select a key. These handles can be adjusted; just center your cursor over the end, and click and drag using the Move Keys tool. Figure 6.9 illustrates how you want the Z Position animation curve to look. This will give the trajectory a nice arc and a good rate of travel.

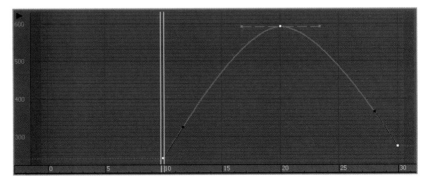

FIGURE 6.9 Adjust the curve for the knife's arc through the air.

5. Now it is time to edit the Rotation keys. In the Curve Editor, scroll to find the X, Y, and Z Rotation tracks. The first thing you can do is add a bit of drama to the knife to make the action more exciting. To this end, you can say that the rotation on the knife is too slow. Select the X Rotation track and select its key at frame 30. In the Key Stats, change the value to –290. The higher the value, the faster the knife will rotate. This will add one full revolution to the animation and some more excitement to the action.

6. Adjust the tangent handles to resemble the curve shown in Figure 6.10. The knife will speed up just a bit as it leaves the first rotation keyframe. The speed will be even as it goes into the last keyframe.

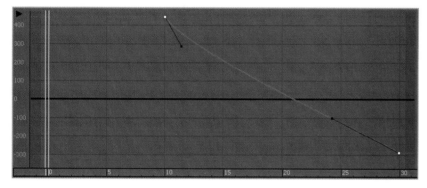

FIGURE 6.10 Match your curve to this one.

With just a little bit of fast rotation as the knife leaves frame 10, you give the animation more spice. The knife should now have a slightly weightier look than before, when it rotated with an ease-in and ease-out.

Adding Anticipation

Now let's animate the knife to create *anticipation,* as if an invisible hand holding the knife pulled back just before throwing it to get more strength in the throw. This anticipation, although it's a small detail, adds a level of nuance to the animation that enhances the total effect. Follow these steps:

1. Move the Time slider to frame 0. Go to the Curve Editor, scroll in the Controller window, and select the X Rotation track for the knife. In the Curve Editor toolbar, click the Insert Keys icon (▦), bring your cursor to frame 0 of the curve, and click to create a keyframe. Doing so creates a key at frame 0 with the same parameters as the next key, as shown in Figure 6.11.

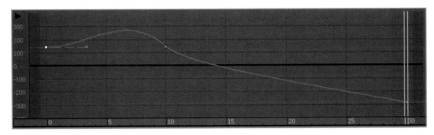

FIGURE 6.11 Add a key to the beginning to create anticipation for the knife throw.

2. Select the Move Keys tool and select the key at frame 10. In the Key Stats type-in box, change the value of that key to **240**. If you play back the animation, it will look weird. The knife will cock back really fast and spin a bit. This is due to the big hump between frames 0 and 10.

3. Keep the tangent at frame 0 set to the default, but change the tangent on the key at frame 10 to Linear (▨). Play back the animation. You'll have a slight bit of anticipation, but the spice will be lost and the knife will look less active and too mechanical.

4. To regain the weight you had in the knife, press Ctrl+Z to undo your change to the tangency on frame 10 and set it back to what you had. You may have to undo more than once. Now, select the Move Keys Vertical tool (⬍) and select the In tangent handle for keyframe 10. This is the tangent handle on the left of the key.

5. Press Shift and drag the tangent handle down to create a curve that is similar to the one shown in Figure 6.12. By pressing Shift as you dragged the tangent handle, you broke the continuity between the In and Out handles, so that only the In handle was affected. Play back the animation. It should look much better now.

It's common to try something and rely on Undo to get back to the starting point. You can use Undo several times when you find yourself at a dead end. You can also save multiple versions of your file to revert back to an earlier one.

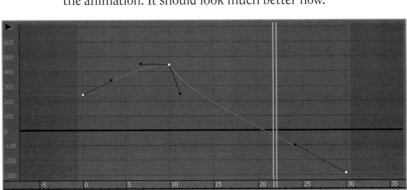

FIGURE 6.12 To create a believable anticipation for the knife throw, set your curve to resemble this one.

Following Through

The knife needs more weight. A great way to show that in animation is by adding follow-through; have the knife sink into the target a little bit and push back the target. To add follow-through to your animation, use these steps:

1. You want to sink the knife into the target after it hits. Select the Time Configuration button and change End Time to 45 to add 15 frames to your frame range. Click OK. Doing so will not affect the animation; it will merely append 15 frames to the current frame range.

2. Select the knife and go to frame 30, where it hits the target. In the Curve Editor, select the X Position track of the knife. Add a keyframe with the Insert Keys tool at frame 35.

3. Note the value of the key in the type-in boxes at the top right of the Curve Editor (*not* the type-in boxes at the bottom of the main UI). In this case, the value in this scene is about –231. You will want to set the value for this key at frame 35 to about –224 to sink it farther into the target. If your values are different, adjust accordingly so you don't add too much movement. Also make sure the movement flows *into* the target and not back out of the target as if the knife were bouncing out.

4. Keep the tangent for this new key set to Auto. With these relative values, scrub the animation between frames 30 and 35. You should see the knife's slight move into the target. The end of your curve should look like the curve in Figure 6.13.

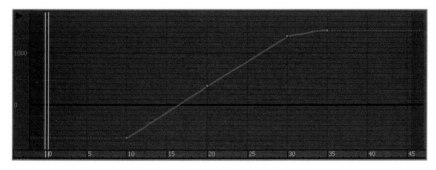

FIGURE 6.13 Your animation should end like this.

5. You still need to add a little bit of follow-through to the rotation of the knife to make it sink into the target better. In the Curve Editor, select the X Rotation track to display its curve. Add a key to the curve at frame 35. The value of the key at frame 30 should already

be about –652. Set the value of the keyframe at frame 35 to be about –655. Keep the tangent set at Auto. If your values are different, adjust accordingly to what works best in your scene.

Be careful about how much the knife sinks into the target. Although it is important to show the weight of the knife, it is also important to show the weight of the target; you do not want the target to look too soft.

Transferring Momentum to the Target

To make the momentum work even better for the knife animation, you will have to push back the target as the knife hits it. The trouble is, if you animate the target moving back, the knife will stay in place, floating in the air. You have to animate the knife *with* the target.

Parent and Child Objects

To animate the knife and target together, the knife has to be linked to the target so that when the target is animated to push back upon impact, the knife will follow precisely since it is stuck in the target. Doing this won't mess up the existing animation of the knife because the knife will be the child in the hierarchy and will retain its own animation separate from the target. Just follow these steps:

1. Go to frame 30, about when the knife impacts. On the far left of the main toolbar, choose the Select And Link tool (⬚). Select the knife and drag it to the target, as shown in Figure 6.14 (left). Nothing should change until you animate the Target object.

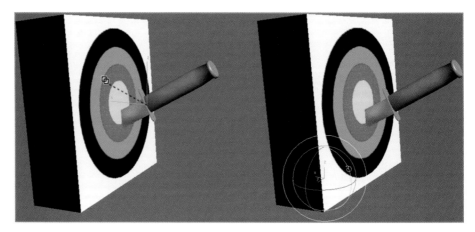

FIGURE 6.14 Link the knife to the target (left), and then rotate the target back slightly (right).

2. Move the Time slider to frame 34 and press the N key to activate the Auto Key tool. With the Select And Rotate tool, select the Target object and rotate it back about 5 degrees, as shown in the second image in Figure 6.14 (right). The pivot of the target has already been placed properly, at the bottom back edge.

3. Go to the Curve Editor, scroll to find the Y Rotation track for the Target object, select the keyframe at frame 0, and move it to frame 30. Then hold the Shift key, and click and drag the keyframe (which will make a copy of it) to frame 37.

4. Change the tangent for the key at frame 30 to Fast and leave the other key tangents alone.

5. Add a little wobble to the target to make the animation even more interesting. This can be done easily in the Curve Editor. Use Insert Keys to add keys at frames 40 and 44. Using the Move Keys Vertical tool, give the key at frame 40 a value of about 1.7. Your curve should resemble the one in Figure 6.15.

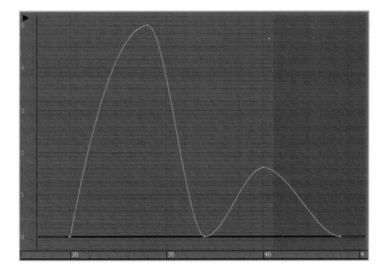

FIGURE 6.15 The Target animation curve

6. Finally, add a little slide to the target. Using the Select And Move tool, move the Time slider to frame 37, and move the target just a bit along the X-axis. Go to the Curve Editor, scroll to the *X* position of the Target object, select the keyframe at frame 0, and move it to frame 30 so the move starts when the knife hits the target. Change the tangent for frame 30 to Fast and leave the other tangent at Auto.

Done! Play back your animation. Experiment and change some of the final timings and values of the target's reaction to the impact to see different weights of the knife and target and how the weight looks to the viewer.

You can see a sample render of the scene in the knife_animation.mov QuickTime file in the RenderOutput folder of the Knife project on the companion web page (or copied onto your hard drive). You can also download the Animation_Knife_01.max scene file from the Scenes folder of the Knife project to check your work.

THE ESSENTIALS AND BEYOND

In this, our second chapter on animation, you further expanded your knowledge of creating and editing animation. You learned about hierarchies and how to link objects together to create a hierarchy useful for the knife animation as well as how pivot points are used. You also learned some key animation terms (such as anticipation, follow-through, and momentum) and how they apply to the animation.

ADDITIONAL EXERCISES

▶ Try animating simple objects like boxes and just play around with anticipation, follow-through, and momentum.

▶ Again using simple primitives, create hierarchies and play around with anticipation, follow-through, and momentum.

▶ Constrain and animate a camera on a path through a nice modeled environment.

▶ Animate planets around the sun using paths.

CHAPTER 7

Character Poly Modeling: Part I

In games, characters are designed and created cleverly to achieve the best look with the lowest amount of mesh detail to keep the polygon count low. With that in mind, this and the next two chapters introduce you to character modeling, focusing on using the Editable Poly toolset to create a relatively low-polygon-count soldier model suitable for character animation and for use in a game engine (though that topic is not covered in this book). This chapter begins with the basic form of the character first.

Topics in this chapter include the following:

▶ **Setting up the scene**

▶ **Creating the soldier**

Setting Up the Scene

You can import and use sketches of the character's front and side as background images as you create the character using the 3ds Max® toolset. Additional sketches of your character from several points of view can be used as quick references to help you target your goal.

HIGH- AND LOW-POLY MODELING

High-polygon-count models are used when a model's level of detail needs to be impeccable, such as when the model is used in close-ups. High-polygon models are also used to generate displacement and normal maps to use on lower resolution models. This technique is used to add needed detail without the issues that come with large model sizes.

Low-polygon-count modeling, also called *low-poly modeling,* refers to a style of modeling that sacrifices some detail in favor of efficient geometry that places a very low load on the system on which it is being created or rendered. The number of triangles needed to consider something low-poly is based on the rendering platform and increases as the technology improves.

Creating Planes and Adding Materials

This exercise begins by creating crossed boxes and applying reference images to them. Set your project to the Soldier project downloaded to your system:

1. In a new scene, go to the Front viewport and create a plane.

2. In the Parameters rollout of the Command panel, set Length to **635** and Width to **622**. The units are in inches, which is the 3ds Max default. The size of the image planes in units is the same size as the reference images in pixels. Therefore, when you apply the image to the plane, it will be proportional, maintaining its width and length with no stretching or squeezing of the images.

3. Rename this box Image_Plane_Front.

4. With the plane still selected, go to the Modify tab and in the Parameters rollout set the Length and Width Segs to **1**. Then select the Move tool (W) in the main toolbar, and in the Transform type-in areas at the bottom of the user interface, move the plane to these coordinates: **0.0, 80, −5**.

5. Click in a blank space in the user interface (UI), and then press Ctrl+ Shift+Z on your keyboard to initiate the shortcut for Zoom Extents All. In the main toolbar, turn on the Angle Snap toggle (![icon]) or press A on your keyboard. Doing so will snap your rotation to every 5 degrees. Select the Rotate tool (E) and hold down the Shift key on the keyboard; then in the Front viewport, rotate the image plane along the Y-axis 90 degrees. Using the Shift key activates the Clone tool, as shown in Figure 7.1.

6. In the Clone Options dialog box, under Object select Copy; name it Image_Plane_Side and click OK.

7. Switch to the Move tool and move the plane to these coordinates: **−82, 0, −5**.

Adding the Materials

At this point, the reference materials are texture-mapped onto the planes to provide a reference inside the scene itself while you model the character. Therefore, it's critical to ensure that the features of the character that appear in both reference images (the front and the side) are at the same height. For instance, the top of the head and the shoulders should be at the same height in both the front and side views to make the modeling process easier.

1. In the Left viewport, press the V key on your keyboard and select Right View from the list. Change the shading in the Right viewport to Consistence Colors (F3).

2. Open an Explorer window and navigate to the Soldier/sceneassets/ images folder on your hard drive from the Soldier project you downloaded from the book's web page at www.sybex.com/ go/3dsmax2013essentials. Drag ImagePlane_Front.jpg from the Explorer window to the image plane in the Front viewport.

3. Drag ImagePlane_Side.jpg onto the image plane in the Right viewport. The image planes should have the two images mapped on them, as shown in Figure 7.2.

FIGURE 7.1 The Clone Options dialog box

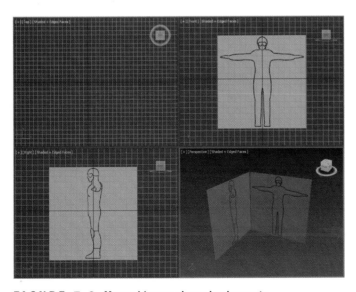

FIGURE 7.2 Mapped image planes in viewports

Creating the Soldier

A good practice is to block out the basic form of the character and focus on the size and crucial shapes of the major elements, and then add detail for the finer features. The following exercises describe the steps required to block out the soldier's major features. Go wild!

Forming the Torso

The basic structure for the torso will begin with a simple box primitive. After converting the box into an editable poly, you will use the Mirror tool on the object so that any manipulations performed on one side are also performed on the other. You will begin forming the basic shape of the torso by moving the editable poly's vertices and extruding its polygons in the following steps.

Continue with the previous exercise's scene file, or open the Soldier_V01.max scene file in the Scenes folder of the Soldier project downloaded from this book's web page.

1. Go to the Shading Viewport Label menu and choose Shaded and then select F4, this will turn on Edged Faces, do this if it isn't already set that way.

2. Start by creating a box primitive in the Perspective viewport with these parameters: Length: **25**, Width: **16**, Height: **53**, Input Height Segs: **8**. Leave the Width and Length Segs at **1**, as shown in Figure 7.3. This is a starting point for the detail needed to create the form of the body. Position the box as shown in Figure 7.4. Press Alt+X to make the box see-through. Change the box's name to **Soldier**.

3. In the Graphite Modeling Tools ribbon on the Poly: Edit ➢ Edit Polygons ➢ Convert To Poly.

FIGURE 7.3
Box parameters

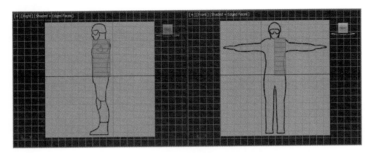

FIGURE 7.4 Box position from the front and side views

4. In the Edit Polygons tab, enter the Vertex sub-object level. In the Right viewport, position the vertices on the right side of the box to match the side outline of the character on the image plane, as shown in Figure 7.5.

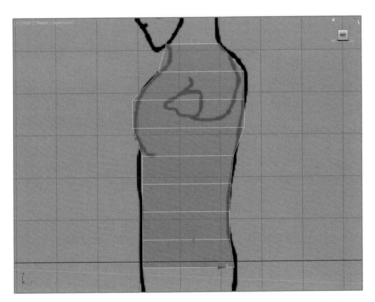

FIGURE 7.5 Move the vertices to match the soldier image in the Right viewport.

5. In the Poly: Edit ➤ Edit Polygons ➤ Favorites ➤ SwiftLoop. Switch to Edge mode, and then use the Swift Loop tool to create two new edge loops that run vertically from the front of the model to the back, as shown in Figure 7.6. The dashed lines show the loop running in the back and bottom of the model.

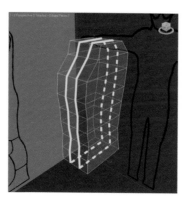

FIGURE 7.6 Create two new edge loops using Swift Loop.

6. Using Swift Loop, create a single new edge on the side of the model running from the left side to the right side, as shown in Figure 7.7. The dashed lines show the loop running across the bottom of the model. Turn off the tool.

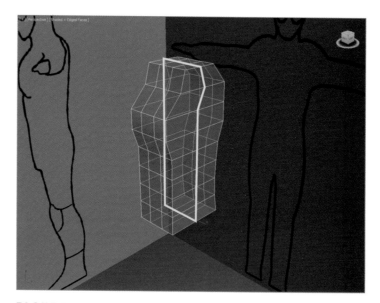

FIGURE 7.7 Create a single new edge on the side of the model using Swift Loop.

7. Now round the side of the torso. You should still be in Edge mode. Double-click on one of the edges running vertically on the side of the torso box, this is a shortcut to the Loop Selection tool in the Poly: Edit ➢ Edit Polygons ➢ Selection ➢ Loop Selection ➢ move the loop of edges toward the back of the model to begin rounding that edge. Then select the loop of edges to the left of the previous one and move them back to form a more rounded front to the torso, as shown in Figure 7.8. While still in Edge mode, select the second edge from the top edge and move it out, as shown in Figure 7.9.

8. Switch to Vertex mode and select the vertex on the left side below the top edge, as shown in Figure 7.10, left image. Select Poly: Edit ➢ Edit Polygons, and click the Chamfer Settings shown in an arrow below the Chamfer button. Doing so opens the Tool caddy. Use a Vertex Chamfer Amount value of **4.808**, and click the green check-mark button (OK) in the caddy to commit the action, as shown in Figure 7.10, right image. This is where the arm will be positioned.

9. Switch to Polygon mode (4), select the new diamond-shaped polygon in the middle, and press Delete to delete the polygon. A hole appears where the arm will be positioned. Also, while in Polygon mode, select all the polygons on the inside edge of the torso model (the side opposite of the new armhole) and delete.

10. Switch to Edge mode (2) and select the four diagonal edges of the diamond-shaped hole and the four edges shown in Figure 7.11.

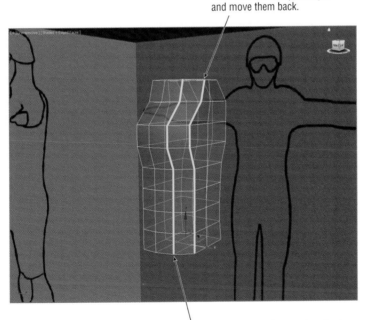

First select this loop of edges and move them back.

Next, select this loop of edges and move them back.

FIGURE 7.8 Select and move edges toward the back of the model.

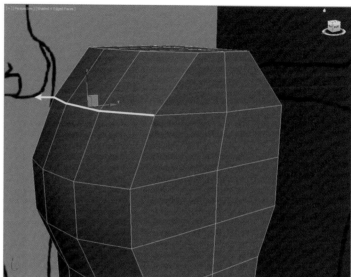

Select these edges and move out.

FIGURE 7.9 Select the edge shown and move out.

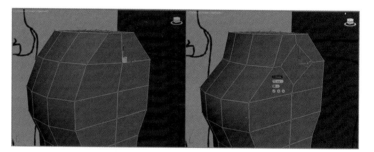

FIGURE 7.10 Select the vertex (left image). Use Chamfer to create a new polygon where the arm will be positioned (right image).

11. Select Poly: Edit ➢ Selction ➢ Ring Selection, and select the ring of edges running across the top of the chest. Again in the Poly: Edit ➢ Edges ➢ Flow Connect to create more horizontal divisions for the upper chest. Flow Connect connects selected edges across one or more edge rings and adjusts the new loop position to fit the shape of the surrounding mesh. The newly created edges are illustrated in Figure 7.12. The diamond-shaped hole in the shoulder is now more rounded (the hole is now an octagon) as well, since more edges were created at the hole. The dashed lines show the loops running behind the model.

Select highlighted edges.

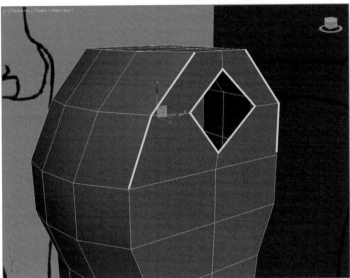

FIGURE 7.11 Select these eight edges.

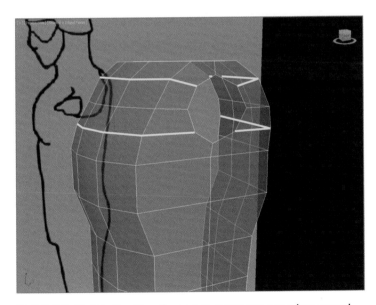

FIGURE 7.12 Use Flow Connect to create two new edges around the model.

12. Select the two horizontal edges under the armhole, as shown in Figure 7.13 (left). Select Poly: Edit ➢ Selction ➢ Ring Selection, and then select the horizontal edges running down the side, top, and bottom of the torso. Again, select Poly: Edit ➢ Edges ➢ Flow Connect to create two new loops of edges, as shown on the right in Figure 7.13.

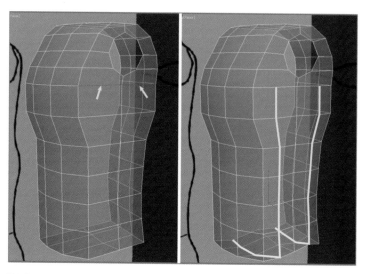

FIGURE 7.13 Select the two horizontal edges under the armhole (left) and use Flow Connect to create more edges (right).

13. The new edge ring does not reach all the way up to the octagon armhole. You will need to cut an edge from the top of the new edges you just made, to the bottom of the armhole. Select Poly: Edit ➢ Favorites Cut ![icon], and click on the first vertex under the armhole, and then click on the second vertex above at the armhole to create the first new edge; right-click to commit the edge. You will still be in the Cut tool, so click on the third vertex and create the second new edge up to the fourth vertex shown in Figure 7.14; right-click to commit the second edge.

14. The armhole isn't great right now; it will be easier to start from a circular shape rather than the uneven octagon form you have now. Enter Border mode (![icon]), select the armhole's border, select Poly: Edit ➢ Geometry (All), and click the Cap Poly tool to create an NGon (a polygon with more than four sides) cap to fill the hole.

15. Go to Polygon mode and select the new NGon. Select Poly: Edit ➢ Polygons, and click the GeoPoly tool to create a symmetrical polygon

from the previous shape, as shown in Figure 7.15. GeoPoly untangles a polygon and organizes the vertices to form a perfect geometric shape. This will make it easier for you when you create the arm later.

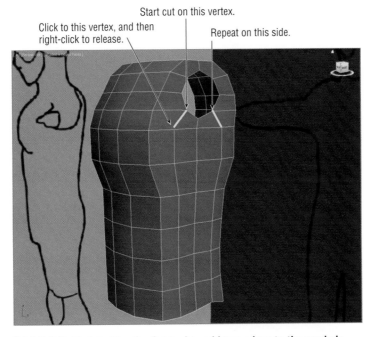

FIGURE 7.14 Use the Cut tool to add two edges to the armhole.

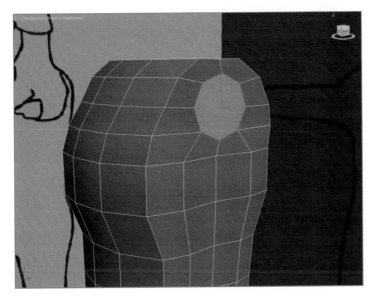

FIGURE 7.15 Use GeoPoly to create a symmetrical shape for the armhole.

16. Select the new NGon cap you created in step 14 and press Delete to delete the NGon. Also select and delete the top and bottom polygons on the model, as shown in Figure 7.16 (left).

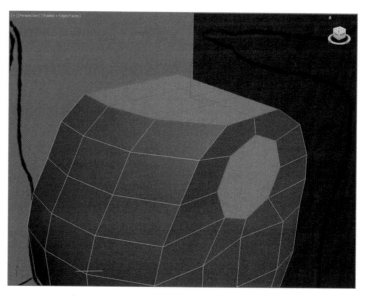

FIGURE 7.16 Delete the NGon as well as the topmost and bottommost polygons of the model.

17. Select Poly: Edit ➢ Selection and turn on Ignore Backfacing ( ). Then select the left-side polygons, as shown in Figure 7.16 (right), and delete them as well. Your torso should now have only a front, side, and back.

18. Now, select the edge loops on the right of the model and move them closer toward the left, and closer to the center of the model, as shown in Figure 7.17. You might want to translate or move them on the Y-axis as well. Your goal is to round out the character for a more organic feel.

19. Notice how the armhole's circle looks neater in Figure 7.18, but the edges on the right and top are a bit awkward. Enter Vertex mode and move the edges to give the armhole a more rounded feel.

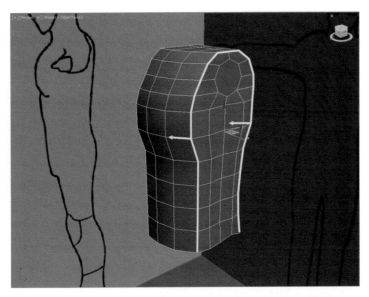

FIGURE 7.17 Select the edge loops and move them to create a more rounded look to the model.

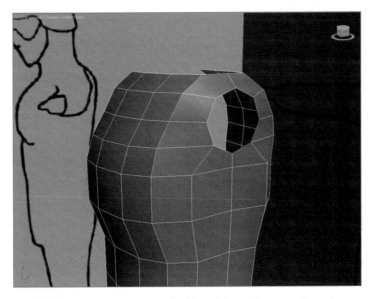

FIGURE 7.18 Adjust the editable poly's vertices to make a cleaner hole for the arm.

20. Go into Edge mode and select the edge running vertically on the right side of the model's back, as shown in Figure 7.19, and move it toward the armhole. This action will make the back rounder.

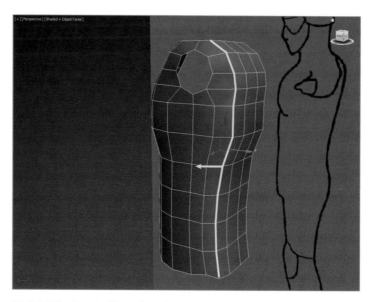

FIGURE 7.19 Move the selected edge toward the front of the torso to round out the back.

Now we are starting to see some shape in the torso. Let's move on to the arms.

Creating the Arms

Continue with the previous exercise's scene file, or open the `Soldier_V02.max` scene file in the `Scenes` file of the Soldier project on the book's web page.

1. In Border mode, select the armhole's border, then hold down the Shift key, and with the Move tool, drag out from the body on the X-axis, extruding polygons as you drag. This method is a form of Border Extrude. This method gives you more control over the extrude process because you can more easily choose the axis along which to extrude. Release the mouse button and view your model in the Front viewport to line up the border to the wrist of the arm in the image plane.

2. From the Poly: Edit ➤ Favorites ➤ SwiftLoop, and create three edge loops on the arm, evenly spaced over the newly created arm; then turn off the tool.

3. Switch to Vertex mode and move the newly created vertices on the Y-axis to fit the form on the image plane. It is okay to select a group of vertices and scale on the Y-axis to taper that part of the arm to create the wrist.

4. In Edge mode, select and use Loop Selection (Poly: Edit ➤ Selection ➤ Loop Selection) on the horizontal edge running around the body under the arm and move the edges down. Repeat the same process with the loop of edges under the previous loop, as shown in Figure 7.20. This ensures the underarm area geometry is lined up properly, as shown later in Figure 7.22.

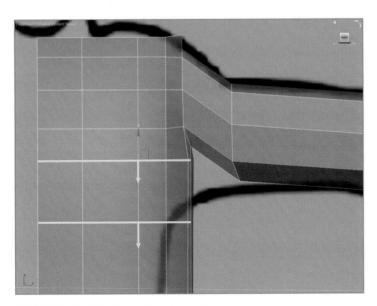

FIGURE 7.20 Move these looped edges down.

5. In Edge mode, select and use Loop Selection on the horizontal edge running directly at the underarm and move the loop down, as shown in Figure 7.21. If Loop Selection doesn't work, just hold down Ctrl and click (Ctrl+click) on the remaining edges to select.

FIGURE 7.21 Select and loop these edges to move them down.

6. In the Front viewport, in Edge mode, select the middle edge on the arm. Select Poly: Edit ➢ Selection ➢ Loop Selection, and then choose Edges ➢ Chamfer ➢ Chamfer Settings from that ribbon and enter an Edge Chamfer Amount of **2** and a Connect Edge Segments value of **2**.

7. Then chamfer the edges to the right and left, using an Edge Chamfer Amount of **3**, with a Connect Edge Segments value of **1**, as shown in Figure 7.22. Keep the middle edge a bit tighter together. Because this is the area where the elbow bends, it is a good idea to include more detail there for deformations at the elbow. Your model should have the vertical edges you see in Figure 7.22.

8. In Border mode, select the wrist border and, while holding down the Shift key, use the Scale tool to scale the wrist border down on the Z- and Y-axes into the center, as shown in Figure 7.23 (left). Using Shift

while performing a Scale operation clones the selected objects much as with an extrusion using the Shift+Move method used earlier. In this case, it makes a copy of the border, effectively closing the open end of the wrist.

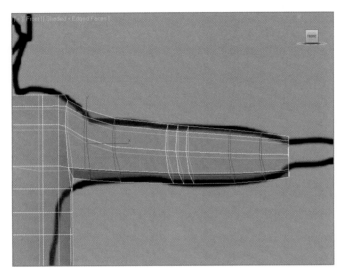

FIGURE 7.22 Chamfer the arm to add more edges for detail.

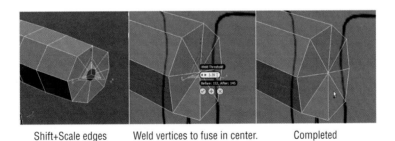

Shift+Scale edges   Weld vertices to fuse in center.   Completed

FIGURE 7.23 Weld the vertices from the wrist edge in toward the center.

9. Switch to Vertex mode, select the vertices of the smaller wrist hole, and select Vertices ➢ Weld ➢ Weld Settings ◢ Weld to open the Weld Vertices caddy, as shown in Figure 7.23 (middle). Use a Weld Threshold of **3.39**, as shown. This creates a completed cap at the end of the arm, as shown in Figure 7.23 (right). You will continue with the hand in a later section.

Creating the Legs

Continue with the previous exercise's scene file, or open the Soldier_V03.max scene file in the Scenes folder of the Soldier project downloaded from the book's web page.

1. In Edge mode, select the bottommost loop of edges on the model's torso. Now hold Shift+Move (hold down the Shift key while moving with the Move tool, as you did in the previous set of steps) to create a new extrusion all the way down to the groin in the reference illustration. You will extrude and move down on the Y-axis, as shown in Figure 7.24.

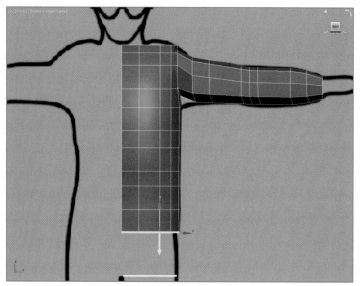

Shift+Move this edge loop down.

FIGURE 7.24 Select the edge loop at the bottom of the model and Shift+Move down.

2. You are starting to prepare the model for the legs and groin area. Use the Cut tool (accessed by selecting Poly: Edit ➢ Favorites ➢ Cut), and cut an edge from about 25 percent to the right from the corner of the bottommost edge of the model, to the top corner on the polygon closest to the groin, as shown in Figure 7.25 (left). Do the same for the polygon at the back of the model in the corresponding corner.

Use the Cut Tool
to cut from here...

Select this vertex,
and move it up.

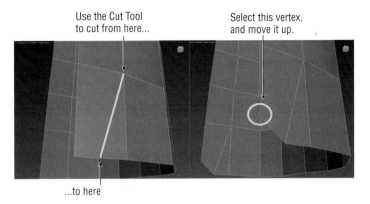

...to here

FIGURE 7.25 Cut the polygon and raise the corners.

3. In Vertex mode, select the lowest inside vertices and move them up a bit to create a diagonal edge. Do this for both the front and back of the model, as shown in Figure 7.25 (right).

4. In Edge mode, select both of the new diagonal edges (front and back), then choose Poly: Edit ➤ Edges ➤ Bridge ➤ Bridge Settings. Use four segments to create a bridge, as shown in Figure 7.26. Doing so creates a bridge between the front and back.

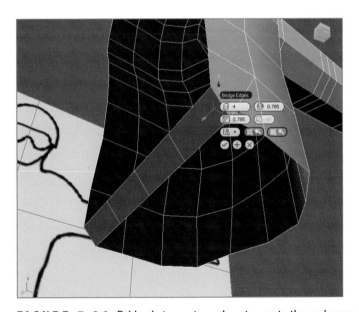

FIGURE 7.26 Bridge between two edges to create the groin area

With the bridge in place, the border edge on the bottom of the torso resembles a capital letter *D*, as shown in Figure 7.26. If you extrude the leg down from here, the inner thigh will be flat. For a better starting point to form the leg, you need to cap the hole as you did with the arm previously.

To begin the upper-thigh extrusion, continue with the following steps to cap the D-shape.

5. Enter Border mode, select the D-shaped border edge, and Shift+Move down on the Z-axis to extrude the upper thigh downward to right above the knee pad, as shown in Figure 7.27 (left). The knee pad's position can be seen better in the side reference image plane. Don't worry; you will adjust the shape to fit the thigh later.

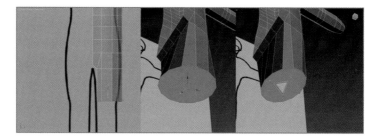

FIGURE 7.27 Creating the upper thigh

6. With the D-shaped border still selected, select Poly: Edit ➢ Geometry (All) ➢ Cap Poly to cap the end of the thigh stump. Enter Poly mode and select the new poly, and then select Poly: Edit ➢ Polygons ➢ GeoPoly to make the end of the thigh a more even shape; see Figure 7.27 (middle).

7. Select the thigh's end polygon and scale on the X-axis, as shown in Figure 7.27 (right), to create a more oval shape. Then delete the cap so the bottom of the leg is open once again.

8. In the Front viewport, switch to Vertex mode and scale and move the vertices on the leg to match the image plane. Check the Right viewport and shape the thigh as needed. Notice the bottom of the geometry should be located at about the top of the knee pad. Use the Perspective viewport often to make sure some of the vertices are not being accidentally moved.

9. On the inside of the groin area where you created the four-segment bridge in step 4, move the edges to make sure the segments are evenly spaced. This step should be repeated throughout the exercise to keep edges evenly spaced and ensure that the model is organized and clean.

10. Switch to Border mode and select the border opening at the bottom of the leg. Then use the Extrude Border method (hold Shift+Move) to extrude the leg down to the ankle, as shown in Figure 7.28 (left).

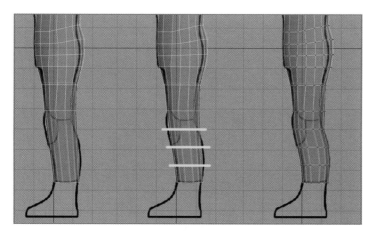

F I G U R E 7 . 2 8 Extrude down to the ankle, use the Swift Loop tool to create three new loops, and fit the new edges to the image plane.

11. Choose Poly: Edit ➢ Favorites ➢ SwiftLoop, and create three new horizontal segments around the leg, as shown in Figure 7.28 (middle). Then fit the vertices to the shape of the soldier's leg in the side image plane in the Right viewport, as shown in Figure 7.28 (right). Go into the Front viewport and do the same to shape the leg properly.

12. In Border mode, select the ankle border, as shown in Figure 7.29 (left) and Shift+Scale the border down on the Z- and Y-axes and in toward the center of the ankle, leaving a small hole; see Figure 7.29 (middle). Then switch to Vertex mode and select the vertices around the resulting small hole, and use Weld (Poly: Edit ➢ Vertices ➢ Weld) to bring the vertices together, as shown in Figure 7.29 (right). Adjust the Weld Threshold setting as needed to weld these vertices together.

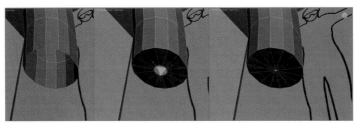

Select the border.   Shift+Scale in to center.   Weld the vertices.

FIGURE 7.29 Closing the ankle's hole

Fixing Up the Body

Continue with the previous exercise's scene file, or open the Soldier_V04.max scene file in the Scenes folder of the Soldier project from the book's web page.

1. The pelvis looks a bit funky. You need to streamline the mesh by combining some edges. Select the vertical edges at the waist (select a single vertical edge from Poly: Edit ➤ Selection ➤ Ring Selection); see Figure 7.30.

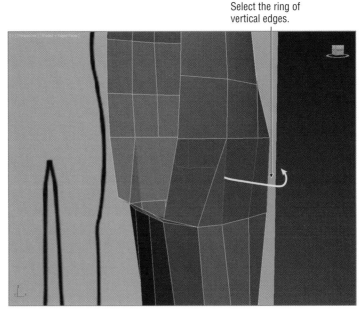

Select the ring of vertical edges.

FIGURE 7.30 Select waist edges and use Ring to prepare for Collapse.

2. Right-click to bring up the Quad menu. In the upper-left quad, in the Tools 1 section, choose Collapse. Doing so brings the two horizontal edge loops at the top and bottom of the selected vertical edges together into one edge loop.

3. In the Perspective viewport, use Orbit (use the ViewCube® 3D navigation control or Alt+MMB) to adjust the view to see under the groin area. In Edge or Vertex mode, move the segments to round out that section, as shown in Figure 7.31.

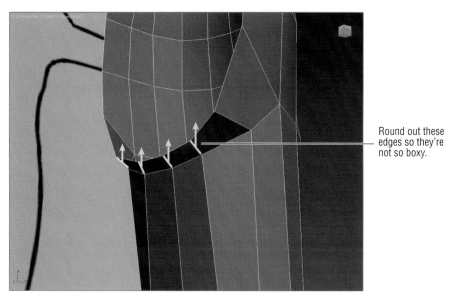

Round out these edges so they're not so boxy.

FIGURE 7.31 Round out the edges in the groin area.

4. In the Perspective viewport, use Orbit again around the leg and look for any spikes or pinches that may have occurred in the model. The goal is to split the difference between edges so that they're as close to 50 percent from another edge as possible.

Save your work! Keep in mind that a joint edge, such as the edges that make up the knee or elbow, need to stay where they are. Figure 7.32 shows the leg with good edge spacing. Take a moment to go back through the model and tweak the rest of it until you feel it is right. When you're modeling for animation, the mesh flow is an important factor.

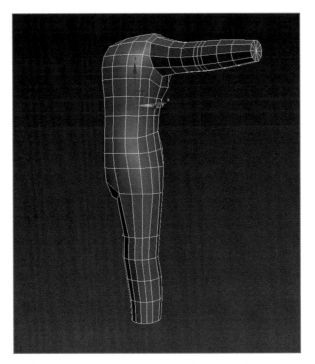

FIGURE 7.32 The leg with good edge spacing

THE ESSENTIALS AND BEYOND

This chapter explored and explained several tools used in modeling, organic and otherwise, to begin the basic form of the soldier character. Reference planes of the soldier design were used at first, and then from a simple box, a torso was formed to match the general shapes shown in the reference images. The arms and legs were extruded and shaped to match as well. As you can see, the more that you model, the easier the process becomes, and the more detailed and finessed your models will turn out.

ADDITIONAL EXERCISES

▶ Try creating a character of your own. A female character or something more edgy like an alien. Get reference images or draw out what you want the character to look like, scan the drawings and use them for reference. Use and expand on the techniques used in this chapter and Chapters 8 and 9.

CHAPTER 8

Character Poly Modeling: Part II

Realistic computer-generated (CG) characters are common in television and films; they appear as stunt doubles, as vast crowds, and as primary characters. Sometimes using a CG character works better than using a real person. Using a CG stunt double is safer and sometimes cheaper than using a live stunt person, and weird creatures can be created with better clarity by using CG rather than using puppetry or special makeup effects.

In this chapter, you will continue with the model of a special operations soldier, focusing on using the Editable Poly toolset to create a relatively low-polygon-count soldier model suitable for character animation and for use in a game engine.

Topics in this chapter include:

▶ **Completing the main body**

▶ **Creating the accessories**

▶ **Putting on the boots**

▶ **Creating the hands**

Completing the Main Body

Continue with the previous chapter's exercise scene file, or open the Soldier_ V05.max scene file in the Scenes folder of the Soldier project from the book's web page at www.sybex.com/go/3dsmax2013essentials.

To create the other half of the model you have so far, as shown in Figure 8.1, you are going to use the Symmetry modifier, which works by mirroring and then automatically welding the vertices along a seam. When the Symmetry modifier is applied to a mesh, any edits you make to the original half of the mesh also occur interactively to the other half of the mesh. This saves time and keeps the two halves of the model consistent.

This mirror technique gives the same results but in a different way. You will mirror the soldier's body in the following steps:

1. In the Front viewport, select the model. Go to the Command panels to the right of the interface, and in the Modify panel, go to the drop-down Modifier List menu. From the list, choose Symmetry. Depending on where the pivot point is on your mesh, the results of the modifier may look a bit strange, as shown in Figure 8.1.

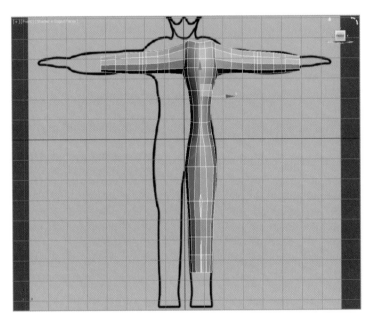

FIGURE 8.1 The results of the Symmetry modifier added when the pivot is not in the center of the model

2. In the Symmetry parameters, set the Mirror Axis to X. In the modifier stack, click the plus-sign icon (■) to expand the Symmetry modifier hierarchy and then highlight Mirror. This will release the slice plane in the modifier and allow you to edit where the mirror takes place.

3. In the Front viewport, select the X-axis arrow of the Transform gizmo and move the slice plane to the left until you get a whole soldier, as shown in Figure 8.2.

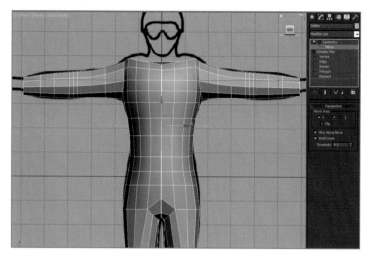

FIGURE 8.2 Using the Symmetry modifier, move the slice plane so the soldier is a complete whole.

When you begin to edit the mesh, the first thing you will do is go back down the modifier stack to the editable poly. It will appear that the symmetry side of the mesh has disappeared. This is not the case. What has occurred is that the 3ds Max® software evaluates the modifiers in the stack from the bottom up, and when you are below a modifier, the software doesn't calculate those modifiers. It is easy enough to fix. In a line of icons below the modifier stack, select Show End Results (▣). This will allow you to see the end results of the Symmetry modifier regardless of where you are in the stack.

4. Enter Edge mode, select the edges at the top of the right side of the torso geometry, as shown in Figure 8.3 (left image), and Shift+Scale them on the X- and Y-axes to extrude the top of the shoulders toward the neck (middle image). The edges all scale in toward the middle of the shoulder area and not the center of the neck at the spine, so switch to Vertex mode and move the vertices to better match the shape shown in Figure 8.3 (right image).

5. Go back to Edge mode and select the inner neck edges, extrude-move them (Shift+Move) to extrude another set of polygons toward the center of the neck, and then move the vertices toward the center of the model.

Select these edges.   Shift+Move to begin the shoulder.   Move vertices toward the center.

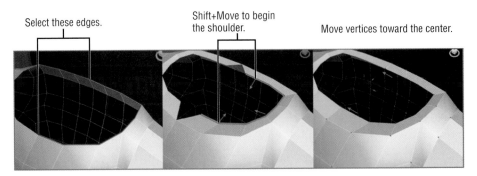

FIGURE 8.3 Drag out the edges around the neck.

6. In Edge mode, select the same inner neck edges again, and extrude-move them down to create a lip downward into the torso (you can see the vertical lip in Figure 8.4). Release the mouse, and then click again to Shift+Move in toward the center of the model to create a cap at the neck area, as shown in red in Figure 8.4.

   Now, go through one last time and fix any edge spacing issues or wonky geometry you may have. When you're ready, you are going to combine the two parts of the model.

   To combine the Symmetry side of the model with the original side, go to the Graphite modeling tools and choose Poly: Edit ➤ Edit Polygons ➤ Collapse Stack. The Symmetry modifier automatically welds the mesh together at the seam.

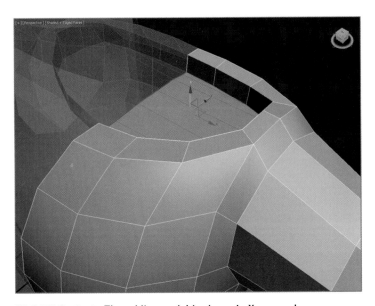

FIGURE 8.4 The soldier model is shown in X-ray mode.

Creating the Accessories

Continue with the previous exercise's scene file, or open the Soldier_V06.max
scene file in the Scenes folder of the Soldier project from the book's web page.
Most of the smaller detail in the model will be added through textures; however,
adding detail such as pouches, elbows, and knee pads into the actual geometry
helps tremendously. This creates a better silhouette for your character.

1. To create the belt, you're going to chamfer and extrude an edge
   loop that's located closest to the belt line on the model. Choose the
   edge in the middle of the soldier's waistline and select Poly: Edit ➢
   Selection ➢ Loop Selection.

2. With the edge loop selected, select Poly: Edit ➢ Edit Polygons ➢
   Edges ➢ Chamfer Settings. Set Edge Chamfer Amount to **1.5** and
   click OK.

3. With the two edges from the chamfer still selected, hold Shift and
   select Poly: Edit ➢ Edit Polygons and then select the Polygon icon.
   Doing so selects the polygons associated with the two selected edges.
   If that doesn't work, hold down the Ctrl key and click on the remaining polygons that need to be selected.

4. Next, select Poly: Edit ➢ Polygons ➢ Extrude Settings, and make
   sure you extrude by Local Normal with a Height value of **0.5**, as
   shown in Figure 8.5.

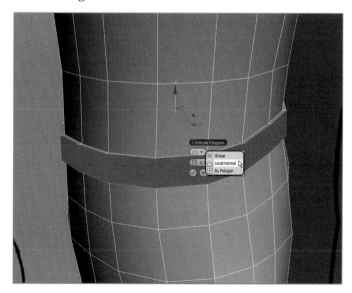

FIGURE 8.5 Extrude polygons for the belt.

5. Next, you're going to block out a pouch on the belt. Delete two sections of the belt on the body's left side, as shown in Figure 8.6.

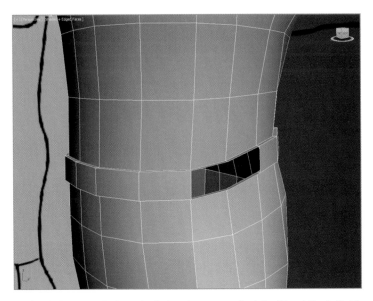

FIGURE 8.6 Delete the belt polygons on the left side of the belt. Then select the indicated polygons for the next step.

6. Select the four polygons above and below the deleted area, also shown in Figure 8.6. Select Poly: Edit ➢ Polygons ➢ Extrude ➢ Extrude Settings, set an amount of **0.5**, and then click Apply and Continue (⊟) to apply one extrusion. Then click OK (⊕) for a second extrusion and to exit the caddy. The pouch is now extruded twice for a total extrusion depth of 1 inch.

7. Select the four polygons on top of the bottom half of the pouch and the four polygons on the bottom of the top half of the pouch, as shown in Figure 8.7, and delete them. Figure 8.7 shows the model in See-Through mode. Press Alt+X to see all eight polygons to be selected and deleted.

8. In Edge mode, select the top and bottom edges around the newly deleted areas, and select Poly: Edit ➢ Edges ➢ Bridge Settings, as shown in Figure 8.8, to open the caddy. Accept the default values, shown in Figure 8.9, and click OK.

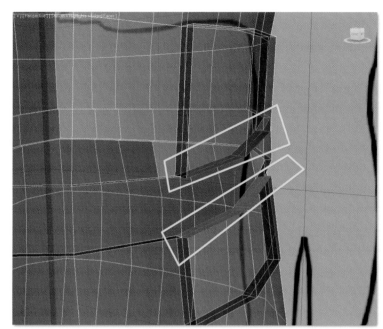

Select and delete these polygons.

FIGURE 8.7 Select and delete polygons.

FIGURE 8.8 The Edge Bridge tool

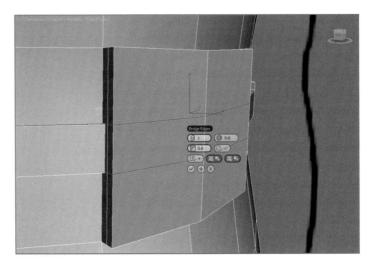

FIGURE 8.9 The Bridge caddy settings

The pouch should look like a box; if it doesn't, move vertices around so it does. Once the pouch has the correct shape, move the top level of polygons farther out away from the belt to give the pouch more depth.

9. To add some depth to the vest that the character will be wearing, you will want to cut out a level of clothing under the arms. Select two columns and three rows of polygons directly underneath the armpit, as shown in Figure 8.10.

10. Select Poly: Edit ➢ Polygons ➢ Bevel Settings, and in the caddy use a Height of **-0.5** and an Outline of **-1.0**.

Adjust any vertices as necessary for an even and smooth look. Do the same for the other side of the model. The final appearance of the area underneath the armpit is shown in Figure 8.11.

11. Next, you're going to add a leg strap to hold a gun holster. Select Poly: Edit ➢ Favorites ➢ SwiftLoop, and add a new horizontal loop of edges below the groin area on both legs. When the loop is created, it is crooked, but you need the new edges to be straight. The Swift Loop tool should still be active when you're doing this. So, after you create the edge, hold Ctrl+Alt and click and drag the edge down, and you will see that it straightens.

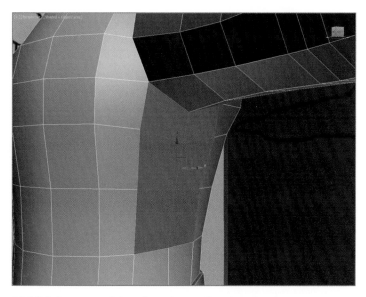

FIGURE 8.10 Select the polygons directly under the armpit.

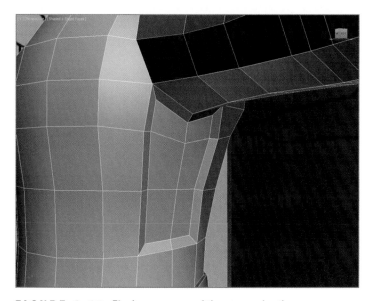

FIGURE 8.11 Final appearance of the area under the arm

12. On the right leg, in Edge mode select one edge of the new edge loop you created in the previous step. Select Poly: Edit ➢ Selection ➢ Loop Selection, and then Edges ➢ Chamfer Settings. Enter an edge chamfer amount of **1.5** and click OK.

13. In Polygon mode, select the loop of new polygons by holding Shift and clicking the Polygon icon in the Polygon Modeling panel. Then select Polygon ➢ Extrude Settings, using a Height value of **0.4**.

14. In Polygon mode, select a strip of polygons that goes from the top of the leg strap to the bottom of the belt, and delete them, as shown in Figure 8.12.

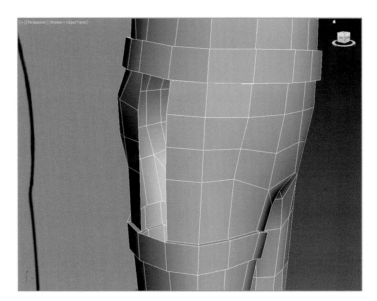

FIGURE 8.12 Deleting polygons

15. Select the edge at the leg strap and at the belt, and use Bridge to create the polygons needed to fill out the strap. The sides of the holster are still open.

16. Select the edges between the new bridged polygons and the model's hip, and then use Bridge again in this area, as shown in Figure 8.13. Be sure to repeat this on the other side of the holster as well.

17. Exit Sub-Object Mode by clicking on the polygon icon or click 6 on your keyboard and then with the soldier model still selected, at the bottom of the interface click the Isolate Selection toggle button (Alt+Q). Now

go back into Edge mode, and in the Left viewport, create a plane with these parameters:

Length: **20**, Width: **7**, Length Segs: **4**, Width Segs: **1**

18. Convert the plane to an editable poly. Position the plane where the holster will be on the soldier. Then in Vertex mode, shape it as shown in Figure 8.14.

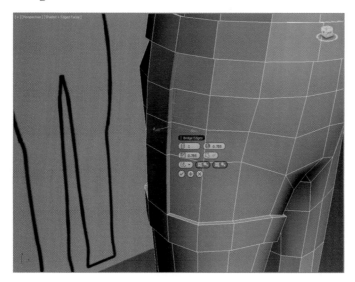

FIGURE 8.13 Use Bridge to fill the gap on the side of the strap.

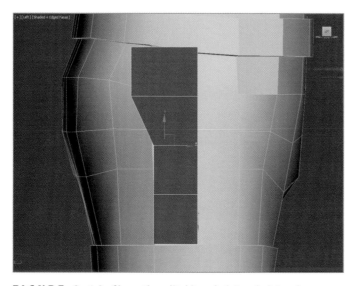

FIGURE 8.14 Shape the editable poly into a holster shape.

19. In the Modify panel, use the modifier list to add a Shell modifier to the plane and give it the following parameters:
Inner Amount: **1.2**, Outer Amount: **1.2**, Segments: **1**

Now, fit this piece in place on the vertical leg strap you created.

20. Select the body and from the Graphite Modeling Tools ribbon, select Geometry (All) ➢ Attach and click on the gun holster.

Putting on the Boots

Continue with the previous exercise's scene file, or open the Soldier_V07.max scene file in the Scenes folder of the Soldier project from the book's web page. At this point, you are probably feeling comfortable with the tools and interface, so we'll pare down the steps somewhat unless the procedures are new to this chapter.

1. To create the boots, start by creating a cylinder in the Perspective viewport. In the Create panel, select Geometry ➢ Cylinder. Set Radius to **5.0**, Height to **8.0**, Height Segments to **1**, Cap Segments to **1**, and Sides to **8**, and make sure the Smooth option is checked. Create the cylinder.

2. Select the cylinder and choose Poly: Edit ➢ Edit Polygons ➢ Convert To Poly. Then position the cylinder under the left leg to be the top part of the boot.

3. Using the Right viewport, move vertices on the cylinder so the shape mimics the form of the top of the boot in the image plane. Delete the topmost and bottommost polygons that were created with the cylinder.

4. Ignore the two bottom-front edges of the cylinder where the top of the foot would be, and select the bottom U-shaped edges of the cylinder. Extrude-move (Shift+Move) the edges of the back half of the boot top to the bottom of the foot in the image plane, as shown in Figure 8.15.

5. Select the two bottom-front edges that you ignored previously, and extrude-move them four times to form the extruded polygons to the image plane, as shown in Figure 8.16. You will need a total of four rows of polygons for the top and front of the foot. As you extrude, you can release the mouse button after one extrusion, and then Shift+Move again for the next extrusion. Repeat for a total of four new strips of polygons, as Figure 8.16 shows. Form the new polygons as needed to fit the top of the foot.

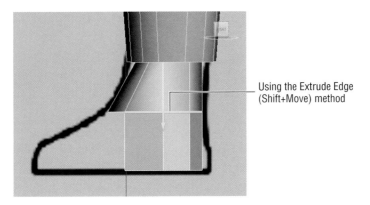

Using the Extrude Edge (Shift+Move) method

FIGURE 8.15 Using Extrude Edge to create another set of polygons for the U-shaped back and side part of the boot

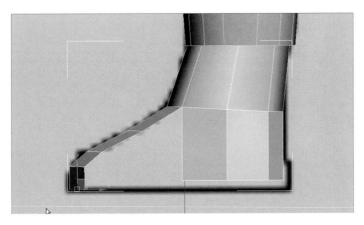

FIGURE 8.16 Using Extrude Edge to create four new polygons that form with the image plane for the top of the foot

6. In Edge mode, select the vertical edges on either side of the gap, as shown in Figure 8.17 (left). Then select Poly: Edit ➤ Edges ➤ Bridge ➤ Bridge Settings, enter three segments, and bridge the gap. Repeat the same on the opposite side of the foot.

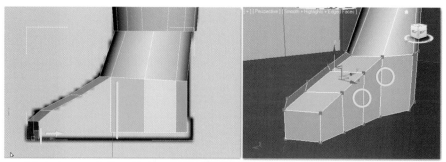

Select edges; use Bridge with three segments.   Select the vertices and weld them.

FIGURE 8.17 Use Bridge to fill the gaps and Weld to close the gaps.

7. Switch to Vertex mode, and from the Edit: Poly ➢ Vertices ➢ Weld, open the caddy, set Threshold to **2.0**, and click OK, as shown in Figure 8.17 (right).

8. Select Poly: Edit ➢ Favorites ➢ SwiftLoop. Create a new horizontal edge loop around the foot from heel to toe on the side of the foot, as shown in Figure 8.18.

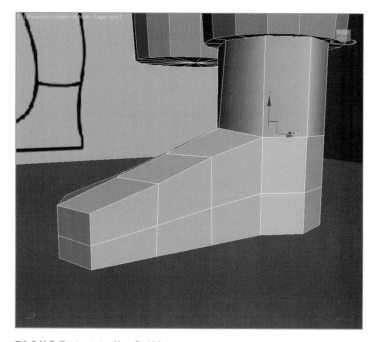

FIGURE 8.18 Use SwiftLoop to create a new horizontal edge around the side of the foot.

The eight segments you defined on the original boot cylinder are not enough, so you need to create more segments for the cylinder.

9. In Edge mode, select the middle vertical edge of the foot, and select Loop. Choose Poly: Edit ➤ Edges ➤ Chamfer ➤ Chamfer Settings, and enter the caddy parameters: Chamfer Amount: **0.667**, Segments: **1**. Click OK.

10. Follow the same process to chamfer the very back vertical edge on the boot (running just below the calf) and use the added vertices to round out the heel. The top of the foot is a bit boxy, so scale in the vertices and smooth out the sides as in Figure 8.19.

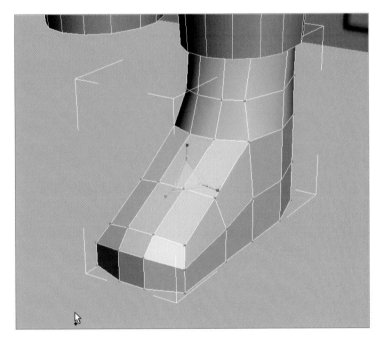

FIGURE 8.19 Smoothing out the sides of the boot

When you are happy with how this looks, center the pivot point to the soldier model and use Symmetry modifier on the X-axis and select Flip in the Symmetry parameters. Attach the boots to the rest of the body, as you did with the gun holster. Figure 8.20 shows the two completed boots, now attached to the body.

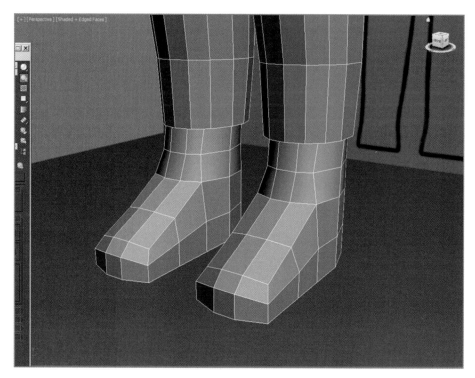

FIGURE 8.20 Boots completed and attached to the body

Creating the Hands

Continue with the previous exercise's scene file, or open the Soldier_V08.max scene file in the Scenes folder of the Soldier project from the book's web page. In this section, you will create simple "mitten hands" for the soldier:

1. To create one of the hands, start with a box. Create a box primitive in the Perspective viewport, and then in the Modify panel, set Length to **7.5**, Width to **16.0**, and Height to **5.0**. All segments should be set to **1**. Position the box in your Top viewport over the wrist. Finish positioning it in the Front viewport and convert it to an editable poly.

2. In the Top viewport, use Swift Loop to create two segments vertically and two segments horizontally. Then, in Vertex mode, move the vertices to create a mitten arc, as shown in Figure 8.21.

FIGURE 8.21 Reshape vertices to create a mitten shape.

3. With the hand selected, go into Polygon mode and select the polygons on the hand where the wrist and the arm meet; then delete them. The result is a hollow hand.

4. In Edge mode, select the outer edge loop running along the top and bottom of the hand lengthwise. Then select Poly: Edit ➢ Edges ➢ Chamfer ➢ Chamfer Settings, and set Edge Chamfer Amount to **0.7**, as shown in Figure 8.22.

5. Use Swift Loop (Poly: Edit ➢ Edit) to create an edge up from the wrist, as shown in Figure 8.23.

6. In Polygon mode, select the three polygons just up from the newly created edge on the side of the hand, where the thumb should be. Choose Poly: Edit ➢ Polygons ➢ Extrude ➢ Extrude Settings and use a Height value of **0.8** to start pulling out the thumb. Then move the corner edges in to round out the beginning shape of the thumb.

7. Bevel the polygons at the end of the thumb for the knuckle. Choose Poly: Edit ➢ Polygons ➢ Bevel Settings. Set Bevel Amount to **3.0** and Outline Amount to **-.55**, and click OK.

8. Repeat step 7 at the tip of the thumb geometry to create another segment for the thumb from the knuckle to the tip of the thumb. Adjust the polygons, vertices, and edges to get the thumb to look like Figure 8.24.

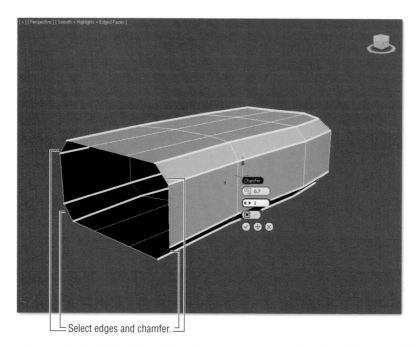

Select edges and chamfer.

FIGURE 8.22 Select and chamfer the edge loops running lengthwise along the top and bottom of the hand.

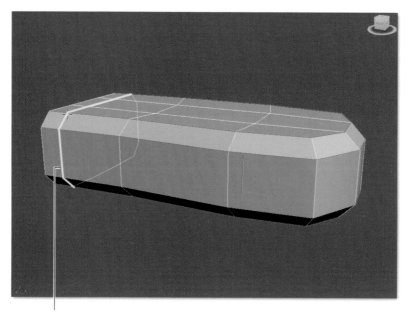

Using SwiftLoop to create a new edge

FIGURE 8.23 Use SwiftLoop to create an edge at the wrist.

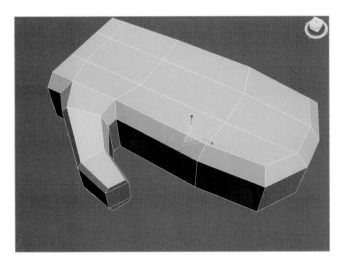

FIGURE 8.24 The thumb with all its joints

9. Select the polygon at the ends of the thumb and fingers. Choose Poly: Edit ➢ Selection, and click the Soft Selection icon (⬤). In the Front viewport, move the thumb and fingers down to give them a slight slope.

10. In the Perspective viewport, scale the wrist down to fit within the sleeve if necessary. Center the pivot point to the model's body, and mirror it as a copy for the other side. Place the hands at the wrists and attach them to the rest of the model. The final gloved hand is shown in Figure 8.25.

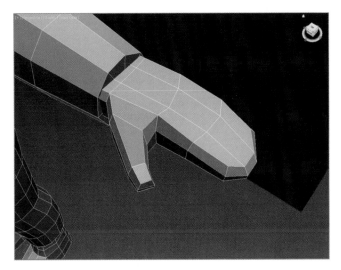

FIGURE 8.25 The final gloved hand

THE ESSENTIALS AND BEYOND

In this chapter, you completed the main body for the soldier and continued using edge loops and vertices to shape the accessories and various parts of the character model.

ADDITIONAL EXERCISES

▶ Create additional pouches or straps for your model. (Keep in mind that any changes you make to the design of the book's model will make your model differ from the one you use for texturing in Chapter 11, "Textures and UV Workflow: The Soldier.")

▶ With the tools you used to create the belt and pouches, create geometry for knee pads and elbow pads.

You can see the extra accessories on Soldier model here:

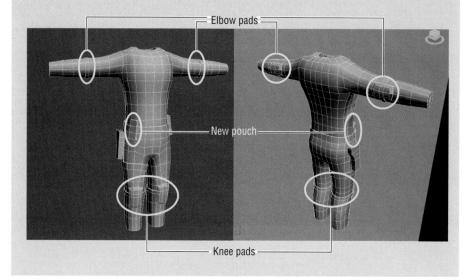

CHAPTER 9

Character Poly Modeling: Part III

Finishing elements are critical to the veracity of a model's design. To make things easier, such elements can be modeled separately and later incorporated into the base model. In this chapter, you will finish the model of the special operations soldier you started in Chapter 7, "Character Poly Modeling: Part I." To do that, you will model the head shape, merge the head shape with elements such as goggles and a face mask, and integrate them into the scene.

Topics in this chapter include the following:

▶ **Creating the head**

▶ **Merging and attaching the head's accessories**

Creating the Head

Continue with the previous exercise's scene file (from Chapter 8, "Character Poly Modeling: Part II"), or open the Soldier_V09.max scene file in the Scenes folder of the Soldier project from the book's web page at www.sybex.com/go/3dsmax2013essentials.

The soldier's head will consist of four parts: a helmet, goggles, a face mask, and a head shape on which they can sit. The easiest way to create and fit these components is to start with the head shape. First, though, you need to adjust the body's neckline so working with it is a bit easier. Right now the neck area is almost a circle shape. You want it to be closer to an oval that follows the contour of the rest of the model.

1. In Polygon mode, select the front of the neckline. Then, from the Graphite Modeling Tools ribbon, choose Poly: Edit ➤ Selection ➤ Use Soft Selection (▣). Then in the Soft floating panel, change the Falloff value to 4.000, as shown in Figure 9.1. Move the polygons down on the Y-axis. Do the same for the back of the model. These actions will smoothly create a lower neckline, giving more definition to the shoulders as well.

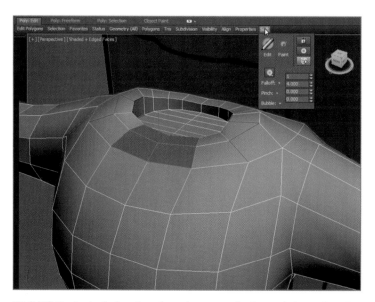

FIGURE 9.1 Soft-select the polygons at the front of the neck and move them down.

2. Under the Object Type rollout, select Create Panel ➢ Geometry and then check AutoGrid. When the box is checked, it activates a construction grid that allows you to create objects on the surface of the soldier. Select Cylinder and click and drag within the neck of the soldier model using these parameters:

   Radius: 5.0

   Height: 3.0

   Height Segments: 1

   Cap Segments: 1

   Sides: 12

3. Convert the cylinder in Poly: Edit ➢ Edit Polygons ➢ Convert to Poly. You'll model half of each part and then use mirroring to save time. In Polygon mode, select and delete the left half, the top, and the bottom of the cylinder, and move the edges and vertices so the new neck geometry is formed better within the neckline, as shown in Figure 9.2.

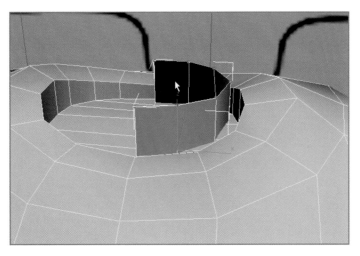

FIGURE 9.2 Delete half of the cylinder and its top and bottom.

4. Select the top edges of the cylinder and extrude-move them (Shift+Move) to create another level of polygons. The neck now has two rows of polygons. Next, select the first edge on the top nearest where the Adam's apple would be, and extrude-move to create a new polygon. Move the edge up along the Z-axis, as shown in Figure 9.3.

Use Extrude Edge (Shift+Move method).

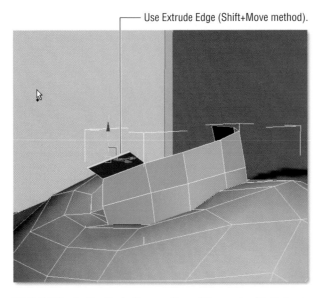

FIGURE 9.3 Begin the creation of the neck with Extrude.

Outlining the Head

In the following steps, you will create an outline of the head by creating one strip of polygons and then forming them to the side image plane. You will extrude 15 times and move the edges to create the general form of a head. Be sure to keep the outer edge of the head inside the edges of the image plane; that way, you'll have room to fit the head accessories.

1. You should still have the edge selected from the previous exercise. Use extrude-move again, but when you finish one polygon, release the mouse button; then click again and move the edge to create another extruded polygon. You'll do this 14 more times, following the form of the head in the image plane, as shown in Figure 9.4.

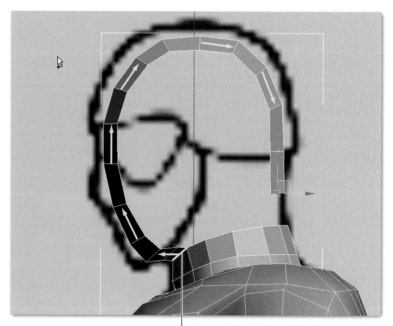

Use the Extrude Edge (Shift+Move method). Do this 15 times, following the form of the head in the image plane.

FIGURE 9.4 Following the image plane, create the head outline using the Shift+Move method.

2. In the Front viewport, select the edge on the top base of the neck about where the ear might be. Using Shift+Move, position a polygon strip as you did in step 1, but this time for the side of the head.

Extrude a total of five segments up from the neck. In Edge mode, use Bridge (on the Poly: Edit ➤ Edges ➤ choose Bridge) to fill the gap between the side of the head and the nearest edge on the top of the head, as shown in Figure 9.5.

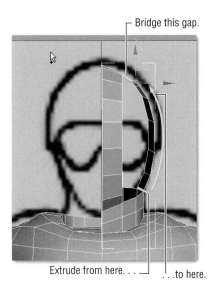

Bridge this gap.

Extrude from here. . . . . .to here.

FIGURE 9.5 Creating polygons for the side of the head

3. To build the front of the face, start by selecting the two edges just under the chin and use Shift+Move to extrude them out to the right, as shown in Figure 9.6. In Vertex mode, select the Graphite Modeling Tools ribbon and choose Vertices ➤ Target Weld. To use Target Weld, click on one vertex and drag a line to the other to fuse the vertices together. So first click the vertex on the new polygon closest to the neck, and then click on the neck vertex, shown in Figure 9.6. This will fuse the new polygons for the jowls to the neck.

4. Back in Edge mode, select the two rightmost edges of the polygons you just created for the jowls, and then use Shift+Move to extrude those edges up on the Z-axis. Match the number of segments with the segments on the outer head strip you already created. The result is shown in Figure 9.7.

5. Select the edges shown on the left side of Figure 9.8. Use Bridge to curve the strip toward the forehead, as shown in Figure 9.8.

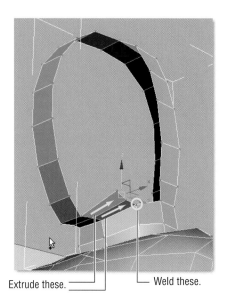

Extrude these. ———————   —— Weld these.

FIGURE 9.6 Extrude edges to the right and weld the neck vertices.

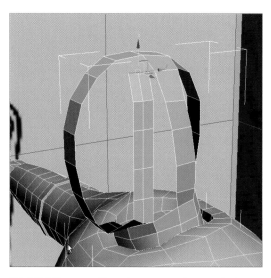

FIGURE 9.7 Extrude a new strip; match the segments.

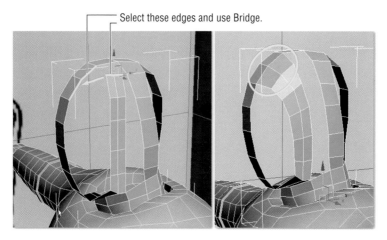

Select these edges and use Bridge.

FIGURE 9.8 Use Bridge to close the gap.

6. As you did in step 5, in Edge mode use Shift+Move to extrude another row of polygons in toward the front of the face. Then in Vertex mode, use Target Weld on either side of the front face strip, as shown in Figure 9.9.

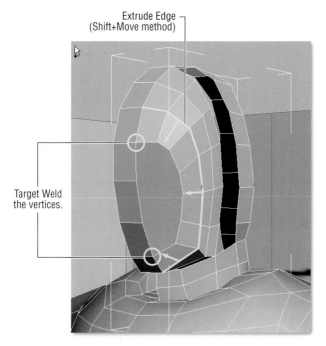

Extrude Edge
(Shift+Move method)

Target Weld
the vertices.

FIGURE 9.9 Use Shift+Move and then use Target Weld.

7. Looking at the ring of edges from the front of the strip of the head to the side of the head, it's clear you don't have enough horizontal edges. Select the edge closest to where the bridge of the nose would be, and then use Chamfer (from the Graphite Modeling Tools ribbon, choose Edges ➤ Chamfer Settings ➤ Chamfer Settings) with an Edge Chamfer Amount value of 1.346, and then click OK. Try to keep the edges equally spaced, as shown in Figure 9.10.

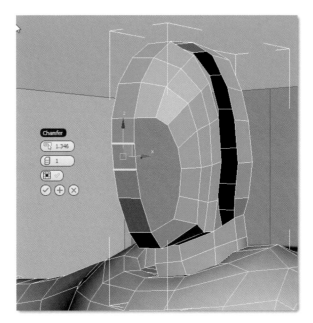

FIGURE 9.10 Chamfer the edge that falls at the bridge of the nose.

8. Select the eight edges on the front of the face and the side of the face, and then use Bridge, as shown in Figure 9.11. Notice that there is nowhere to weld to on the vertical edge on the top of the head. You need to create another edge running down the front of the face and then weld the vertices together to close the head.

9. From the Graphite Modeling Tools ribbon, choose Edit to access the Cut tool. Then cut from the dead-end edge at the top of the head down to the bottom of the neck, as shown in Figure 9.12. Make sure you start and end the cut directly on the vertices.

10. In Vertex mode, select the two vertices at the top of the cut; from the Graphite Modeling Tools ribbon, choose Vertices ➤ Weld and modify the Weld Threshold setting until the two vertices are welded together.

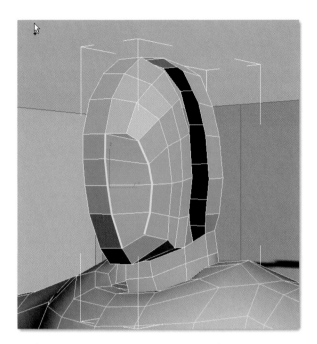

FIGURE 9.11 Select edges and use Bridge.

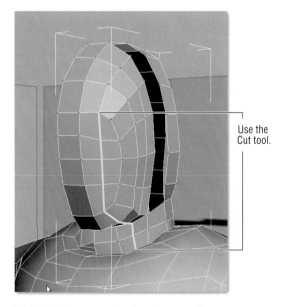

Use the
Cut tool.

FIGURE 9.12 Cutting the new edge

Rounding Out the Face

Now it is time to round out the face a bit. The face doesn't have to be perfectly round, but it will help if the face is close to a round shape. The majority of the head mesh you will create will be covered with the goggles, helmet, and face mask. However, you can use the geometry you create to fit and form those accessories.

1. In Edge mode, select the edges around the ear and use Bridge to close the gap, as shown in Figure 9.13.

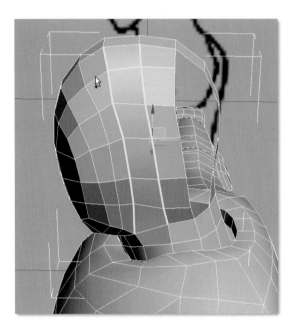

FIGURE 9.13 Bridging the edges

2. Looking at the back of the head, you can see an edge open on the bottom. Use the Cut tool to add another vertical edge, as shown in Figure 9.14.

3. Select the edges on the inside of the gap closest to the back of the head and use Shift+Move to extrude more faces toward the ears, as shown in Figure 9.15. Then switch to Vertex mode and use Target Weld to weld the loose vertices at the top and bottom, also shown in Figure 9.15.

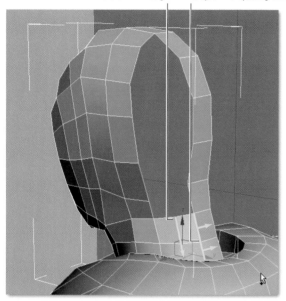

FIGURE 9.14 Create a new edge for the back of the head/neck using the Cut tool.

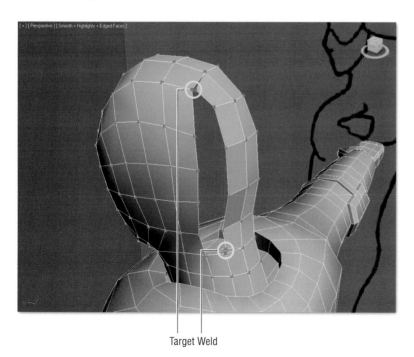

FIGURE 9.15 Extrude edges and use Target Weld on the loose vertices.

Creating the Back of the Head

You have the same problem with the back of the head as you did with the front of the face: There are not enough horizontal edges.

1. Chamfer a horizontal edge near the top of the back of the head, as shown in Figure 9.16. In the figure, you can visualize how the polygons will bridge over. In this case, after you create the chamfer, you will have five segments that can bridge in the next step.

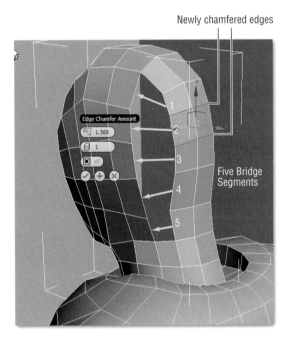

FIGURE 9.16 Chamfer the edges.

2. Bridge the vertical edges of the gap, as Figure 9.17 shows. This time you have the exact amount needed to create a solid head shape.

3. Go into the Right viewport and notice how the edges are closer to the front of the head than the back, as shown in Figure 9.18 (left). Select and move edges or vertices until the vertices are more evenly spaced (Figure 9.18, right).

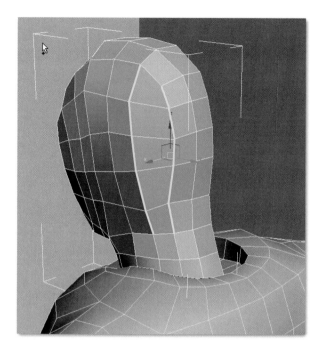

FIGURE 9.17 Bridge the vertical edges to fill the last hole.

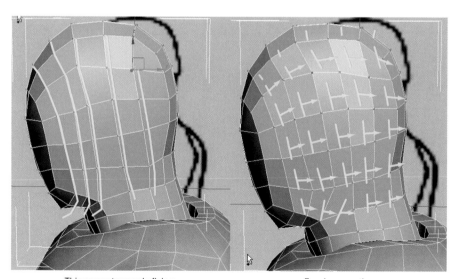

This geometry needs fixing.   Evenly space these.

FIGURE 9.18 Move edges or vertices to evenly space the edges.

Mirroring the Head

Now make any necessary adjustments to your mesh to get it just right. Again, it's not terribly vital that this part be perfect because you will cover it up with accessories in the upcoming steps. Once you're satisfied, continue with these steps:

1. With the Head selected, go to the Modify panel and from the modifier list, choose Symmetry. When you add the Symmetry modifier, the soldier's head may appear warped or even as if it disappeared. It depends on where the pivot point is sitting; the pivot point defines the center from which the modifier mirrors.

2. In the modify stack, click the plus sign icon (+) next to the Symmetry modifier to expand the gizmo. This adjusts the Symmetry so it appears that the head is whole. If the mesh doesn't appear even when you move the gizmo, click the box next to Flip in the Symmetry parameters.

3. When the head looks correct, in the Poly: Edit ➢ Edit Polygons ➢ Collapse Stack. This integrates the Symmetry modifier into the editable polygon, making the head a whole mesh.

Merging and Attaching the Head's Accessories

The remaining accessories for the soldier are the helmet, goggles, and face mask. To create these objects, you can repeat the same methods you've already used, so we'll save a little time and merge the finished pieces.

The finished models for the helmet, goggles, and face mask have been created separately and can be merged into your final model. Keep in mind that if you changed the design of the soldier as you built him in your scene, these premade accessories for the head may not perfectly fit your particular model. If this is the case, you may want to use the scene file of the soldier provided in the following steps, or create your own accessories to fit your design.

Continue with the previous exercise's scene file, or open the `Soldier_v10.max` scene file in the Soldier project's `Scenes` folder from the book's web page.

1. Click the Applications menu and select Import ➢ Merge. In the Merge File dialog box, choose the file `Soldier_Accessories.max`

in the Scenes folder of the Soldier project from the web page. Click
Open. In the Merge dialog box, select all the objects in the list and
click OK. You might see a warning about materials, as shown in
Figure 9.19, so just click Use Scene Material. The object will appear
in the scene, lined up with the model.

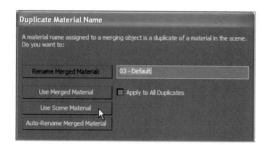

FIGURE 9.19 You might see this warning.

Now you need to attach all the accessories to the main body. This
means the entire soldier model will be a single mesh and can be used
to create the UVW mapping for the model in Chapter 11, "Textures
and UV Workflow: The Soldier."

2. Select the body, and from Poly: Edit choose Geometry (All) ➢
   Attach (Arrow) ➢ Attach From List to open the Attach List dialog
   box. Using this dialog box makes it easier to attach when you have
   multiple objects.

3. Because you selected the body when you opened the Attach List dialog box, the window won't show the body as an object that you can
   select. Select the four objects, but not the image planes, in the list
   and click Attach.

The soldier is complete—well, at least the model. Now that the head objects
are attached to the body, they cannot be selected individually. As a matter of
fact, the entire soldier is one object, from the boots to the helmet. You have
to select the boots, hands, or any accessories you added to the model by using
Element mode from the modifier stack. You will see this approach in action
in Chapter 11 as you lay out UVs for the soldier. Figure 9.20 shows the completed model of the special operations soldier with some added accessories,
elbow and knee pads, and with the head's accessories.

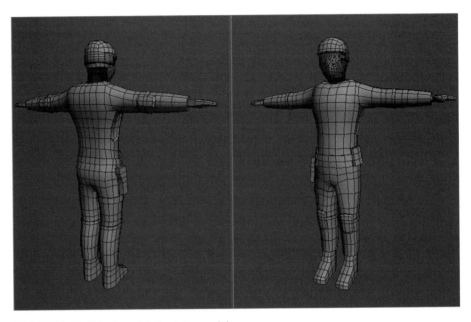

FIGURE 9.20 Completed soldier model

Go grab a frosty beverage; you've earned it!

THE ESSENTIALS AND BEYOND

This chapter explored several tools used in modeling. From a simple box, you formed a torso to match the general shapes shown in the images. The arms and legs were extruded and shaped. Using Mirror required you to model only half of the soldier character at a time. The head modeling came next, and then you merged the already completed accessories from another scene file to add detail to the model's head.

ADDITIONAL EXERCISES

Although we used a fairly low-polygon-count soldier character in this chapter, this toolset can be utilized for any type of model. Try variations on the same themes, such as:

▶ Design and build another special operations soldier to form a team.

▶ Build different accessories for the soldier, such as a rifle.

CHAPTER 10

Introduction to Materials: Interiors and Furniture

A material defines an object's look—its color, tactile texture, transparency, luminescence, glow, and so on. *Mapping* is the term used to describe how the materials are wrapped or projected onto the geometry (for example, adding wood grain to a wooden object). After you create your objects, the Autodesk® 3ds Max® program assigns a simple color to them, as you've already seen.

You define a material with the 3ds Max software by setting values for its parameters or by applying textures or maps. These parameters define the way an object will look when rendered. Much of an object's appearance when rendered also depends on the lighting. In this chapter and in Chapter 14, "Introduction to Lighting: Interior Lighting," you will discover that materials and lights work closely together.

Topics in this chapter include the following:

► **Slate Material Editor**

► **Standard material types**

► **mental ray material types**

► **Shaders**

► **Mapping the couch and chair**

► **Mapping the windows and doors**

The Slate Material Editor

The Material Editor is the central place where you do all of your material creation and editing. You can assign materials to any number of objects, as well as have multiple materials assigned to different parts of the same object.

The 3ds Max® 2013 program has two interfaces to the Material Editor: the Slate Material Editor (or Slate) and the Compact Material Editor.

The Slate Material Editor is the interface you will use in this book: it is far superior to the compact version and is especially nice when you are first learning mapping because you can see the material structure, as shown in Figure 10.1.

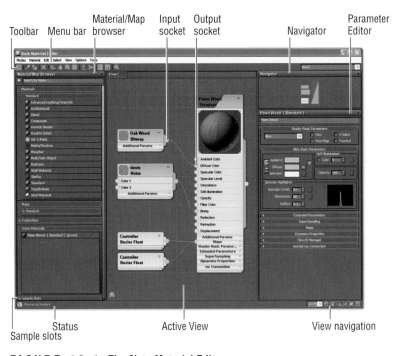

FIGURE 10.1 The Slate Material Editor

You can access the Material Editor by choosing Rendering ➤ Material Editor ➤ Slate Material Editor. There is also an icon for it on the main toolbar (▣), and the keyboard shortcut to open the Material Editor is the M key. The Slate Material Editor is the default Material Editor, but if it opens as the Compact Material Editor, you can switch it in the menu bar at the top of the Material Editor by selecting Modes ➤ Slate Material Editor. The Slate Material Editor has an interface that uses nodes and wiring to display the structure of materials. It has a simple and elegant layout with the Material/Map browser on the left for choosing material and map types. The center area is the Active View area where you build materials by connecting maps or controllers to material components. The area on the right is the Parameter Editor; within that area is a Navigator for moving within the Active View area.

Material Types

Different materials have different uses. The Standard material is fine for most uses. However, when you require a more complex material, you can change the material type to one that will fit your needs. To change a material type in the Slate Material Editor, just choose from the list under Materials in the Material/ Map browser. You should see the rollout for Standard. If you are using the mental ray renderer, you will also see a rollout for mental ray and MetaSL. As you can see, the list is extensive; there are not enough pages in this book to cover the multitude of material types so we will touch on some of the best for an introduction. You will also see some examples using the Slate Material Editor.

Standard Materials

Standard materials typically use a four-color model to simulate a surface of a "single" color reflecting many colors. The four colors are known as the material's color components. Ambient color appears where the surface is in shadow, diffuse color appears where light falls directly on the surface, specular color appears in highlights, and filter color appears as light shining through an object. Along with the color components, there are parameters that control highlights, transparency, and self-illumination. Some of these parameters are different depending on the shader you are using. With the Standard material you can imitate just about any surface type you can imagine, as shown in Figure 10.2.

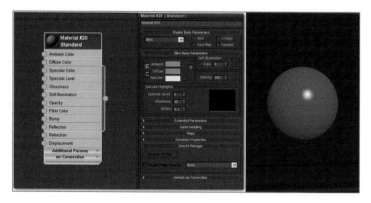

FIGURE 10.2 The Standard Material type shown in Slate Material Editor

Compound Materials

Compound materials combine two or more submaterials for a variegated look, especially when used with maps. Compound materials are similar to compositor maps, but they exist at the material level, as shown in Figure 10.3. You load or create compound materials using the Material/Map browser.

Matte/Shadow   Use Matte/Shadow material when you want to isolate the shadow. The material will receive shadows, but it will remain transparent for everything else. It is useful for rendering objects onto a photo or video background because it creates a separate shadow that you can composite on top of the background. Rendering in separate passes, such as a separate shadow, is very useful because you can have total control of the image by compositing just the right amount of any particular pass.

Raytrace   The Raytrace material is a powerful material that expands the available parameters to give you more control over photo-real renderings. The material uses more system resources than the Standard material at render time, but it can produce more accurate renders—especially when true reflections and refractions are concerned.

Ink 'n Paint   Ink 'n Paint is a powerful Cartoon material that creates outlines and flat cartoon shading for 3D objects based on Falloff parameters, as shown in Figure 10.4.

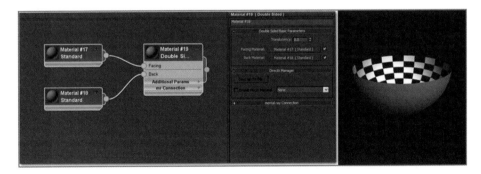

FIGURE 10.3 Double-Sided material is one of the many Compound materials.

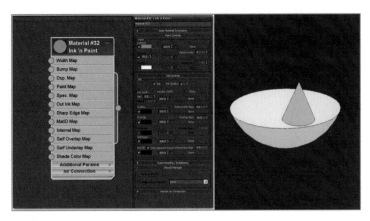

FIGURE 10.4 The Ink 'n Paint material is shown with parameters in the Slate Material Editor.

mental ray Material Types

The 3ds Max program comes with several materials created specifically for use with the mental ray renderer. These materials are visible in the Material/Map browser when mental ray is the active renderer. For the sake of time and space we are only going to cover one here.

Arch & Design   The mental ray Arch (architectural) & Design material improves the image quality of architectural renderings. It improves workflow and performance in general, and performance for glossy surfaces (such as floors) in particular.

Special features of the Arch & Design material include self-illumination, advanced options for reflectivity and transparency, ambient occlusion settings, and the ability to round off sharp corners and edges as a rendering effect. These material types will be further explored in Chapter 16, "mental ray and HDRI."

Shaders

The way light reflects from a surface defines that surface to your eye. With the 3ds Max program, you can control what kind of surface you work with by changing the shader type for a material. In either the Compact or Slate Material Editor, you will find the shader type in the material parameters in the Shader

Basic Parameters. This option will let you mimic different types of surfaces, such as dull wood, shiny paint, or metal. The following descriptions outline the differences in how the shader types react to light, as shown in Figure 10.5.

Shader Types

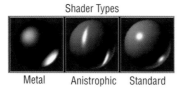

Metal   Anistrophic   Standard

FIGURE 10.5 Shader types shown on a rendered sphere

Anisotropic   Most of the surface types that you will see in this section typically create rounded specular highlights that spread evenly across a surface. By contrast, *anisotropic* surfaces have properties that differ according to direction. This creates a specular highlight that is elliptical in shape and uneven across the surface, changing according to the direction you specify on the surface. The Anisotropic shader is good for surfaces such as foil wrappers or hair. Notice the extra controls for the specular highlights. They allow you to control how the specular will fall across the surface.

Blinn   This is the default material because it is a general-purpose, flexible shader. The Blinn shader creates a smooth surface with some shininess. If you set the specular color to black, however, this shader will not display a specular and will lose its shininess, making it perfect for regular dull surfaces, such as paper or an indoor wall.

Metal   The Metal shader is not too different from the Blinn shader. Metal creates a lustrous metallic effect, with much the same controls as a Blinn shader, but without the effect of any specular highlights. When you are first starting, it's best to create most of your material looks with the Blinn shader until you're at a point where Blinn simply cannot do what you need. The black areas of the shader may throw you off at first, but keep in mind that a metallic surface is ideally black when it has nothing to reflect. Metals are best seen when they reflect the environment. As such, this shader requires a lot of reflection work to make the metal look just right.

Mapping the Couch and Chair

Now let's dive into creating material for the couch we modeled in Chapter 4, "Modeling in 3ds Max: Architectural Model Part II," to get it ready for lighting and rendering in later chapters.

Study the full-color image of the couch shown in Chapter 4 in Figure 4.1. That will give you an idea of how the couch is to be textured. The couch's material is basically all the same; once you create the material, it can be added to all the couch pieces.

Creating a Standard Material

Start by opening your final couch model from your work in Chapter 4, or open the `ArchModel_furniture_01.max` file from the `Scenes` folder of the Arch Model project downloaded from the book's web page at `www.sybex.com/go/3dsmax2013essentials`. This file has the room with the spline chair and couch set up. When you open this file, select the couch and press Alt+Q to enter Isolate Selection mode.

1. Open the Slate Material Editor, in the Material/Map browser in the Materials ➢ Standard rollout, double-click on Standard. This adds the Standard Material node to the Active View area. Double-click on the thumbnail with the sphere showing. This enlarges it and makes your material easier to view.

2. Double-click again on the node title bar; this adds the node parameters to the Parameter Editor.

3. In the Parameter Editor, at the top of the rollout change the name to **Gray/Green Woven Fabric**. It is always best to name your materials precisely. Calling the material "Couch" might be confusing if you want to use the same material on the curtains or a chair.

4. In the Blinn Basic Parameters rollout, select the color swatch next to Diffuse. This brings up the Color Selector; set the settings to Red: 108, Green: 92, Blue: 8, and select OK. In the Material node, the sphere in the thumbnail will change color.

Applying the Material to the Couch

In the scene, select the couch. In Chapter 4, when the couch was merged into the room file, it was grouped. You can add materials to objects that are grouped; it can save time by applying the materials to all the pieces at the same time.

1. In the Slate Material Editor toolbar, click on the Apply Material to Selection icon (▣).

   The material may look slightly different in the viewport compared to in the Material Editor thumbnail, as shown in Figure 10.6. The best way

The Active View area uses the same navigation tools as the viewports. At the lower right of the Slate interface are the Navigation tools. Keyboard shortcuts and the middle mouse button and wheel also work the same as in the viewports. The Navigator is another way to navigate in the Active View area. The Navigator panel changes the view of your material nodes; the colored box called the Proxy View area corresponds to the currently viewable area in the Active View area.

to view the material is by rendering the viewport. Select the Perspective viewport and in the main toolbar, click the Render button (⬛), or press F9 for Render Last. The render looks a bit flat. This is something you can edit by changing the color values until the color looks the way you want. Always judge your colors using the render.

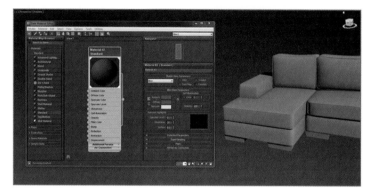

FIGURE 10.6 Compare the material color in the Material Editor to the viewport.

2. In the Slate Material Editor, select the color swatch next to Diffuse. To match the color of the couch better, you will darken the diffuse color.

3. Change the Saturation (Sat:) to **90** and the Value: to **70**, or just edit until the color is to your liking, as shown in Figure 10.7.

FIGURE 10.7 The render of the couch with a Standard material applied

Adding a Bitmap

The couch material needs some refinement. It looks flat and too perfect, which in this instance isn't a good thing. A material with just color is not enough; what is needed is a map. Two map types are available: 2D and 3D. 2D maps are two-dimensional images that are mapped onto the surface of 3D objects; the simplest 2D maps are bitmaps (aka image files). 3D maps are patterns generated procedurally in three dimensions using the 3ds Max software. Using a map to replace the diffuse color is a way to create a more realistic material because you are using actual images. Using maps in other material components can have various effects, such as making a material look bumpy and controlling its transparency.

1. In the Slate Material Editor, click on the Maps rollout to expand.

2. Select the bar with None written in for Diffuse Color. This brings up a separate Material/Map browser; in the Maps rollout, choose Bitmap. In the Explore window, navigate to the SceneAssets\Images folder in the Arch Model project, and select the GrayGreenWovenFabric.tif image file. If you don't see this map, make sure the Files of Type field is set to TIF.

   In the Active view, two additional nodes have been added to the main material node. The green node is the Bitmap node, which holds the fabric image. The yellow node is a Controller node and provides a number of ways to animate the settings of a material or map. Animating material components will not be addressed in this book.

3. In the Slate Material Editor's toolbar, select the Show Shaded Map in Viewport icon (▨). In the viewport, the couch shows the fabric image applied, as shown in Figure 10.8. This improves the color and adds some color variations.

FIGURE 10.8 The couch with the fabric image applied

Introduction to Mapping Coordinates

An image map is two-dimensional; it has length and width but no depth. 3ds Max geometry, however, extends in all three axes. Mapping coordinates define how and where image maps are projected onto an object's surfaces and whether the maps are repeated across those surfaces.

Mapping coordinates can be applied to objects in several ways. When primitive objects are created and the Generate Mapping Coords option is checked at the bottom of the Parameters rollout, the appropriate mapping coordinates are created automatically. The next way is by applying a UVW Mapping modifier, which is commonly used to apply and control mapping coordinates. You select the type of mapping projection, regardless of the shape of the object, and then set the amount of tiling in the modifier's parameters. The mapping coordinates applied through the UVW Mapping modifier override any other mapping coordinates applied to an object, and the Tiling values set for the modifier are multiplied by the Tiling value set in the assigned material.

Using a UVW Mapping Modifier

You are going to use a modifier to replace those coordinates on the geometry. The UVW Mapping modifier allows you to change the bitmap by transforming the UVW Mapping modifier gizmo. In Chapter 4 you grouped the couch when you merged it into the room; for this part of the chapter, you need it to be ungrouped.

1. Select the couch and in the Group menu select Open. This will keep the group intact but allow you to select and edit the items within the group. There are now pink brackets surrounding the couch, representing the group.

2. Select the main seat cushion on the couch. Enter Isolate Selection mode (; the icon is under the timeline at the bottom of the interface (or press Alt+Q). You can also access Isolate Selection by right-clicking on the selected object and choosing Isolate Selection from the Quad menu.

3. In the Modify panel, select UVW Map from the Modifier List drop-down.

4. In the modifier stack, you can see the UVW Map modifier stacked on top of the editable poly. You will also see an orange gizmo around the seat cushion.

5. Go to the UVW Mapping modifier parameters, and in the Mapping section select Box for the projection type.

6. In the Alignment section, click the Bitmap Fit button, as shown in Figure 10.9.

FIGURE 10.9
The Alignment section
for the UVW Mapping
Modifier parameters

7. This will take you to the Select Image dialog box. Navigate to the SceneAssets\Images folder in the Arch Model project and select the GrayGreenWovenFabric.tif file. This will change the size of the UVW Mapping gizmo to the size and aspect of the image rather than the geometry.

The UVW Mapping modifier has also changed the image on the couch. The size is more consistent throughout the couch, but the size of the fabric texture is too big. Now let's adjust the UVW Mapping gizmo:

1. In the modifier stack, click the plus sign in the black box next to the UVW Mapping modifier and select Gizmo.

2. Now look at the seat cushion in the viewport, and you should see the cube-shaped Modifier gizmo. You will now be able to transform the gizmo to the correct size.

3. Switch to the Scale tool (press R), and scale down the gizmo to 70 percent. Click on the UVW Map modifier again to exit.
   Now that the couch fabric is where it should be, it is time to add the UVW Mapping modifier to the remaining pieces of the couch.

4. Exit Isolate Selection mode.

5. Select one of the back couch cushions and repeat steps 1 through 3.

6. Once the UVW Mapping modifier is applied, go to the Alignment section, and click the Acquire button. Then click on the couch seat cushion. Acquire takes the UVW information from the seat cushion and copies it onto the back cushion. This is a great time saver.

7. Repeat the same process on the remaining cushions. The final results are shown in Figure 10.10.

FIGURE 10.10 The final results of the couch mapping

The couch is not finished just yet; look closely at the couch feet. If you compare the current scene couch to the image of the real couch, the feet should be a dark wood, not the fabric that is on them now. Continue with your current file or open ArchModel_furniture_02.max file from the Scenes folder of the Arch Model project downloaded from the book's web page at www.sybex.com/go/3dsmax2013essentials.

1. Open the Slate Material Editor if it isn't already open.

2. In the Material/Map browser, choose Materials. Click and drag a Standard material into the Active View area.

3. Double-click on the title bar of the material to add it to the Parameter Editor. Change the name to **Dark Wood**.

4. Select the bar with None across from Diffuse Color. This brings up a separate Material/Map browser in the Maps rollout. Then choose Bitmap. In the Explore window, navigate to `SceneAssets\Images` folder in the Arch Model project, and select the `DarkWood_Grain.jpg` image file.

5. Apply the material by clicking from the node's output socket to the couch foot, as shown in Figure 10.11.

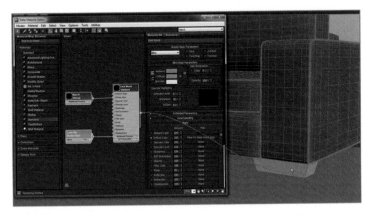

FIGURE 10.11 Apply the Dark Wood material by clicking and dragging from the nodes output socket to the couch foot.

6. In the Material Editor, click the Show Map in Viewport icon (◼). The material shows now, but the image has no detail. This is because it needs to have UVW Mapping applied.

7. In the Modify panel's modifier list, add a UVW Map modifier to the couch foot. Change the Mapping Type to Box. Select Bitmap Fit under Alignment, navigate to the `dark wood.tif` image file. The material now looks correct on the couch foot.

8. Apply the Dark Wood material to the remaining couch feet.

Applying a Bump Map

You are almost but not totally done with the couch. One important feature of the couch is the bumpiness on the surface of the fabric of the couch, as shown in Figure 10.12. This bumpiness changes all the specular and reflective properties on a surface. Bump mapping is very common in CG. It adds a level of detail to an object fairly easily by creating bumps and grooves in the surface and giving the object a tactile element. Bump mapping uses the intensity values (the brightness values) of an image or procedural map to simulate bumpiness on the surface of the model, without changing the actual topology of the model itself. You can create some surface texture with a bump map; however, you will not be able to create extreme depth in the model. For that, you may want to model the surface depth manually or use displacement mapping instead. To add a bump map to the couch, follow these steps:

1. In the Slate Material Editor's Active View area, locate the Couch Fabric material. Double-click the title bar to load the material into the Parameters Editor.

2. In the Maps rollout, click the None button next to the bump map. In the Material/Map Browser, choose Bitmap. Navigate to SceneAssets\Images folder in the Arch Model project, and select the GrayGreenWovenFabric_bmp.tif image file.

3. In the Maps rollout, increase Bump Amount from 30 (the default) to 60.

4. Render to see the results; you should now see a texture on the couch that resembles the real bumpiness of the couch, as shown in Figure 10.13.

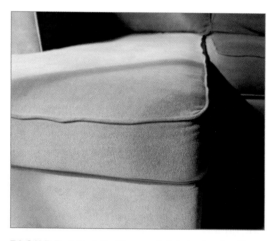

FIGURE 10.12 The couch fabric showing the subtle surface bumpiness

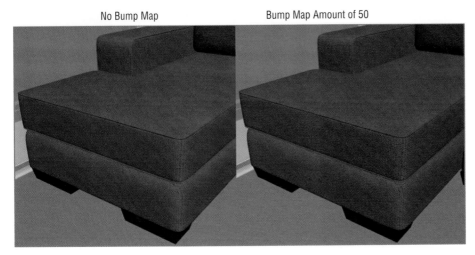

No Bump Map   Bump Map Amount of 50

FIGURE 10.13 The couch fabric without the bump map (left); the couch fabric with the bump map (right)

Applying the Material to the Chair

Mapping the chair is in some ways very much like mapping the couch. Continue with your current file or open the ArchModel_furniture_03.max file from the Scenes folder of the Arch Model project downloaded from the book's web page at www.sybex.com/go/3dsmax2013essentials. The file has the chair centered in the viewports, and the chairs group is open so you can select the individual pieces. The Cushion material has also been applied using the same techniques outlined in the previous section. If you are continuing with your file, create the Cushion material using the techniques discussed in the previous section. Add the BrownWovenFabric.tif for the Diffuse and the BrownWoven Fabric_bmp.tif as the bump. Set the Bump Amount to **60**. When you're mapping images onto a surface, the important thing to remember is to match the scale of the original fabric, as shown in Figure 10.14.

Let's also create the base material for the chair frame.

1. In the Slate Material Editor, add a Standard material to the Active View area. If you double-click on the input socket of the diffuse map on the Standard Material node, the Material/Map browser will open.

2. Choose Bitmap from the Material/Map browser and navigate to the SceneAssets\Images folder in the Arch Design project. Select the file LightWood.tif. Then, on the Material Editor toolbar, click the Show Shaded material in Viewport icon. Rename the material to **Light Wood**.

FIGURE 10.14 Compare the real texture on the left to the created material on the right to get it similar.

3. Select the chair frame. There are two pieces: the seat frame and arm, and the back frame. Apply the Light Wood material to the chair frame by clicking on the Assign Material to Selected button in the toolbar.

Don't worry if the map doesn't look correct. The mapping coordinates need to be applied.

4. In the Modify panel's modifier list, add a UVW Mapping modifier. Change the Mapping to Box, and in Alignment select Bitmap Fit and navigate to the LightWood.tif bitmap to change the size of the UVW Map modifier.

5. The size of the map is now proportional but it is too large, so in the modifier stack, click on the plus sign in the black box and then select the gizmo. Using the Scale tool, scale the wood bitmap until it looks correct, as shown in Figure 10.15.

Applying a Reflection

Reflection occurs when light changes direction as a result of "bouncing off" a surface like a mirror. In the following steps, you will create reflections in the chair's wood frame.

1. In the Light Wood Materials Parameter Editor click to open the Maps rollout. Then click on the None button to the right of Reflections. This will open the Material/Map Browser, from the Maps>Standard rollout, choose Raytrace.

A reflection creates the illusion of chrome, glass, or metal by applying a map to the geometry so the image looks like a reflection on the surface. A reflect/refract map is a way to provide reflections on a material.

2. Render to see the results, as shown in Figure 10.16. There is a bit too much reflection, which makes the chair frame look too smooth and too shiny.

3. Back in the Maps rollout, turn down the Amount to **10**. Render again to see the results. That is much better, as shown in Figure 10.17.

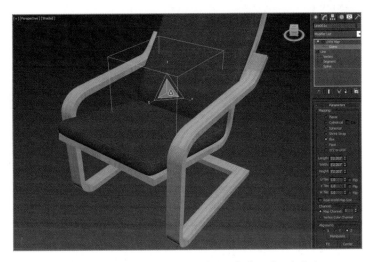

FIGURE 10.15 The wood texture is applied to the chair frame.

FIGURE 10.16 Results of adding the reflect/refract map added to the reflection map

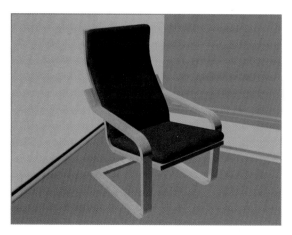

FIGURE 10.17 Final reflections on the chair

Mapping the Window and Doors

The window and doors are special 3D primitive objects. They are a collection of multiple objects attached together: a frame, mullions, and glass. You can edit those objects within the AEC objects parameters. They also give you the ability to add materials to the individual pieces within the attached whole.

Creating a Multi/Sub-Object Material

The Multi/Sub-Object material, which is in the Compound Materials category, lets you assign different materials at the sub-object level of your geometry. In the case of the AEC window, it is already divided into separate sub-object levels so you just have to apply the material and identify the different parts. Continue with your current file or open ArchModel_furniture_04.max file from the Scenes folder of the Arch Model project downloaded from the book's web page at www.sybex.com/go/3dsmax2013essentials.

1. In the Slate Material Editor, drag a Multi/Sub-Object material from the Material/Map browser into the Active View area. The material itself is nothing; it is just a node that gathers other nodes together. It has very simple parameters, as shown in Figure 10.18.

   The parameters allow you to control how many materials can be plugged into the Multi/Sub-Object Material (MSOM).

FIGURE 10.18 Multi/Sub-Object node and parameters

2. Drag a Standard material from the Material/Map browser to the Active View area, and then from the output socket of the Standard material, drag it to the input socket of the MSOM, as shown in Figure 10.19.

FIGURE 10.19 Adding a Standard material to the Multi/Sub-Object Material node

3. Double-click on the new Standard Materials title bar to add it to the Parameter Editor, click on the color swatch to open the color selector, create a red color, and click OK.

4. Repeat the same process until you have five Standard materials with five different diffuse colors plugged into the 1 through 5 input sockets of the MSOM.

5. Double-click on the MSOM node title bar to load it into the Parameter Editor, click on the Set Number button and change it from 10 to 5, and then press OK. The finished node is shown in Figure 10.20.

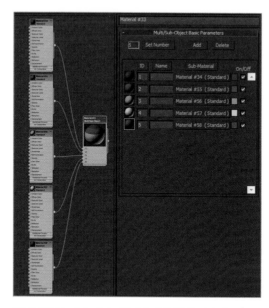

FIGURE 10.20 Finished MSOM with five Standard materials added

The numbers in the MSOM parameters are material IDs. Most objects do not have material IDs by default. They have to be created by converting the object to an editable polygon and selecting a group of polygons and adding a material to that selected group of polygons. AEC objects like the window and doors already have them assigned; they just have to be identified.

6. Apply the MSOM to the main window in the living room area, as shown in Figure 10.21. The colors show clearly which section of the window is which ID number.

7. Start with the glass, click on the material bar for ID #3 in the MSOM parameters. This loads those materials parameters. Rename the Material **Window Glass.**

8. In the Blinn Basic Parameters, change Opacity to 0. If you render, you will see a black hole where the green used to be. That is because you are seeing the default color applied to the background in a render. That means the glass is see-through now.

9. In the Maps rollout, click the Reflection Map button. From the Material/Map browser, choose Reflect/Refract, and then change the Reflection Amount to 10.

FIGURE 10.21 The Multi/Sub-Object Material applied to the window object shows the different colors applied to the different parts of the window.

When the scene renders, the Reflection amount will appear to be very high; this is a bit of an illusion because of the black in the background. In Chapter 14, lighting will be covered and this issue will be addressed more thoroughly; but for now, you will just change the background color. In the Rendering menu, choose Environment, click on the color swatch under Background ➤ Color, and change it to a light gray. Now the reflection looks more appropriate. Eventually, an image of an outdoor scene will be placed behind the glass. For now, let's continue with the MSOM for the window. Window frames and mullions come in many colors and textures, but for this example you are going to use a shiny, white plastic.

10. Double-click the MSOM title bar to load the material into the Parameter Editor and then select any of the material IDs (other than #3). Rename the material as **Shiny White Plastic**.

11. Change the Diffuse Color to White, and then in the Maps rollout add a Raytrace node to the reflection map and change the amount to 10, as you did in step 9.

12. In the Active View area, select and delete all the remaining Standard Material nodes. Keep the newly created Shiny White Plastic and the Glass.

13. Drag from the output socket of the Shiny White Plastic material to the input of the Multi/Sub-Object material's IDs that were deleted, as shown in Figure 10.22.

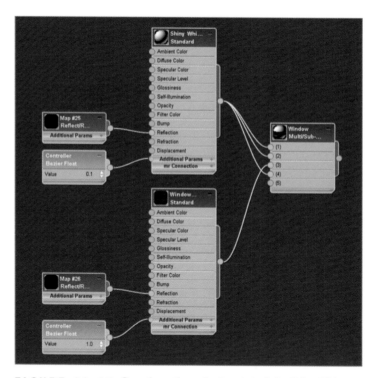

FIGURE 10.22 Drag from the output socket of the Shiny White Plastic into the input socket of the remaining ID slots of the Multi/Sub-Object material.

This places a clone of the Shiny White Plastic into the three remaining material slots and completes the Window material, as shown in a render in Figure 10.23.

The same technique used for the window can be used for the doors, but if you want the doors to be just a plain solid color or simple wood, apply a Standard material to the entire Door object. We'll return to this room in Chapter 14 when we look at lighting. Meanwhile, finish assigning materials to the rest of the scene.

FIGURE 10.23 The completed window

THE ESSENTIALS AND BEYOND

Creating materials can give you a sense of accomplishment because it is essentially the last step in making the object look as you envisioned—aside from lighting and rendering.

Finding the right combination of maps, shader types, and material types can make a world of difference in the look of your scenes. In this chapter, you learned the basics of materials, you mapped part of the room and furniture you modeled in Chapter 3 and Chapter 4, and you readied it for its next step: lighting in Chapter 14.

ADDITIONAL EXERCISES

▶ Using the collection of images in the Sceneassets/Images Folder of the Arch Model project, add materials to the floor and ceiling.

▶ Merge in furniture from the Scenes ➢ Furniture folder from the Arch Model Project. Create materials for these items. Try to match as closely as possible the real furniture in the reference images of the room. These models were built for you to use to practice texturing and lighting.

▶ Create a MSOM for the walls and use the colors you want. The actual colors can be seen in Figure 3.1 in Chapter 3, "Modeling in 3ds Max: Architectural Model Part I." Now the walls will take an extra step. The Wall object has IDs because it is an AEC object, but the IDs are not where you want them. You need to a convert the object to an editable polygon.

CHAPTER 11

Textures and UV Workflow: The Soldier

3ds Max® materials simulate the natural physics of how we see things by regulating how objects reflect and/or transmit light. You define a material by setting values for its parameters or by applying textures or maps. These parameters define the way an object will look when rendered. In this chapter and in Chapter 14, "Introduction to Lighting: Interior Lighting," you will discover that materials and lights work closely together.

Topics in this chapter include:

▶ **Mapping the soldier**

▶ **UV unwrapping**

▶ **Seaming the rest of the body**

▶ **Applying the color map**

▶ **Applying the bump map**

▶ **Applying the specular map**

Mapping the Soldier

In this chapter, you will apply materials and maps to the soldier model from Chapters 7 through 9. You will first set up the model to accept textures properly through a process called *UV-unwrap*. This allows you to lay out the colors and patterns for the soldier's uniform and general look. This process essentially creates a flat map that can be used to paint the textures in a program such as Photoshop.

You have already used Adobe Photoshop to create the textures (i.e., the maps) you'll use for the soldier. We will show you how to prepare the model for proper UVs and how to apply the maps you have already painted. We will not demonstrate the actual painting process in Photoshop because that discussion goes beyond the scope of this book.

UV Unwrapping

Set your project to the Soldier project downloaded from the companion web page at www.sybex.com/go/3dsmax2013essentials. Open the scene file SoldierTexture_ v01.max from the Scenes folder of the project, or use your own final model scene files from Chapter 9, "Character Poly Modeling: Part III." Keep in mind that any design changes you made to your own soldier model may cause discrepancies in the UV unwrapping and mapping steps in the following sections.

You will begin by creating seams to define the shapes of the arms, so you know where in Photoshop to paint the sleeves of the uniform. In this file, the image planes are hidden; if you want them back, right-click in the viewport and choose Unhide All from the context menu.

Begin defining UVs with the following steps:

1. Change the viewport rendering type to Shaded + Edged Faces (F4) in your viewports.

2. With your model selected, go to the Modify panel and from the modifier list choose Unwrap UVW from the modifier list.

3. Expand the Unwrap UVW modifier in the modifier stack by clicking on the plus sign in the black box next to the Unwrap UWV title. Enter Face mode.

4. At the bottom of the Configure rollout, uncheck Map Seams, as shown in Figure 11.1. Doing so turns off the green highlight on the edges; it is generated by default and is not useful in its current state.

5. In the Peel rollout, click the Point To Point Seam button, as shown in Figure 11.2. This tool lets you reroute the seams to where you want them.

FIGURE 11.1
Uncheck Map Seam in the Configure rollout.

FIGURE 11.2
Click the Point To
Point Seam button.

6. With Point To Seam enabled, click on the center of a pair of intersecting edges about where you want to define the left shoulder, as shown in Figure 11.3 (left image). A dashed-line "rubber band" appears next to your cursor, letting you know that the tool is waiting for the next point to be selected.

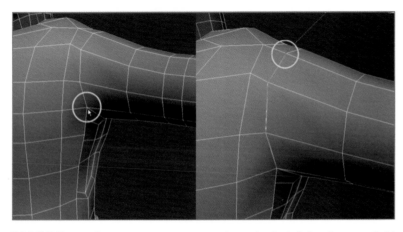

FIGURE 11.3 Pick this edge intersection to begin defining the seam (left). Choose the next point at the upper shoulder (right).

7. Select the next intersecting edges in the loop around the shoulder. This creates a blue highlight across the edges, as shown in Figure 11.3 (right image).

8. Continue around the shoulder until you have a complete loop, ending with the intersection you started with in step 6. Also, you can right-click and then start or continue the picks without overlapping them.

9. Select the bottommost edge intersection on the underarm and continue selecting edge intersections all the way to the middle point of the wrist, as shown in Figure 11.4. You will have to switch to Wireframe view (press F3) or See-Through mode (Alt+X) to pick the last point, as shown in Figure 11.5, at the end of the forearm.

While Point To Point Seam is active, you can navigate using all the viewport navigation tools to look around the model. The 3ds Max software remembers the last intersection you clicked and draws an accurate seam at the next click.

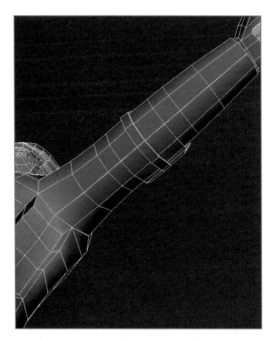

FIGURE 11.4   Select the intersections under the arm.

FIGURE 11.5   Switch to Wireframe view to pick the last intersection for the forearm/wrist.

10. Right-click to deactivate the Point To Point Seam tool's rubber banding but still keep the button active; then continue cutting a new set of UVs for the right arm, just as you did for the left arm.

11. Right-click and box out areas under the arms on both sides, as shown in Figure 11.6. In Figure 11.6, you can see the seams block out the area under the arm and continue down to the belt line and across the top of the belt line around the waist. If you pick a point by mistake, you can use the Undo button.

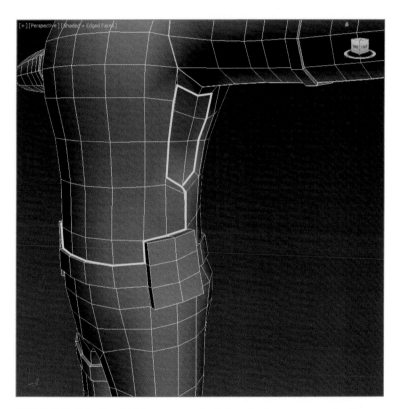

FIGURE 11.6   Add these seams to define the torso areas under the arm.

12. Using the Point To Point Seam tool, cut seams for the two gloves lengthwise down the middle from wrist to wrist. You can see this progression for the left-hand glove start in Figure 11.7. Begin at the wrist on the side of the thumb and work your way around to the opposite side of the wrist. Remember, you may need to enter Wireframe view (press F3) to select the proper edge intersection points. Figure 11.8 shows the seam working around the hand.

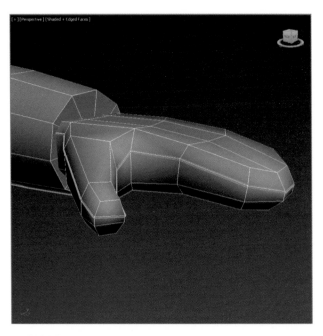

FIGURE 11.7   Cut a new seam along the glove, starting as shown.

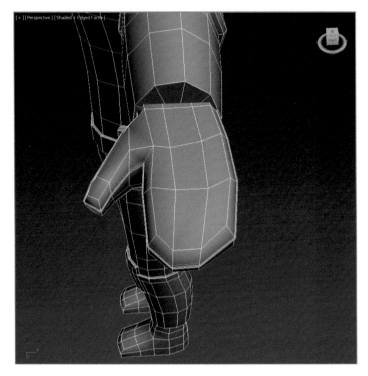

FIGURE 11.8   Work your way around the glove.

13. In the Edit UVs rollout, select the Open UV Editor button. In the top right of the window, in the drop-down menu, choose CheckerPattern (Checker) from the list, even if it already appears in the menu as shown in Figure 11.9. This will apply a low-contrast checker map to the soldier, as shown in Figure 11.10. The checker pattern will disappear when the Open UV Editor is closed.

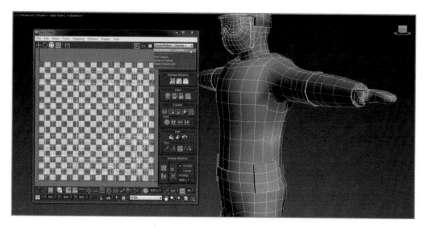

F I G U R E 1 1 . 9 Choose the CheckerPattern (Checker) from the drop-down list.

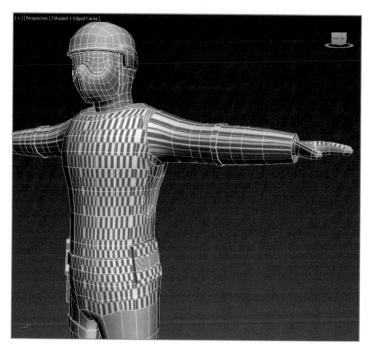

F I G U R E 1 1 . 1 0 Low-contrast checker pattern is added to the soldier model.

Pelting the Left Arm UVs

Save your work now before continuing with the next set of steps to unfold the UVs for the arms into usable patterns to paint the textures. You can pick up with the scene file SoldierTexture_v02.max from the Scenes folder of the Soldier project from the book's companion web page to check your work so far or to skip to this point. In this file the image planes are hidden; if you want them back, right-click in the viewport and choose Unhide All from the context menu. Also remember the checker pattern applied to the soldier will only show if the Open UV Editor is open.

1. With Face mode selected in your Unwrap UVW modifier and Point To Point Seam toggled off, click on a polygon on the left forearm of your model. Then in the Peel rollout, click the Expand Face Selection To Seams icon (■), as shown in Figure 11.11. This will select all the faces that were included when creating seams for the arm.

2. You need to unfold the UVs to create the pattern to paint on in Photoshop (or another image editor). To unfold the UVs into a usable pattern, click the Pelt Map icon (■) in the Peel rollout.

Area within the red shading is what is selected.

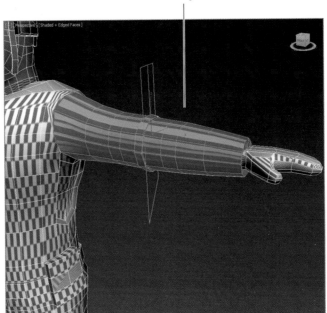

FIGURE 11.11   The arm's faces are selected.

3. The Pelt Map dialog box will open. In the Edit UVWs dialog box, click the View menu and toggle off Show Grid and Show Map to simplify the UV view, as shown in Figure 11.12.

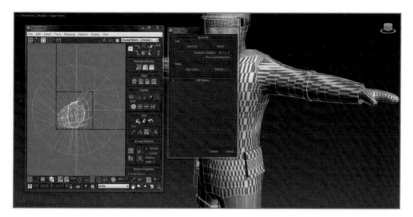

FIGURE 11.12 The Edit UVWs and Pelt Map dialog boxes showing the arm UVs

4. To unfold the map, click the Start Pelt button in the Pelt Map dialog box. Doing so moves the UVs in the Edit UVWs dialog box in real time. This procedure keeps unfolding the UVs until you stop it, so wait a couple of seconds for the UVs to stop moving and then click Stop Pelt.

5. You're almost done with the arm; however, if you check the checkerboard texture in your viewport, you can see that some of the checks are bigger than others. To fix this, click the Settings box next to the Relax button in the Pelt Map dialog box, and change the drop-down option to Relax By Face Angles, as shown in Figure 11.13.

FIGURE 11.13 Set the drop-down menu to Relax By Face Angles.

6. Now, click Start Relax. Wait until the UVs stop moving and then click Stop Relax; then click Apply. Close the Relax Tool dialog box. Checking your texture in the viewport now shows the checkerboard the way you want it.

7. Click the Commit button at the bottom of the Pelt Map dialog box, or your changes won't take effect. Also, you want to close the Edit UVWs dialog box.

Pelting the Right Arm UVs

Repeat steps 1–7 for the right arm. You can see in Figure 11.14 that both arms are now laid out—pelted and relaxed.

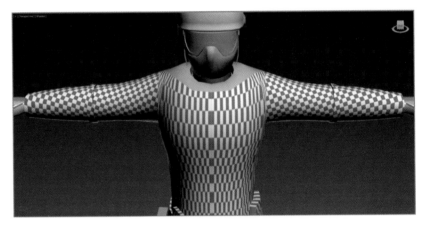

FIGURE 11.14   Both arms are pelted and relaxed.

Unwrapping and Using Pelt for the Head

Save your work now before continuing with the next set of steps to unfold the UVs for the head. You can pick up with the scene file SoldierTexture_v03.max from the Scenes folder of the Soldier project downloaded from the book's web page to check your work so far or to skip to this point.

For this section, since it is a bit hard to see where to seam, the file has the Edit UV Editor closed.

The head poses a problem: Each part (helmet, goggles, and mask) is a separate object that was merged together with the head in "Chapter 9: Character Poly Modeling: Part III" and then attached into one editable polygon. That means when you look closely at the geometry, there is some object penetration, making it difficult to clearly see some of the areas you need to seam. You will use a sub-object visibility technique to control what you are viewing in the following steps:

1. Select the Soldier, and in the Modify panel's modifier stack, choose Editable Poly and select Element. Element mode allows you to select separate objects that are attached together into a single object.

   When you do this, you will get the warning shown in Figure 11.15. Select Yes. Every time you move between the Unwrap UVW modifier and the Editable Poly modifier, you will see this warning; if that gets annoying, check the Do Not Show This Message Again option. The warning tells you that any changes you make to that level of the model will ripple throughout the rest of the stack and may mess up other parts of your work. Since you are simply using Element mode to hide parts of the head of the model to make the seaming easier to see, you need not worry that anything will change.

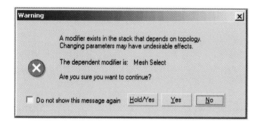

FIGURE 11.15   Topology dependency warning

2. Select the helmet, select Poly: Edit ➤ Visibility and click Hide Unselected. Doing so hides all unselected elements in the model, leaving the helmet as the only visible object.

3. Exit Element mode by clicking Editable Poly in the modifier stack. Now go back up to the Unwrap UVW modifier and click Face. Move down to the Peel rollout and click the Point To Point Seam button. Following the line in Figure 11.16, create a new seam on the helmet.

4. When the seam has been created, click Editable Poly and select Element mode in the modifier stack; in the Visibility tab, click the Unhide All button. Then select the goggles, click the Visibility tab, and click the Hide Unselected button. Repeat step 3 on the goggles using Figure 11.17 as your guide for the seams.

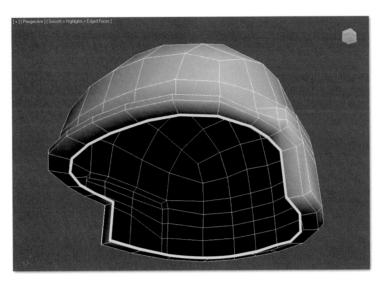

FIGURE 11.16 Create a new seam on the helmet.

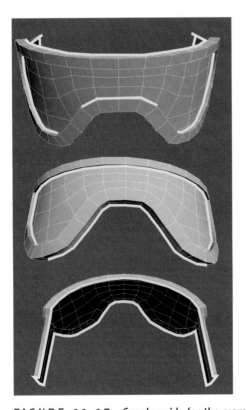

FIGURE 11.17 Goggle guide for the seams

5. Repeat the process individually for the mask, the head, and the helmet straps, using Hide Unselected to isolate each of the three elements as you work on them. Then follow the same process as before to create the seams shown in Figure 11.18 for the face mask, Figure 11.19 for the head, and Figure 11.20 for the helmet strap.

6. Open UV Editor.

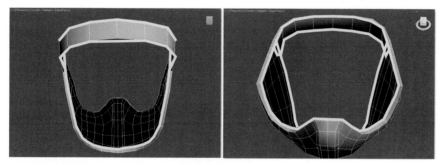

FIGURE 11.18   Seams for soldier face mask

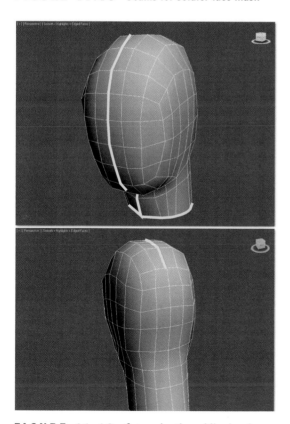

FIGURE 11.19   Seams for the soldier head

FIGURE 11.20   Seams
for the soldier helmet strap

Seaming the Rest of the Body

Use the Point To Point Seam tool to block out the rest of the model's parts and then use the Pelt Map steps as you did for the arms. Refer to Figure 11.21 and Figure 11.22 for the placement of seams on the model's body.

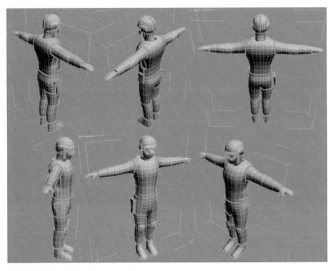

FIGURE 11.21   Follow these outlines to create the rest of the model's seams.

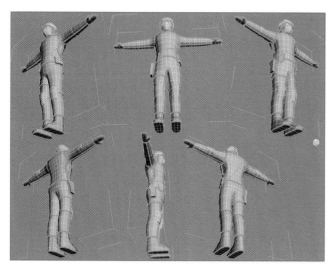

FIGURE 11.22   Follow these outlines taken from a different vantage point to create the rest of the model's seams.

Unfolding the Rest of the Body

Save your work. You can pick up with the scene file SoldierTexture_v04.max from the Scenes folder of the Soldier project downloaded from the book's web page to check your work so far or to skip to this point.

1. With the soldier selected, go to the Modify panel and click the Face button. Then click a single polygon on the helmet. Then in the Peel rollout, click the Expand Face Selection To Seams icon (🖼). Doing so selects all the polygons associated with the seams you created for the helmet.

2. Click the Pelt Map icon (🖼) to open the Edit UVWs dialog box and the Pelt Map dialog box. First, click Start Pelt. You will see the UVs moving around; when they stop moving, click the Stop Pelt button.

3. Now, click the Settings button next to the Start Relax button. Make sure the drop-down menu is set to Relax By Face Angles, click Apply, and then close the Relax Tool dialog box.

4. Click the Start Relax button again, and when the UVs stop moving, click Stop Relax. For the remaining objects, you don't have to go into the Settings box—just click Start Relax.

5. Click the Commit button. The checkers pattern on the helmet should look organized and even.

Now that you are finished with the helmet, make your way down the body using Pelt and Relax to lay out the UVs on the remaining parts of the body, checking each one off as you go.

Save your work. You can pick up with the scene file SoldierTexture_v05.max from the Scenes folder of the Soldier project to check your work so far or to skip to this point.

As you can see in Figure 11.23, when the UVs are finished, the checker pattern for each separate part of the soldier is a different size. In the following steps, you will set all the sizes to be the same, showing that the UVs are now uniform.

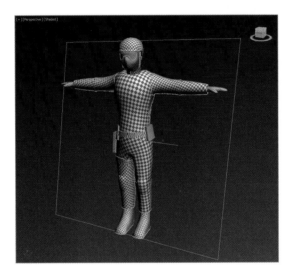

FIGURE 11.23   Soldier model with all the polygons selected

1. In the Modify panel, click the Face button if it isn't already selected. Then click away from the soldier model and drag a selection box around the whole model to select all the polygons, as shown in Figure 11.23.

2. In the Unwrap UVW modifier, go to the Edit UVs rollout and click the Open UV Editor button. What you will see is a mess; these are all the unwrapped UVs piled on top of each other.

3. In the Edit UVWs menu, choose Tools ➢ Relax. Click Start Relax. Be patient and wait for the movement to slow down or stop before clicking Stop Relax. Then close the Relax Tool dialog box. This will relax all of your UVs together uniformly, ensuring that they all have the same UV real estate. This is important so that all the elements carry the same relative texture space, as shown in Figure 11.24.

4. Keep the Edit UVWs dialog box open. Deselect the UVs by clicking away from the model. Figure 11.25 shows what you should see now.

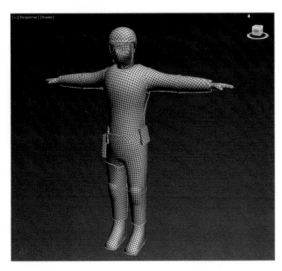

FIGURE 11.24   Soldier model with all UVs relaxed uniformly

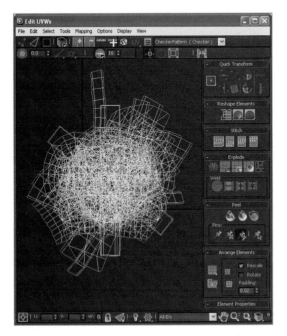

FIGURE 11.25   The Edit UVWs dialog box with the soldier UVs in a pile

Because you are still in Face mode in the Unwrap UVW modifier, if you click anywhere on the pile of UVs you will select a face. What you want to do now is select an individual element's full set of UVs so that you can lay them out separately, giving them some space on the flat blank canvas that can be used later for painting the textures for those parts of the body. The easiest way is to select a face, then go to the toolbar at the top of the Edit UVWs dialog box and click Select By Element, as shown in Figure 11.26.

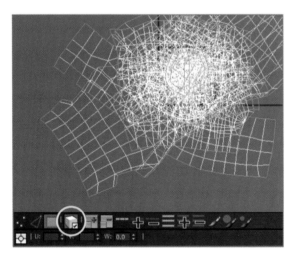

FIGURE 11.26 Clicking Select By Element

At this point, you can select all the UVs associated with an element (such as the helmet only), as shown in Figure 11.27. This will help you know what parts you are moving around in the Edit UVWs dialog box. Also in the Edit UVWs dialog box, you can use all the navigation tools you use in the viewports to pan and zoom. In the following steps, you will start placing the UVs for each element within the thick blue-bordered box in the Edit UVWs dialog box to lay out the entire soldier's UVs for textures.

1. In the Edit UVWs dialog box, drag a selection box around all the UVs. From the Arrange Elements rollout on the right side of the Edit UVWs dialog box, change the Padding type-in selection to **0.0** and then click the Pack Normalize button, as shown in Figure 11.28. Now you should be able to see the blue-bordered box in the Edit UVWs dialog box with the UVs laid out correctly, as shown in Figure 11.29.

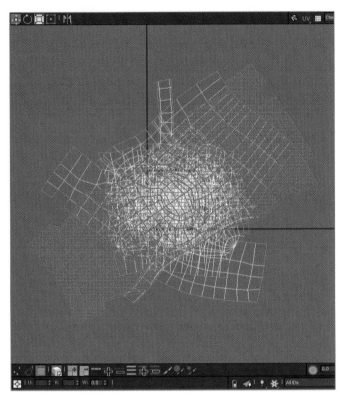

FIGURE 11.27 Select an element in the Edit UVWs dialog box, and it will appear as selected on the model.

Pack Normalize
button

Padding type-in

FIGURE 11.28 The
Arrange Elements rollout

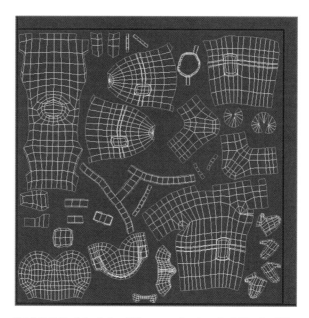

FIGURE 11.29 UVs correctly placed within the UV space

The goal is to fit the UVs into this box without going outside of it and without overlapping any of the UVs. Anything outside this box ends up tiling (or having no texture at all), and any overlapping UVs share parts of the texture from another element. Either way, that's not good. Once you have the layout, you can select and move UVs around.

2. In the Edit UVWs dialog box, select Tools ➢ Render UV Template to open the Render UVs dialog box. In that dialog box, click the Render UV Template button to create an image of your UVs, as shown in the Render Map dialog box in Figure 11.30.

3. Save the UV layout image by clicking the Save Image icon in the Render Map dialog box, as shown in Figure 11.31. Once saved, this image can be opened in your favorite image editor and you can use the pieces as guides to paint the soldier's textures.

With the UV layout image saved, you can go into Photoshop (or the image-editing software of your choice) and create a texture to place on your model. For the example, we took the UV image into Photoshop, and with a combination of painting and cutting and pasting of photos we created the final map for the soldier, as shown in Figure 11.32.

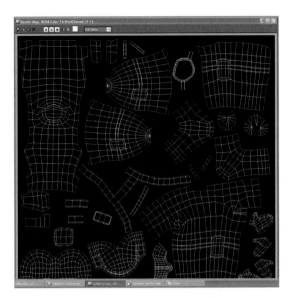

FIGURE 11.30 The UV rendered image

FIGURE 11.31
Save the UV image.

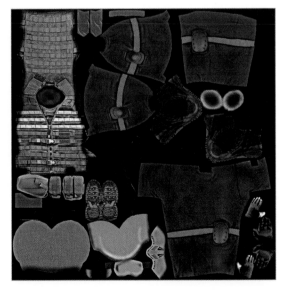

FIGURE 11.32 The final map for the soldier

The texture map, as you can see, places painted parts of the soldier's body according to the UV layout you just created. For example, you can clearly see the soldier's vest painted in the upper-left corner of the texture image file.

The more you unwrap UVs for models, the easier it becomes to anticipate how to paint the textures.

Applying the Color Map

Save your work before continuing with the next set of steps. You can pick up with the scene file SoldierTexture_v05.max from the Scenes folder of the Soldier project to check your work so far or to skip to this point.

Now it is time to use the map you put so much effort into creating.

1. Open the Slate Material Editor (M). You should see the checker material you created for the soldier to help with the UVs. In the Material/Map browser, choose the Materials rollout. On the Standard rollout, drag and drop a Standard material to the Active View area.

2. Double-click on the Diffuse Color input socket of the material to open the Material/Map browser. In the Maps rollout, select the Standard rollout and click Bitmap. When the Select Bitmap Image File dialog box appears, navigate to the \SceneAssets\images folder for the Soldier project and select the Soldier_Color_V04.tif file.

3. Apply the material to the soldier and click Show Standard Map In Viewport; the result is shown in Figure 11.33. Bam! Now wasn't all that hard UV work worth it?

FIGURE 11.33 The soldier with the material applied

Applying the Bump Map

Bump mapping makes an object appear to have a bumpy or irregular surface by simulating surface definition. When you render an object with a bump-mapped material, lighter (whiter) areas of the map appear to be raised on the object's surface, and darker (blacker) areas appear to be lower on the object's surface, as shown in Figure 11.34.

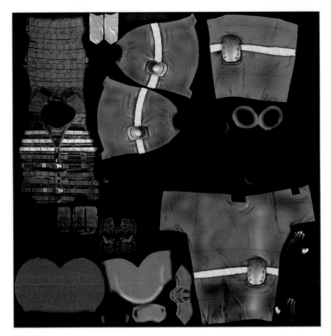

FIGURE 11.34 Bump map created in Photoshop by desaturating the original color map to create light and dark areas that conform to the original color texture

Normal mapping is a technique used for faking the lighting of bumps and dents. A normal map is usually used to fake high-resolution geometry detail while it's actually mapped onto a low-resolution mesh for efficiency. This vector is called a *normal* (or simply, a direction) that describes a high-resolution surface's slope at that very point on the surface. The RGB channels of a normal map control the direction of each pixel's normal, enabling you to fake a high degree of surface resolution when applied to a low-polygon mesh. A normal map for the soldier is shown in Figure 11.35.

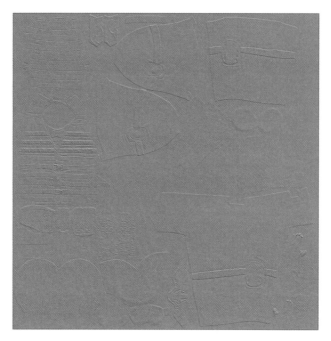

FIGURE 11.35 Normal map created in Photoshop and based on the original color map

You can use one or both of these mapping techniques to create additional surface detail. Bump maps are simpler to create, since you can usually take the color map and just desaturate it to make a grayscale image file. We have both a normal map and bump map for you to use. You will continue with the Soldier material you created in the previous exercise as you add these new maps in the following steps:

1. Double-click on the Bump input socket of the material to open the Material/Map browser. Under the Maps rollout, select the Standard rollout and choose Normal Bump.

2. Click on the title bar of the Normal Bump node to bring up the Parameters rollout shown in Figure 11.36. Click the None button next to Normal. Doing so once again brings up the Material/ Map browser. Under the Maps rollout, select the Standard rollout and choose Bitmap. When the Select Bitmap Image File dialog box appears, navigate to the /SceneAssets/images folder of the Soldier project and select the Soldier_Normal_V01.tif file.

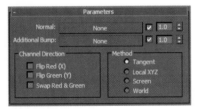

FIGURE 11.36 The Normal
Bump node's Parameters rollout

3. Back in the Normal Map parameters, click None next to Additional Bump to open the Material/Map browser. Under the Maps rollout, select the Standard rollout and choose Bitmap. When the Select Bitmap Image File dialog box appears, navigate to the /SceneAssets/images folder of the Soldier project and select the Soldier_BS_V01.tif file.

4. Double-click on the Materials title bar to show the main material parameters. In the Maps rollout, set the Bump Amount to **100**.

The normal map is applied and finished. See Figure 11.37 for images that compare the soldier rendered with and without the normal map. You may notice that the normal and bump maps have created a lot more detail in the soldier's body, particularly in his vest. You will notice the difference even better in your own renders.

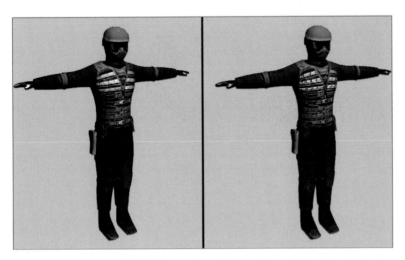

FIGURE 11.37 The left image is a render of the soldier without the normal and bump maps. The right image is rendered with the normal and bump maps.

Applying the Specular Map

Highlights in objects are reflections of a light source. *Specular* maps are maps you use to define a surface's shininess and highlight color, without the complex calculations of reflections in the render. The higher a pixel's value (from black to white, or 0 to 1, respectively), the shinier the surface will appear at that location.

You will be adding a specular map to the soldier to further the amount of detail you can get from the render. You are going to reuse the image that you used for the bump map to give the soldier a bit of bling on his vest and buckles.

In the Slate, drag from the output socket of the Additional Bump bitmap to the Specular Color input socket of the Soldier material already in your scene, as shown in Figure 11.38. Placing the Bump into the Specular color slot allows for iridescence and the flexibility to use the Specular Level spinner to increase or decrease the shininess as much as desired.

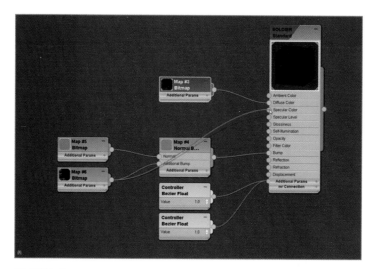

FIGURE 11.38 Dragging from the bump map to the Specular Color slot

The final render of the soldier is shown in Figure 11.39. You can see the improvement to the look of the soldier's vest with the added specular color map.

FIGURE 11.39   Final render of the soldier

You will use the soldier for rigging and animation with Character Studio in Chapter 12, "Character Studio: Rigging."

THE ESSENTIALS AND BEYOND

In this chapter you set up the soldier's UV layout using UV unwrapping and the Pelt toolset. Then you assigned materials and maps created specifically for the soldier, all the while getting to know the Slate Material Editor.

ADDITIONAL EXERCISE

▶ Create a new uniform color scheme for the soldier to make him/her more suitable for jungle camouflage and map it.

CHAPTER 12

Character Studio: Rigging

At one time or another, almost everyone in the 3D community wants to animate a character. This chapter examines the 3ds Max® 2013 toolsets used in the process of setting up for character animation using Character Studio, a full-featured package incorporated into the 3ds Max software that is used mostly for animating bipedal characters, including humans, aliens, robots, and anything else that walks on two feet—though you can have characters with more than two feet in certain situations.

Topics in this chapter include the following:

▶ **Character Studio workflow**

▶ **Associating a biped with the soldier model**

Character Studio Workflow

Character Studio is a system built into the 3ds Max program to help automate the creation and animation of a character, who may or may not be exactly a *biped* (two-footed creature). Character Studio consists of three basic components: the Biped system, the Physique and Skin modifiers, and the Crowd system. Biped and Physique are used to pose and animate a single character, and the Crowd system is used to assign similar movements and behaviors to multiple objects in your 3ds Max scene. This chapter covers the Biped and Physique features; the Crowd system is beyond the scope of this book.

The first step in the Character Studio workflow is to build or acquire a suitable character model. The second step is to *skin* (bind) the character model to the skeleton so the animation drives the model properly.

Models should typically be in the reference position known as the "da Vinci pose," where the feet are shoulder width apart and the arms are extended to the sides with the palms down, as shown in Figure 12.1. This allows the animator to observe all of the model's features, unobstructed by the model itself, in at least two viewports.

FIGURE 12.1   A bipedal character in the reference position

In 3ds Max parlance, a *biped* is a predefined, initially humanoid structure. It is important to understand that you animate the biped that is associated with your model and not the model itself. Once the model is bound to the skeleton, the biped structure *drives* the model. You use the Skin modifier to create that relationship between the skeleton and the model.

General Workflow

There are four different bipeds you can choose from: the Skeleton, Male, Female, and Classic biped (see Figure 12.2). They all consist of legs, feet, toes, arms, hands, fingers, pelvis, spine, neck, and head. After your model is ready, you will create a biped and, using its parameters and the Scale transform, fit the biped closely to the model. The better the biped-to-model relationship, the easier the animation will be.

Once the biped is fit snugly to the model, you select all the components of the model, not the biped skeleton, and apply the Skin modifier in a process often referred to as *skinning*. It may take a while to properly test and refine the relationship between the model and the biped to get it to an acceptable level.

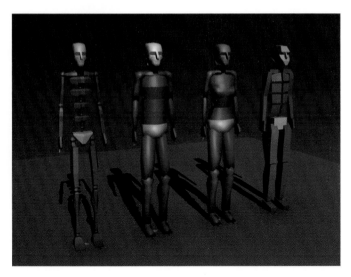

FIGURE 12.2 Skeleton, Male, Female, and Classic biped (from left to right)

BONES AND SKIN

The Bones system has capabilities similar to those found in Character Studio. Bones is a series of linked, hierarchical components that are used to control the displacement of a model similar to the Biped method. The Bones system requires a more tedious setup process to create a skeleton than the Biped method and is not covered.

The final step is animating your character. You can accomplish this by adding to the biped any combination of default walk, run, and jump cycles included with Character Studio, and then applying any freeform animation to the character, and finally refining the animation keyframes in the Dope Sheet. Don't expect the default walk, run, and jump cycles to create realistic motion, though. They are just starting points and must be tweaked to achieve acceptable movements.

The best way to start is to jump in and examine the tools available. In the next section, you will work with a biped and adjust the parameters and components to modify it.

Associating a Biped with the Soldier Model

The purpose of a biped is to be the portal through which you add animation to your model, rather than animating the model itself using direct vertex manipulation or deforming modifiers. Any motion assigned to a biped is passed through it to the nearest vertices of the associated model, essentially driving the surfaces of the model. For this reason, it is important that the biped fit as closely as possible to the model.

Creating and Modifying the Biped

In the following steps, you'll create and adjust a biped to fit to a character model. Set your project to the Soldier project available for download from this book's web page at www.sybex.com/go/3dsmax2013essentials. You can then open the CSSoldier01.max file from the Scenes folder of the Soldier project. It contains a completed soldier model in the reference position. Be sure to set the project folder to the root folder for the CSSoldier project.

With the soldier model file open, set the viewport rendering type to Edged faces (F4), select the character, and use Alt+X to make the model see-through. Also, right-click in a viewport and choose Freeze Selection. This will prevent you from inadvertently selecting the soldier instead of the biped.

VIEWING FROZEN OBJECTS

If your background color is similar to the default shade of gray used to depict frozen objects, the model may seem to disappear against the background. There are several solutions to this situation:

- ▶ You can go to Object Properties, turn off Show Frozen As Gray, turn on See-Through, and set all viewports to Realistic or Shaded mode.

- ▶ You can change the shaded color in the Customize User Interface dialog box (Customize ➢ Customize User Interface ➢ Colors).

- ▶ You can change the viewport background color in the Customize User Interface dialog box (Customize ➢ Customize User Interface ➢ Colors).

Follow these steps to create and adjust a biped:

1. From the Command panel, select Create ➢ Systems (▣) ➢ Biped. When you click on Biped, the parameters will appear below. Go to Body Type, and from the drop-down menu choose Male.

2. In the Perspective viewport, click at the soldier's feet and drag to create the biped. The first click sets the insertion point. Dragging defines the height of the biped system and defines all of the components. All of the biped's components are sized relative to the biped's Height parameter.

3. Create a biped with a height about the same as the soldier's. This will size most of the biped's parts similar to those of the soldier, as shown in Figure 12.3.

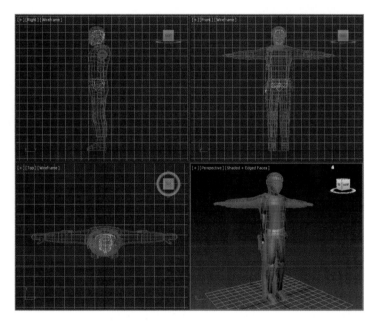

FIGURE 12.3 Create a biped about the same height as the soldier model.

Click any part of your biped to select it. Bipeds react differently than other objects. Selecting any single component of the biped opens the entire Biped object for editing.

4. With the biped still selected, click the Motion tab (⚙) of the Command panel and enter Figure mode, as shown in Figure 12.4. Changes to the biped's features or pose must be made in Figure mode to be retained by the system. Then in the Structure rollout, change the parameters to match Figure 12.5. The number of spine links should be set to 3. Change the number of toes to 1, and toe links to 2. Because the soldier is wearing boots, a single, wide toe will suffice. Change the Fingers to 2 because with mittens you only need one finger and a thumb.

FIGURE 12.4
Enter Figure mode in
the Biped rollout.

FIGURE 12.5
Change the biped from
the Structure rollout.

5. Use the Body Vertical and Body Horizontal buttons in the Track
   Selection rollout and the Move Transform gizmo to position the
   biped's pelvis in the same location as the model's pelvis, as shown
   in Figure 12.6. With the pelvis located properly, scaling the legs or
   spine to match the model's proportions will be much easier. Check
   to make sure the location is correct in all of the viewports.

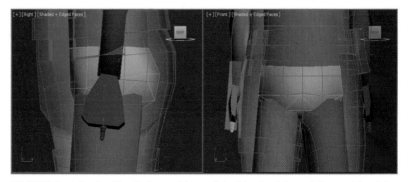

FIGURE 12.6 Match the positions of the biped pelvis and the model pelvis.

There are two important factors when creating a rig. The first is to place the joints accurately at the 3d mesh's joints. The other is to modify only one side of the model, and then use mirroring to copy to the other side.

6. Select Scale in the main toolbar; make sure the coordinate system is set to Local, as shown in Figure 12.7. In the Front viewport, select the pelvis and scale its width so that the biped's legs fit inside the soldier's legs. Scale the pelvis in the Right viewport so that it roughly encompasses the soldier's lower region, as shown in Figure 12.8.

FIGURE 12.7
Set the coordinate
system to Local.

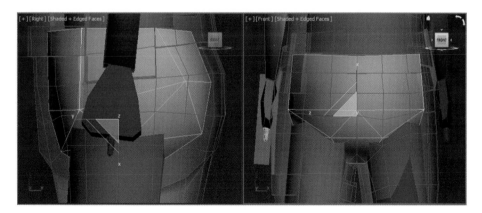

FIGURE 12.8 Scale the pelvis to fit.

7. Select the biped's left thigh, and then scale it along the X-axis until the knee aligns with the soldier's knee. Scale it on the Y- and Z-axes until it is similar in size to the soldier's thigh.

8. Select the biped's left calf. In the Right viewport, rotate the calf to match the model and then scale it on the X-axis until the biped's ankle matches the soldier's ankle. You may need to select the left foot and use the Move transform, in the Front viewport, to orient the calf to the model. Scale the calf to match the proportions of the soldier's calf.

9. Continue working down the leg by scaling the biped's foot to match the soldier's. Be sure to check the orientation of the foot in the Top viewport.

10. Scale and move the biped's toe to match the model's boot. Be sure to scale the toe links on the Z-axis, as shown in Figure 12.9.

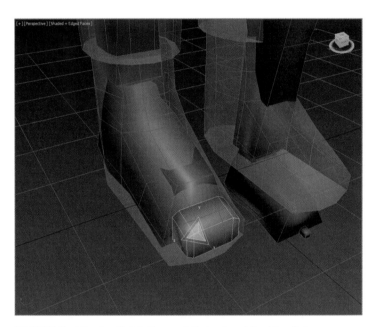

FIGURE 12.9 Match the model's boot and the biped's toe.

11. Double-click the left upper leg to select it and all of the objects below it in the hierarchy, from the thigh down to the toe.

12. In the Biped parameters, open the Copy/Paste rollout.

13. Postures must be saved as collections prior to being pasted. Click the Create Collection button, as shown in Figure 12.10, and then rename the collection from the default Col01 to **Left Leg**.

FIGURE 12.10
Create the collection in
order to paste the left
leg hierarchy.

14. Click the Copy Posture button just below the Posture button to copy
the selected posture to the Clipboard. A preview of the copied posture
will appear in the Copied Postures area of the Command panel, as
shown in Figure 12.11.

FIGURE 12.11
Copy the posture. The
selected objects will show
in red in the preview.

15. Click the Paste Posture Opposite button (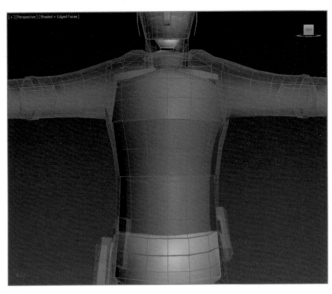). The size, scale, and orientation of the selected objects will be applied to the reciprocal objects on the opposite side of the biped.

Adjusting the Torso and Arms

Similar to the method used to adjust the legs, you will use the Scale and Rotate transforms to fit the biped to the model. The locations of the arms rely on the scale of the spine links. You can continue with your file from the previous exercise or open CSSoldier02.max from the Scenes folder of the Soldier project available on the book's web page. Just make sure your project is set to the Soldier project.

1. In your scene (or the one from the web page), select the biped and then access Figure mode if needed.

2. To add to the selection without losing the previous one, Ctrl+click to select each of the spine links in turn, and then rotate and scale them to fit the soldier's torso. Only the lowest spine link can be moved, and this will move all of the links above it as well. Each spine link should be scaled up slightly on the X- and Y-axes to move the biped's clavicles to match the model's, as shown in Figure 12.12. (For this image only, the arms have been hidden so the placement of the clavicles can be seen clearly.)

FIGURE 12.12 Scale the spine links up to place the clavicles in position.

3. Move, rotate, and scale the left clavicle as required, placing the biped's shoulder joint in the proper location.

4. Scale and rotate the left upper arm and left forearm using the same techniques you used to adjust the biped's legs to fit the arm with the model. Pay close attention to the placement of the elbow and wrist joint, as shown in Figure 12.13

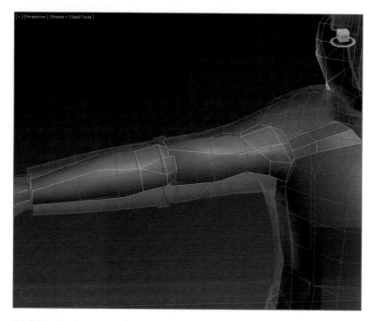

FIGURE 12.13 Arm positioned within the 3d mesh

5. Scale and rotate the left hand as required to fit the model.

6. The hands need only two fingers (the second finger is actually the thumb) and two links each. Adjust the biped's fingers to match the model's fingers, as shown in Figure 12.14. This can be one of the most tedious tasks in character animation, depending on the complexity and orientation of the model's fingers. Take your time and get it right. (Would you rather do it right or do it over?)

7. When you are done, paste the posture to the right side of the biped and make any required changes.

Once the fingers have been adjusted, you cannot go back and change the number of fingers or finger links. If you do, all modifications to the fingers will be lost.

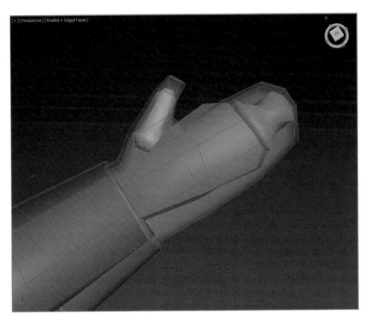

FIGURE 12.14 Match the biped's fingers to the model fingers.

Adjusting the Neck and Head

The neck and head will seem easy to adjust when compared to the hands. You need to make sure the neck link fill the soldier's neck area, and scale the head to fit. Follow along here:

1. In the Structure rollout, increase the number of neck links to 2.

2. Move, scale, and rotate the neck links to match the proportions of the model's neck.

3. Move and scale the head to the approximate size of the soldier's head, as shown in Figure 12.15.

That's it. The biped has been created and adjusted to fit the 3D model, and half the battle is over. Next, you will tie the biped to the model and make adjustments to the skinning process. Now would be a good time to save your work and take a break.

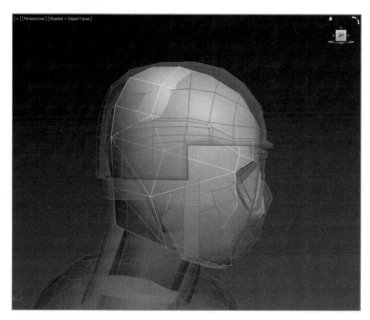

FIGURE 12.15   Matching the head

Applying the Skin Modifier

The Skin modifier is the tool used to skin the 3D model to the biped so that all of the biped's animation is passed through to the model. It's important to remember that the modifier is applied to the model and not to the biped. Continue with the previous exercises file or open CSSoldier03.max from the Scenes folder of the Soldier project on the book's web page to follow these steps:

1. Right-click in any viewport and select Unfreeze All from the Quad menu to unfreeze the soldier model. Then select the Soldier and use Alt+X to exit See-Through mode and turn off Edged Faces (F4).

2. In the Modify panel, expand the modifier list and select the Skin modifier.

3. In the Skin parameters, choose the Bones: Add button and load all bones. Be careful not to add non-Bones objects (in the scene from the web page, you will see a few lights in the list; do not select them).

Testing the Model

The most time-consuming part of the process is complete. You have created a biped and adjusted all of its component parts to fit your model. The next step is to add animation that will allow you to test the skinning once it has been applied.

Before we get into fixing the skin, you need to add a little extra animation. Select the soldier model and right-click in the viewport to get the Quad menu. Choose Hide Selected.

1. To unfreeze the soldier model, right-click in any viewport and select Unfreeze All from the Quad menu. Select the model, right-click again, and from the Quad menu choose Hide Selected.

2. Move the timeline to frame 0. Turn on the Auto Key button ([Auto Key]) below the timeline.

3. Select the entire biped. The best way to do this is to select the Select from Scene tool from the main toolbar (⊞); and from the dialog, select all the Biped objects and press OK. Go to the Motion panel (⊙), and click the Figure Mode button (⬚) to exit. You cannot animate a biped in Figure mode.

4. Select the Move tool and move the biped just a bit. The purpose of this is to create a keyframe of this original pose, so that when you add animation this pose won't be lost. The biped should still be in the same position as before—just give the Move tool a wiggle.

5. Select the right upper arm and then Ctrl+click the left upper arm on the biped and then set the Coordinate System menu to Local, as shown earlier in Figure 12.7.

6. Move the timeline to frame 15, rotate the arms −55 degrees on the Z-axis (the blue wire in the rotate gizmo).

7. Now select the right and left lower arms on the biped and rotate −55 degrees on the Z-axis.

8. Move the timeline to frame 30 and select the upper arms again, but this time rotate 45 degrees on the Y-axis (green wire).

9. Now move to frame 50 and select the lower arms and upper arms. In the timeline Shift+click on the keyframe at frame 0, and then move it to frame 50. This copies the keyframe at frame 0 to frame 50.

Using the same technique, add animation to the legs, chest, and head. The animation does not have to be elaborate. The purpose of the animation is to test the skinning when applied to the model. When you are finished, turn off the AutoKey button and Unhide the soldier and play the animation. Most likely you will see some problem with the mesh—mostly around the feet, upper arms, and groin, as shown in Figure 12.16.

FIGURE 12.16   The problem areas with the skin

Tweaking the Skin Modifier

Each element in the biped has an area of influence, called an *envelope*. It determines which parts of the model it affects. The biped's left foot, for instance, should control the movement of only the model's left foot and the lower part of the ankle. In this case, the envelopes extend to affect some of the vertices on the opposite side. You can continue with your file from the previous exercise or open CSSoldier04.max from the Scenes folder of the Soldier project available on the book's web page.

To fix the envelopes, follow this procedure:

1. Select the soldier model and in the Skin parameters, select the Edit Envelopes button.

The model turns gray except for a color gradient around the pelvis. The gradient shows how heavily weighted vertices on your mesh are to a given envelope, as shown in Figure 12.17. The Biped bone is represented in the viewport as a straight line with vertices at either end. Envelopes are represented by two concentric capsule-shaped volumes; vertices within the inner volume are fully affected by that bone, and then the weighting falls off increasingly for vertices that lie outside the inner volume and inside the outer volume. The weight values appear as a colored gradient with red representing higher weights, decreasing to orange, yellow, green, and then blue for the lowest values.

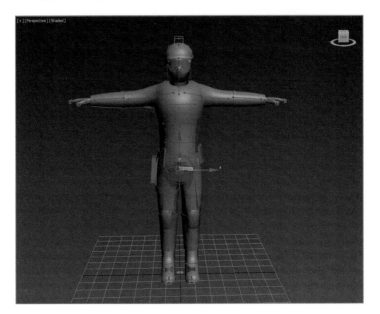

FIGURE 12.17   The soldier after the Edit Envelopes button is active

2. Select the Bip001 R UpperArm object. You can select the object from the name list in the Skin parameters or just click on the representation of the bone on the model. Select the vertices at the end of the bone and move in to make the envelope smaller, as shown in Figure 12.18.

   As the vertex moves, the gradient that represents the influence changes so the yellow-red color is moving up the arm. You want the influence to be on the upper arm only. Repeat the same on the other side of the bone, bringing it in toward the center of the bone.

3. Select and move the points on the outer envelope and move them in on both sides of the bone, as shown in Figure 12.19. The final result is shown in Figure 12.20.

Move this point in. This will scale
the size of the envelopes influence.

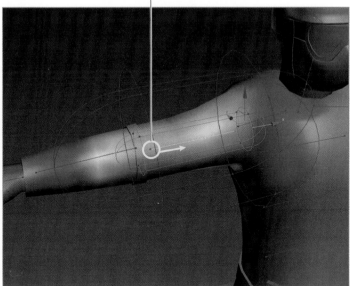

FIGURE 12.18   Select the bone vertex and move in to make the
envelope smaller.

Move these points to change
the weight of the envelope.

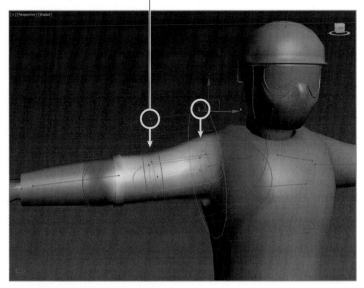

FIGURE 12.19   Make the outer envelope smaller by selecting and
moving the points.

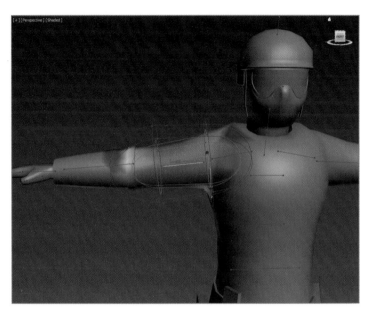

FIGURE 12.20 The edited envelope for upper arm

Move to frame 30 in the animation; in this frame you can really see the problem with the arm. Even though you edited the envelope for the upper arm, you can't see any improvement in the deformity. The previous exercise showed how to edit the envelope; now let's figure out where the trouble really lies with the upper arm. There is one bone that is affecting the upper arm: Bip001 Spine 2 bone.

4. Select the Spine 2 bone. This bone's envelope is huge! It is influencing almost the whole upper body. Select a vertex on either end of the bone and move it in; immediately you will see the arms reacting. Now scale down the size of the outer envelope so that the gradient has some yellow on the inside and blue between the capsules, as shown in Figure 12.21. Now select and edit the remaining two Spine bones.

   The feet are the next area with problems and a bit more of a challenge to fix. Move to frame 88 in the animation. This frame shows that the part of the mesh on the inside of the feet is getting pulled.

5. Select the Bip001. Move the Time slider back to frame 1; it will be easier to edit the envelope when the foot isn't so distorted.

6. Look closely at the bone. As shown in Figure 12.22, the bone is actually sideways. Move the points on the bone so they run from the toe to the heel. Then edit the envelopes so that the gradients are isolated on the foot, as shown in Figure 12.23.

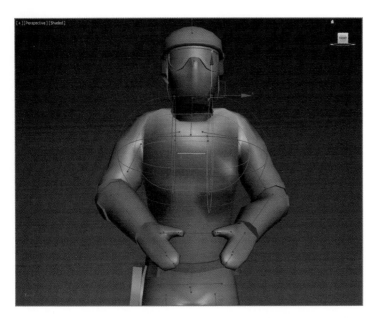

FIGURE 12.21 The Spine bone after the envelope has been edited

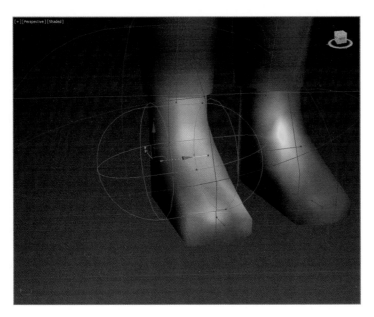

FIGURE 12.22 The envelope at the foot is set horizontal to the foot instead of lengthwise.

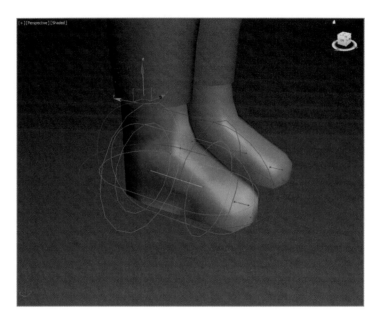

FIGURE 12.23 The edited envelope on right foot

Continue editing the bones and envelopes for the right side and middle of the model. Once you are finished, the next step is to mirror the results to the left side of the body.

7. Select the Foot bone. In the Mirror parameters of the Skin modifier, select the Mirror Mode button. Then set the Mirror Offset to –8.3, as shown in Figure 12.24. This splits the body into half, blue side and green side. Then click on the Paste Blue to Green Bones button (◧).

FIGURE 12.24
In the Mirror
Parameters rollout, set
the Offset to –8.3.

In the Skin parameters, select the Edit Envelope button to exit. Play the animation again and pay attention to any areas where you see parts of the mesh pulling or distorting. Go back to that area's envelope and edit until you are happy with the results.

Weighting the Accessories

Now let's improve the skinning on the accessories, the gun holster on the right side belt of the soldier, by adjusting the weight setting for the vertices. This technique is another way of editing the skinning on a character. You can choose to use the vertex weighting technique in conjunction with editing envelopes or use it exclusively. You can continue with your file from the previous exercise or open CSSoldier05.max from the Scenes folder of the Soldier project available on the book's web page.

1. In the Skin Parameters rollout's Select section, uncheck Envelopes and Cross Sections. Check Vertices and Select Element, as shown in Figure 12.25. You are selecting elements because you are working with the accessories that are individual objects attached to the overall soldier model.

FIGURE 12.25
Uncheck the Envelopes and Cross Sections boxes and check the Vertices and Select Element boxes.

2. Drag a selection box around the gun holster; the selected vertices appear as white hollow boxes. If any other element is selected, then Alt+click or Alt+drag to deselect those vertices.

3. In the Weight Properties rollout, click on the Weight Table button; this will open the Weight Table dialog box.

4. In the Weight Table dialog box, in the Options menu, choose Show Affected Bones. At the bottom of the dialog box is a drop-down menu; choose Selected Vertices.

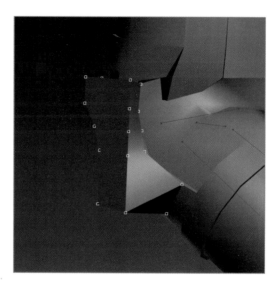

FIGURE 12.26   The Gun Holster element is selected, showing the vertices for weighting.

5. On the left of the Weight Table dialog box under Vertex ID, drag from the top of the list down to the bottom to highlight all the vertices in the list. Then highlight at the top of the dialog box Bip001 Pelvis. Click on one of the numbers in the list below Bip001 Pelvis, type in **1**, and then press Enter. All the numbers in the list change to 1, while the numbers in the other lists change to 0, as shown in Figure 12.27. You just put all the weight of the gun holster on the pelvis, and removed it from the thigh and spine.

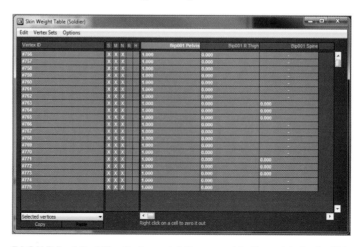

FIGURE 12.27   Vertex weighting moved to the pelvis in the Skin Weight Table

Now if you play the animation, you will see the gun holster looks stiff and doesn't move with the leg. Continue using the Skin Weight Table to edit the various soldier accessories, including the face mask, belt pouches, and anything that looks deformed and shouldn't.

Testing the Model

The most time-consuming part of the process is complete. You have created a biped, adjusted all of its component parts to fit your model, and applied the Skin modifier to link the model to the biped. Let's really put the rig to the test and add some animation. Continue with your file from the previous exercise or open CSSoldier06.max from the Scenes folder of the Soldier project available on the book's web page. This file has the completed rig with all the animation deleted. These were done by selecting all the Biped bones, and dragging a selection around the keyframes and deleting them in the timeline.

1. Select any element of the biped and click the Motion tab of the Command panel.

2. Enter Footstep mode (🔳).
   The rollouts change to display the tools for adding and controlling a biped's motion. The Footstep mode and Figure mode are exclusive; you cannot be in both modes at the same time.

3. In the Footstep Creation rollout, make sure that the walk gait is selected and then click the Create Multiple Footsteps button (🔳) to open the Create Multiple Footsteps dialog box.

4. In the dialog box that appears, you will assign Footstep properties for the number of steps you want, the width and length of each step, and which foot to step with first. Set the number of footsteps to 8, leave the other parameters at their default values, and click OK.

5. Zoom out in the Perspective viewport to see the footsteps you just created. Look at the Time slider, and note that the scene now ends at frame 123; that's 23 more frames than the 100 frames the scene had at the beginning of this chapter. The 3ds Max software recognized that it would take the biped 123 frames, or just over 4 seconds, to move through the eight steps that it was given.

6. Click the Play Animation button in the Playback Controls area. What happens? Nothing. The biped must be told explicitly to create animation keys for the steps that you have just added to the scene. Drag the Time slider back to frame 0.

7. In the Footstep Operations rollout in the Command panel, click the Create Keys For Inactive Footsteps button (🖭). The biped will drop its arms and prepare to walk through the footsteps that are now associated with it.

8. Click the Play Animation button again. This time the biped walks through the footsteps with its arms swinging and its hips swaying back and forth.

Controlling the View

Now the problem is that if you zoom in on the biped and play the animation, it walks off the screen so you cannot see the end of the walk cycle. What good is that? Motion cycles can be very linear and difficult to track, so Character Studio contains the In Place mode to follow a biped's animation. In the In Place mode, the biped will appear to stay in place while the scene moves around it in relation. The In Place mode cannot be used in a Camera viewport, however.

1. Go to frame 0 and then zoom in on the biped in the Perspective viewport.

2. At the bottom of the Biped rollout, click the Modes and Display text with the plus sign to the left of it. This is a small rollout located inside of another rollout that expands to show additional display-related tools.

3. In the Modes And Display rollout, click the In Place Mode button, as shown in Figure 12.28.

FIGURE 12.28
Click the In Place Mode button.

4. Click the Play Animation button again. This time the biped will appear to be walking in place while the footsteps move underneath it. Stop the animation playback when you're ready.

Using the In Place mode helps you work out the way a character moves without having to navigate throughout 3D space with your viewport, so you won't need to hunt down your biped. The In Place mode is great for tweaking your animation cycle because the viewport moves with the character in 3D space and you can concentrate on how its body is moving.

5. Exit Footstep mode, and then select the entire soldier biped by double-clicking on the Bip001.

6. Right-click in any viewport and choose Hide Selection from the Quad menu to hide the biped and obtain an unobstructed view of the model.

7. Click the Play Animation button. Your soldier will walk through the scene. It should be similar to the rendered soldier shown in Figure 12.29.

FIGURE 12.29 The rendered soldier during a walk cycle

Skinning a character is a detail-oriented task, and it requires lots of experimentation and trial-and-error—and patience. Character Studio is a complete character-animation package, and we've barely scratched the surface here. There are tools for saving biped configurations and sequences of animation. You can mix animation sequences from different files to create an entirely new motion. When the model does not skin as well as you need, you can use envelopes to refine the skinning process further, define vertices to be excluded from a specific Biped object's influence, or include bulge conditions to define the model's behavior depending on the angle between subsequent biped elements.

The list goes on, but the good news is that the Character Studio tutorials and help system that ship with the 3ds Max program are very thorough, and you should find the information there to expand your skills once you have a solid footing with the basics. It's important to realize that animation requires nuance, and the best animation with the simplest rig and setup will beat a mediocre animation created with a more wonderful, complicated, and ingenious setup.

THE ESSENTIALS AND BEYOND

This chapter introduced you to the basics of Character Studio and Biped setup for the soldier character. You used Skin to apply the Biped setup to the geometry of the soldier and adjusted the envelopes for the best animation results.

ADDITIONAL EXERCISES

▶ Try adjusting the proportions of the soldier model to create a new character design and adjust the biped accordingly.

▶ Try adding a tail to the biped for an interesting creature.

CHAPTER 13

Character Studio: Animation

Character animation *is a* broad and complex field. This chapter introduces you to the basics of using Character Studio and bones for animation. Further investigation into these tools is a must if you want your animation to be full of life and character.

Topics in this chapter include the following:

▶ **Character animation**

▶ **Animating the soldier**

▶ **Using Inverse Kinematics**

Character Animation

The character animation CG specialty is one of the toughest specialties to master. To use one word, good character animation comes down to *nuance*.

When you animate a character, you have to have a keen eye for detail and an understanding of how proportions move on a person's body. Setting up a CG character to walk *exactly* like a human being is amazingly complicated.

Character systems such as Character Studio make it a breeze to outfit characters with biped setups and have them moving in a walk cycle very quickly.

Animating the Soldier

Bipeds can be animated in several ways, including footstep-driven animation and freeform animation. With *footstep-driven animation,* you add visible Footstep objects to your scene and direct the biped to step onto those footsteps at particular points in time. Footsteps can be added individually or as a set of walk, run, or jump steps; they can be moved or rotated to achieve the desired result and direction. When you use footstep-driven animation, the legs and feet of the biped are not the only things animated; the hips, arms, tails, and all other components are animated as well. However, this approach is rarely the complete solution to your animation needs.

Freeform animation is when you animate the components of the biped manually, as you would animate any other object, such as a bouncing ball.

Animation keys that are added to the selected Biped objects appear in the track bar, just like other objects, where they can be moved, modified, or deleted to adjust the animation.

Adding a Run-and-Jump Sequence

At the end of the previous chapter, you finished rigging the soldier model and added footsteps to check the model. New footsteps can be appended to any existing footsteps. In the next exercise, you will add footsteps to the existing animation cycle.

Continue with the previous soldier model or open the CSSoldierComplete00 .max file in the Scenes folder of the Soldier project on the book's web page at www .sybex.com/go/3dsmax2013essentials. This file has the Biped bones hidden with the soldier model, Bip001, and footsteps showing.

1. Select the Bip001 object. If you have trouble, you can either press the H key or open the Select By Name dialog icon (⬚) found on the main toolbar. Once you've selected the Bip001 object, click Select. Then on the Motion panel, choose Footstep mode (⬚).

2. Click the Run icon (⬚) in the Footstep Creation rollout. This will apply a run gait to any footsteps you add to your current footsteps in the Create Multiple Footsteps dialog box.

3. Click the Create Multiple Footsteps icon (⬚) to open the Create Multiple Footsteps dialog box.

4. Change the number of footsteps to **10** and click OK.

5. In the Footstep Operations rollout, click the Create Keys For Inactive Footsteps icon (⬚) to associate the new footsteps with the biped.

6. Click the Play Animation button. The biped walks through the first 8 steps and then runs through the next 10. As you can see, the run sequence meets the definition of a run, but it is far from realistic. In the next exercise, you'll learn how to add to or modify a biped's motion with freeform animation to make a better cycle. For now, click the Play Animation button again to turn off play.

7. Click the Jump button in the Footstep Creation rollout, and then click the Create Multiple Footsteps button.

8. In the Create Multiple Footsteps dialog box, set the number of footsteps to 4 and click OK. Because a jump is defined as a sequence with either two feet or zero feet on the ground at a time, four jump steps will equal two actual jumps.

9. Click the Create Keys For Inactive Footsteps icon to associate the new jump footsteps with the biped.

10. Click the Play Animation button. The biped will walk, run, and then end the sequence with two jumps, as shown in Figure 13.1.

◀

The Actual Stride Height parameter in the Create Multiple Footsteps dialog box determines the height difference from one footstep to the next.

FIGURE 13.1 Soldier model with the Jump biped applied

Adding Freeform Animation

When you set your keys initially, you will need to edit them to suit good timing and form. When one part of the body is in one movement, another part of the body is in an accompanying or supportive or even opposite form of movement. When you are walking and your right leg swings forward in a step, your right arm swings back and your left arm swings out to compensate.

You can easily add or modify the biped's existing animation keys with freeform animation using the Auto Key button and the Dope Sheet. The following exercises contain examples of freeform animation.

Moving the Head

The following steps will guide you through the process of creating head movement for your biped. Continue with the previous soldier model or open the CSSoldierComplete01.max file in the Scenes folder of the Soldier project on the book's web page at www.sybex.com/go/3dsmax2013essentials. Because you will be working with the biped a lot in this exercise, the biped components have been unhidden and the soldier model has been hidden.

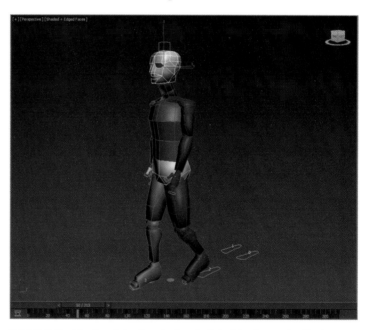

Footsteps are numbered, starting with the number 0 and initially alternating from the left to the right side. They are also color-coded, with blue footsteps on the left and green footsteps on the right.

1. Select the Bip001 object and, if necessary, exit the Footstep mode by clicking the Footstep Mode icon.

2. Drag the Time slider to frame 50, approximately the point when the biped lifts its left foot off footstep number 2.

3. Select the biped's head and note the animation keys that appear in the track bar, as shown in Figure 13.2.

F I G U R E   1 3 . 2   Selecting the head of the biped reveals all of that object's animation keys in the track bar.

4. In the track bar, select the two keys on either side of the current frame. You can do that by dragging a selection box around both keys

directly on the track bar; or by selecting one key, then holding the Ctrl key and selecting the other key. Once you do that, right-click either one and then delete them as shown in Figure 13.3.

FIGURE 13.3 Delete the keys on either side of frame 50.

5. Click the Auto Key button or press the N key to turn it on. This will allow you to begin creating the animation.

6. Click the Rotate Transform button and rotate the head, as shown in Figure 13.4, to the left and up, as if the character sees somebody in a second floor window off-screen. A new key will be created at frame 50, recording the time and value of the head's rotation.

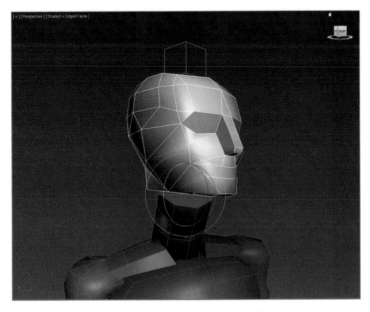

FIGURE 13.4 Rotate the head to the left and up.

7. Scrub through the Time slider by moving it back and forth. Watch the head rotate from a neutral position to the orientation that you created and then rotate back to the neutral position.

8. Select all the keys between frame 50 and frame 100 (but not keys at frames 50 and 100). Delete them. Doing so will make room for the new key that you are about to create. If animation keys are too close together, the animation could appear jerky.

9. Select the key at frame 50, hold down the Shift key, and drag a copy of the key to frame 90, as shown in Figure 13.5. Use the readout at the bottom of the 3ds Max® window to drag the key with precision. Copying the key will cause your biped to hold that neck pose for 40 frames, or about 1⅓ seconds. Scrub the Time slider to review the animation.

FIGURE 13.5
Drag to copy the key.

10. Select the biped's left upper arm.

11. In the track bar, select and delete all keys between frames 50 and 100. The animation keys for the arms define their swing motion. If you scrub the Time slider or play the animation, the biped will hold its arm unnaturally stiff for 60 frames because you deleted the animation keys between two points where it holds its hand forward. That's okay; you're just making room for some new keys.

12. Move the Time slider to frame 60. This is the location for the first new animation key.

Moving the Arms

Now it's time to animate the arms, which are essential components in any walk cycle. To do so, follow these steps:

1. Rotate the upper arm upward, so that it points to the same location at which the head is looking.

2. Continue adjusting the biped's left arm, hand, and finger until they appear to be pointing at something, as shown in Figure 13.6.

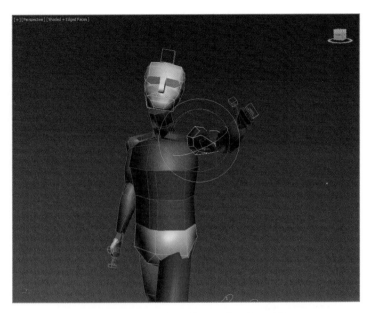

FIGURE 13.6 Rotate the biped's arm, hand, and fingers to assume a pointing posture.

3. Double-click on the left upper arm to select it and all of the components below it in the hierarchy.

4. In the track bar, select the key at frame 60, hold down the Shift key, and drag it to frame 85 to create a copy of that key.

5. Drag the Time slider and watch the Perspective viewport. The biped will walk for a bit, notice something off-screen, point at it, and drop its arm while looking forward again before breaking into a run and then a jump.

6. Click the Auto Key button to turn it off.

Completing the Motion Sequence

Continue with the previous soldier model or open the CSSoldierComplete02 .max file in the Scenes folder of the Soldier project on the book's web page at www.sybex.com/go/3dsmax2013essentials.

For additional practice, add keys to the animation of the biped's arms when it jogs through the run cycle. For example, when the left foot is fully extended and the heel plants on the ground, the right arm should be bent at the elbow and swung forward and slightly in front of the biped's body. As the right foot swings forward during the next step, the right arm should swing backward and assume a nearly straight posture. Bend each of the spine links and swing both arms backward to prepare the biped for each of the jumps. Use the Body Vertical button in the Track Selection rollout to lower the pelvis into a prelaunch position, as shown in Figure 13.7, before the biped launches into its upward motion. Remember to make sure the Auto Key button is turned on to record all the changes that you make as animation keys.

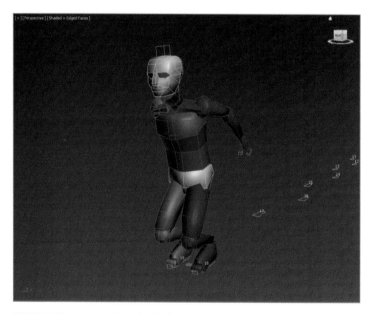

FIGURE 13.7   Use the Body Vertical button to position the biped for a jump.

Modifying Animation in the Dope Sheet

To change the animation that is generated with Character Studio, you will edit the keyframes of the biped once you are happy with the base animation cycle. For this, you need to use the Track View–Dope Sheet. The Track View–Curve Editor, as you have already seen in Chapter 5, "Animating a Bouncing Ball," is used to edit the function curves between animation keys; however, the Track View–Dope Sheet interface is cleaner and is used to edit the specific value and position of the keys. It is not a different set of keyframes or animation; it's just a different way of editing them. Furthermore, access to editing the footstep keys is available only in the Dope Sheet. In the next exercise, you will add individual footsteps and modify the footstep timing in the Dope Sheet to make the biped dance and jump.

Adding Footsteps Manually

In the following steps, you will manually add footsteps to your biped character. Continue with the previous soldier model or open the CSSoldierComplete03 .max file in the Scenes folder of the Soldier project on the book's web page at www.sybex.com/go/3dsmax2013essentials. This is the rigged and skinned soldier biped with no footsteps applied.

1. Select a biped component and enter the Footstep mode.

2. In the Footstep Creation rollout, click the Walk button and then the Create Footsteps (At Current Frame) icon (▣).

3. In the Top viewport, click in several locations around the biped to place alternating left and right footsteps to your liking.

4. Change the gait to a jump, and then click the Create Footsteps (Append) icon (▣) to create additional footsteps. Create about 16 footsteps in all.

5. When you are done, use the Move and Rotate transforms to adjust the footstep locations and orientations as desired. Your Top viewport should look similar to Figure 13.8.

6. In the Footstep Operations rollout, click the Create Keys For Inactive Footsteps icon and then play the animation.

7. Character Studio doesn't have a collision-detection feature, so it is very possible that limbs will pass through one another, which is quite uncomfortable in real life. If this happens, the footsteps must be modified to eliminate these conditions. If necessary, move any footsteps that cause collisions or other unwanted conditions during the playback.

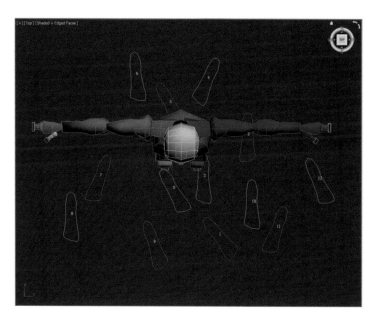

FIGURE 13.8   Manually place the footsteps in the Top viewport.

Using the Dope Sheet

In Chapter 5, you experimented with the Track View–Curve Editor and learned how to adjust the values of animation keyframes. When the Track View is in Dope Sheet mode, frames are displayed as individual blocks of time that may or may not contain keys. Although you cannot see the flow from key to key that the Curve Editor displays with its curves, the Dope Sheet mode has its advantages. For one, the Dope Sheet has the ability to add Visibility tracks to control the display of an object, as well as Note tracks for adding text information regarding the keys as reminders.

Using the Track View–Dope Sheet, you can adjust the point in time when a foot plants on or lifts off the ground, how long the foot is on the ground, and how long the foot is airborne. Rather than appearing as single-frame blocks in the Dope Sheet as other keys do, footstep keys appear as multiframe rectangles that identify each foot's impact time with the footstep. Let's try the Dope Sheet on for size here:

1. Make sure you are in Footstep mode. This will select the biped's footsteps.

2. In the main toolbar, choose Graph Editors ➢ Track View–Dope Sheet. The Dope Sheet will open.

3. In the Navigation pane on the left, scroll down until you find the Bip001 Footsteps entry. Expand the Bip001 Footsteps entries. The footstep keys appear as rectangles in the Key pane. As expected, the left keys are colored blue and the right keys are colored green. If necessary, click the Zoom Region icon () in the lower-right corner of the Dope Sheet window and drag a zoom window around the footstep keys, as shown in Figure 13.9. The region will expand to fit the Key pane.

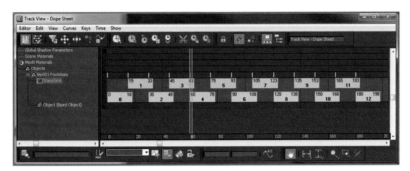

FIGURE 13.9 Zoom to the Footstep keys.

4. Select a few footsteps in the viewport or select the green- and blue-colored rectangles (holding Ctrl to select multiple footsteps).

The white dot on the left side of a selected key identifies the frame when the heel of the biped's foot first impacts the footstep. The white dot on the right side of a selected key identifies when the biped's foot lifts off a footstep, as shown in Figure 13.10. A blue key (rectangle) overlapping a green key (rectangle) indicates that both feet are on the ground. A vertical gray area with no footstep indicates that the biped is airborne and neither foot is on the ground.

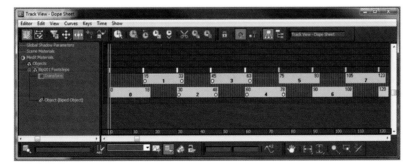

FIGURE 13.10 The dots indicate when contact begins and ends. You can drag a dot to change the duration of contact.

> You can't move the end of one footstep key beyond the beginning of another one, and you must maintain a one-frame gap between same-side footsteps.

> It is possible to move a footstep beyond the limits of the active time segment in the Dope Sheet. Use the Alt+R key combination to extend the active time segment to include all existing keys.

5. Select the first key (numbered 0), place the cursor over the right edge of the key, and then drag the dot to the right to extend the length of time that the biped's foot is on the ground.

6. The double vertical line in the Dope Sheet's Key pane is another Time slider that allows you to scrub through the animation. Drag the Dope Sheet's Time slider to a point in time when the biped is airborne.

   Increasing the airborne time by increasing the gap between footsteps will also boost the height to which the biped rises, acting against the gravitational force pushing it downward.

7. Select the last four jump keys and drag them to the right to create a gap approximately 30 frames wide, as shown in Figure 13.11. Doing so will cause the biped to be airborne for about one second.

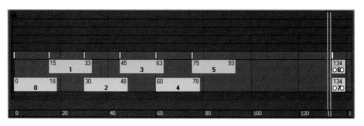

FIGURE 13.11   Create a key gap to get your biped airborne.

8. Move the Time slider to the frame when both feet are planted before the jump starts. Turn on the Auto Key button.

9. Deselect any keys by clicking a blank area in the Key pane.

10. To prepare the biped to leap, turn on Auto Key and then select the Bip001 object and move it downward, causing the biped to bend its knees more. Rotate the spine links, neck, and head to bend the torso forward and tuck the chin. Rotate both arms backward into a pre-jump posture, as shown in Figure 13.12. Be sure to choose Local as the reference coordinate system for the Rotate transform.

11. Move the Time slider forward until the biped is at the apex of the jump. Rotate the biped's components into positions you like, such as the split shown in Figure 13.13. Delete any animation keys that may interfere with your desired motion, and turn off Auto Key.

FIGURE 13.12   Prepare your biped to jump.

FIGURE 13.13   Position your biped in mid-jump.

The CSSoldierComplete04.max file in the Biped Scene Files folder on the book's web page contains the completed exercise so you can check your work. This file has the soldier model unhidden and the biped hidden. Play the animation and see how it looks; modify where needed.

As you saw in this section, there are several ways to animate a biped, including the footstep-driven method, the freeform method, and a combination of techniques. You can also modify the animation in the track bar, with the Auto Key button, and with Track View–Dope Sheet.

Using Inverse Kinematics

When a hierarchy is set up through linking, the result is a kinematic chain. Transforms are passed from a parent object to all of the child objects down the chain. Imagine your arm is a system of linked 3ds Max objects; when you pivot your forearm (the parent) at the elbow, your hand (the child) and your fingers (the descendants) are also transformed to maintain the relationship between the objects. This is known as Forward Kinematics (FK) and is the default method of passing transforms in a hierarchy.

When Inverse Kinematics (IK) is used, the child object is transformed while the parent and ancestor objects maintain their relationships throughout the chain. Using the same arm analogy, lifting your arm by grabbing and pulling up on a finger would raise the hand, which would raise the forearm, causing a curl at the elbow. With IK, the end of the chain, the child, is positioned in your animation and the rest of the chain upstream rotates and pivots to fit the new layout of the chain to achieve a possible pose. IK setups require the use of an IK solver to determine how the parent objects react to the child transforms and joint constraints to prevent unnecessary twists in the motion.

In the following exercise, you will play some more with toys of war by linking a machine gun mounted on a tank model. Here, the goal is to arrange the IK setup so that the gun pivots vertically at the joints only and then pivots at the turret.

Linking the Objects

Open the IKGun1.max file in the Scenes folder of the Soldier project on the book's web page at www.sybex.com/go/3dsmax2013essentials. The machine gun unit consists of the gun itself, two two-component pivot assemblies, two shafts, and the turret ring. The gun is at the top of the hierarchy, and the turret is at the bottom

1. In the main toolbar, click on the Select and Link tool (![link icon]). Begin by dragging and linking the Gun object to the PivotTop object, the small, blue cylindrical object near the gun. The PivotTop object will flash briefly to signify that is has been linked.

2. Continue creating the hierarchy by also linking the PivotTopRing to PivotTop, PivotTop to Shaft1, and then Shaft1 to PivotBottom.

3. Complete the setup by linking PivotBottomRing to PivotBottom, PivotBottom to Shaft2, and Shaft2 to Turret.

4. Go to the main toolbar and select Tools ➤ New Scene Explorer. This opens a Scene Explorer, as shown in Figure 13.14.

FIGURE 13.14 The Scene Explorer window showing the hierarchy

The Scene Explorer is for viewing, sorting, filtering, and selecting objects as well as additional functionality for renaming, deleting, hiding, and freezing objects, creating and modifying object hierarchies, and editing object properties. The

Scene Explorer looks just like the Select From Scene dialog box (⊞); the difference is the Scene Explorer allows you to edit your scene while keeping the Scene Explorer open.

Creating Joint Constraints

The gun assembly should only be able to rotate in certain ways. The gun itself should only pivot perpendicular to the PivotTop object, for example. This is accomplished by constraining the Rotate transform for the PivotTop object, the parent of the gun, to a single axis. The transforms can further be restricted by limiting the range of motion an object can rotate within an acceptable axis. This method is used to prevent the gun barrel from rotating to the point where it disappears within the tank body. Both of these tasks are accomplished under the Hierarchy tab of the Command panel, as you will see in the following steps:

1. In the Command panel, click the Hierarchy tab (▦).

2. Click the IK button and then, in the Inverse Kinematics rollout, click the Interactive IK button, as shown in Figure 13.15. The Interactive IK button will turn blue to indicate that this feature is active and any transforms applied to objects in the hierarchy are applied in IK mode.

3. In the Perspective viewport, select and move the Gun object along the X-axis. The gun's orientation changes and all of the hierarchy elements, including the turret, change to maintain the connection, but they all rotate oddly. This is because the orientation at the joints is not constrained to a single axis or limit of degrees.

4. Undo any transforms that were applied (↩).

5. In the Scene Explorer, select the PivotTop object. Then in the Hierarchy panel, Rotational Joints rollout, uncheck the X Axis and Z Axis Active check boxes.

6. Check the Limited check box in the Y-axis section. Increase the From parameter to approximately –65 by dragging the spinners. The Pivot and its children will rotate in the viewport and then snap back to their original orientations when the mouse is released. Drag the To spinner to approximately –40, as shown in Figure 13.15. Limiting the orientation restricts how far the object can rotate in a particular axis, and dragging the spinners instead of typing in the values gives visual feedback regarding the axis about which the object is rotating.

FIGURE 13.15
In the Rotational Joints
rollout, change the From
spinner to −65 and the
To spinner to −40.

7. Select Shaft1 and uncheck the Active option for the X-, Y-, and Z-axes in the Rotational Joints rollout. Repeat the process for the Shaft2 and Gun objects. None of these objects needs to rotate on their own; they just need to follow their parent objects.

8. Select the PivotBottom object. Check the Active and Limited options in the Y-axis area. Set the From value to −4 and the To value to 30. Uncheck the X-axis and Z-axis Active options.

9. Select the Turret object. Only the Z-axis option should be checked, so the turret can only rotate laterally and not flip over. Do not check the Limited option; the turret should be able to rotate freely.

10. In the Object Parameters rollout, check the Terminator option to identify the turret as the top object in the IK structure, as shown in Figure 13.16.

11. Select the Gun object and then click the Link Info button at the top of the Hierarchy panel. In the Rotate section of the Locks rollout,

check the X option. The gun should not rotate in any axis except the
local X-axis.

FIGURE 13.16
In the Object Parameters
rollout, check the
Terminator option.

12. Select the Turret object and in the Link Info rollout, check the X,
Y, and Z options in the Move section, to lock any movement for the
turret. The turret should be fixed in place. In a complete 3ds Max
scene, the turret would be linked to a larger structure to define its
transforms.

13. Click the IK button at the top of the Hierarchy panel, and then click
the Interactive IK button again to turn it on if necessary. Test your IK
chain by moving the gun. As it moves, the other objects in the chain
will reorient to maintain the proper relationships with their parent
objects. Turn off the Interactive IK button when you are done.

Applying the IK Solver

An IK solver calculates the controls required to position and orient the members
of an IK chain when one or more members is moved or rotated. The IK solver
defines the top of the chain and identifies the goal, or the base of the chain.
The IK solver precludes the need to activate the Interactive IK mode in the
Hierarchy panel whenever IK is required.

   The two appropriate IK solvers for this situation are the HI (History Independent)
solver and the HD (History Dependent) solver. The HI solver is better suited for
long animation sequences and character animation, and the HD solver is better
suited for machine animation. Because the goal for this animation for this setup is
for a machine, in this case a tank, the HD solver will be used here.

   Open the IKGun2.max file in the Scenes folder of the Soldier project on the
book's web page at www.sybex.com/go/3dsmax2013essentials.

1. Undo any transforms that were applied in your own scene during the
previous exercise if necessary. You can undo a string of commands
easily by right-clicking the Undo button in the main toolbar.

N O T E   Right-click the Undo button in the main toolbar to see a list of the recent changes to the scene, with the most recent changes at the top of the list. Click on the entry in the list that defines the last command that you want undone. That command and all of the commands above it will highlight. Press the Enter key to undo all the selected commands.

2. Choose Edit ➢ Hold from the main menu. A few IK operations, including applying an IK solver, are not always undoable through the Undo command. If the result of the IK solve is not correct, choose Edit ➢ Fetch to restore your scene to the point just before you executed the Edit ➢ Hold.

3. Turn off Interactive IK.

4. Select the gun and choose Animation ➢ IK Solvers ➢ HD Solver. A rubber-band line will stretch from the gun's pivot point to the cursor, as you can see in Figure 13.17. Place the cursor over the Shaft2 object and click to define it as the end of the IK chain. The IK chain should now be bound to the object that has been designated as the Terminator.

 N O T E   When the cursor is moved over the other viewports while an IK solver is being assigned, the view will update to show the rubber-banding line projecting from the object to the cursor in that particular viewport. The viewport does not have to be the active viewport for this viewport change to occur.

5. The End Effectors behaves as the pivot point of the Terminator object and can be used to straighten out the chain without actually moving the child object. On the Motion panel, in the IK Controller Parameters rollout, click the Link button in the End Effectors area and then click on the turret. Turret appears in the End Effector Parent field, as shown in Figure 13.18.

6. Select the gun and use the Move Transform to test your IK setup. Moving the gun forward, backward, up, or down will now cause the two pivots to rotate within their limits.

The HD solver's IK components are not listed in the Select Objects dialog box because they act on behalf of the objects to which they are assigned. To modify any of its properties, select the object and open the Motion panel of the Command panel. The IK Controller Properties rollout contains the options for modifying the IK chain.

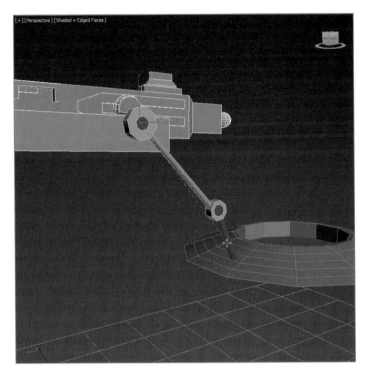

FIGURE 13.17 A line stretches from the gun's pivot to the cursor.

FIGURE 13.18
Click the Link button
in the End Effectors
area and then select the
Turret.

THE ESSENTIALS AND BEYOND

This chapter introduced you to animating characters with Character Studio. Using the Biped system, you can quickly create and adjust the substructure that controls a 3D model. Once the Physique modifier associates or skins the model to the biped, character animation can be added using footstep-driven or freeform animation.

IK is used throughout mechanical design and character animation, and it is another 3ds Max tool that you may find invaluable once its workflow becomes second nature to you. The exercises in this chapter examined the basics of an IK setup and the basic use of an IK solver for a mechanical animation of the tank. The IK setups can include several IK chains controlling the transforms for different components of the same model. Easily selected controls can be placed in the scene for simple selection and manipulation of a complex model's components. IK can also be used for organic character animation, because the 3ds Max program has different types of IK for character work as well (such as the HI IK or Limb Solver IK). This chapter covered only one type of IK (using the HD solver) for a simple use of IK. Most practical applications will use the HI system; however, for the purposes of this book, familiarizing yourself with the simpler HD solver primes you for further study in 3ds Max IK systems.

ADDITIONAL EXERCISES

- ► Add different head or arm movements to the current footsteps on your soldier.
- ► Animate the soldier character running and dodging enemy fire.
- ► Create other object hierarchies to link together and create Inverse Kinematics.

CHAPTER 14

Introduction to Lighting: Interior Lighting

Light reveals the world around us and defines shape, color, and texture. Lighting is the most important aspect of CG, and it simply cannot be mastered at a snap of the fingers. The trick to correctly lighting a CG scene is to understand how light works and to see the visual nuances it has to offer.

In this chapter, you will study the various tools used to light in Autodesk® 3ds Max® software. This chapter will serve as a primer on this important aspect of CG. It will start you on the path by showing you the tools available and giving you opportunities to begin using them.

Topics in this chapter include the following:

▶ **Three-point lighting**

▶ **3ds Max lights**

▶ **Standard lights**

▶ **Lighting a still life in the interior space**

▶ **Selecting a shadow type**

▶ **Atmospheres and effects**

▶ **Light Lister**

Three-Point Lighting

Three-point lighting is a traditional approach to lighting a television shot. After all these years, the concepts still carry over to CG lighting. In this setup, three distinct roles are used to light the subject of a shot. The scene should, in effect, seem to have only one primary or *key* light to define lighting direction and create primary shadows, a softer light to fill the scene and soften the shadows a bit, and a back light to make the subject pop out from the background.

This does not mean there are only three lights in the scene. Three-point lighting suggests that there are three primary angles of light for your shot, dependent on where the camera is located.

Three-point lighting ensures that your scene's main subject for a particular shot is well lit and has highlights and a sense of lighting direction using shadow and tone. Figure 14.1 shows a plan view of the three-point lighting layout. The subject is in the middle of the image.

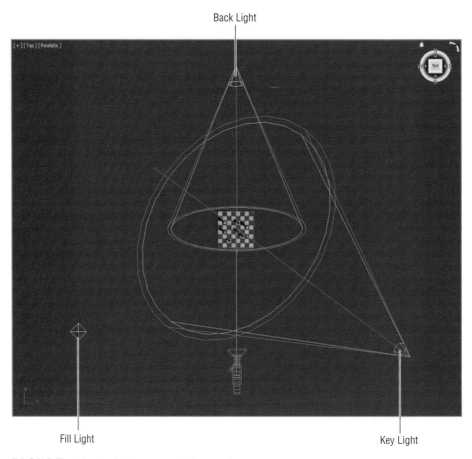

FIGURE 14.1   A three-point lighting schematic

3ds Max Lights

The 3ds Max program has two types of light objects: photometric and standard. *Photometric lights* are lights that possess specific features to enable a more accurate definition of lighting, as you would see in the real world. Photometric lights have physically based intensity values that closely mimic the behavior of real light. *Standard lights* are extremely powerful and capable of realism, but they are more straightforward to use than photometric lights and less taxing on the system at render time. In this book, we will discuss only standard lights.

Standard Lights

The 3ds Max lights attempt to mimic the way real lights work. For example, a lightbulb that emits light all around itself would be an *omni* light in 3ds Max terminology. A desk lamp that shines light in a specific direction in a cone shape would be a spotlight. Each of the different standard lights casts light differently. We will look at the most commonly used lights.

The 3ds Max program has a total of eight light types in its Standard Light collection. The following lights are in the collection:

> Target spotlight
>
> Target direct light
>
> Free spotlight
>
> Free direct light
>
> Omni light
>
> Skylight
>
> mr area omni light
>
> mr area spotlight

The last two on this list have the prefix "mr" to signify that they are mental ray–specific lights (see Chapter 16, "mental ray and HDRI," for more about mental ray). An advanced renderer, mental ray is commonly used in production today. It offers many sophisticated and frequently complex methods of lighting that enhance the realism of a rendered scene. In this chapter, we will cover only the first five standard lights.

◄

In the absence of lights, a 3ds Max scene is automatically lit by *default lighting* so you can easily view an object in Shaded mode and test render without creating a light first. Default lighting is replaced by any lights added to the scene.

Target Spotlight

A *target spotlight,* as shown in Figure 14.2, is one of the most commonly used lights because it is extremely versatile. A spotlight casts light in a focused beam, similar to a flashlight. This type of lighting allows you to light specific areas of a scene without casting any unwanted light on areas that may not need that light. You can control the size of the *hotspot,* which is the size of the cast beam.

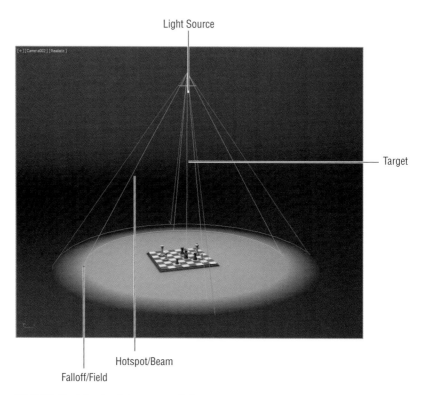

FIGURE 14.2 A target spotlight

The light is created with two nodes, the light itself (*light source*) and the Target node, at which the light points at all times. This way, you easily are able to animate the light following the subject of the scene, as a spotlight would follow a singer on stage. Select the target and move it as you would any other object. The target spot rotates to follow the target.

Similarly, you can animate the light source, and it will orient itself accordingly to aim at the stationary target. Select the box at the end (the target) to point the light. Move (and animate) the entire light by selecting the line that connects the light source and the target. To access the parameters of the light, you have to select the top of the light (tip of the cone).

Create a target spot by going to the Create panel and clicking the Lights icon (◤) to access the Light Creation tools.

In any scene, click the Target Spot button, and in the Top viewport, click and drag to create a target spotlight.

To create a *falloff,* select the light source of the target spot. Go to the Modify panel and open the Spotlight Parameters rollout, shown in Figure 14.3.

FIGURE 14.3
The Spotlight
Parameters rollout

The falloff, which pertains to standard lights in 3ds Max software, is represented in the viewport by the area between the inner, lighter yellow cone and the outer, darker yellow cone. The light diminishes to 0 by the outer region, creating a soft area around the hotspot circle (where the light is the brightest), as shown in Figure 14.4.

FIGURE 14.4   **The falloff**
of a hotspot

Target Direct Light

A *target direct light* has Target and Light nodes to help you control the direction and animation of the light. It also has a hotspot and beam, as well as a falloff, much like the target spot. However, where the target spot emits light rays from a single point (the light source) outward in a cone shape, the target direct light casts parallel rays of light within its beam area. This helps simulate the lighting effect of the sun, because its light rays (for all practical purposes on Earth) are parallel. Figure 14.5 shows a target direct light in a viewport.

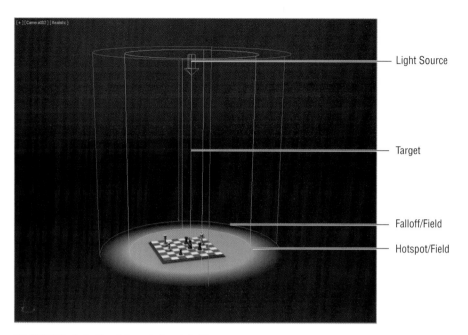

FIGURE 14.5 A target direct light

Because the directional rays are parallel, the target direct lights have a beam in a straight cylindrical or rectangular box shape instead of a cone.

You can create and select/move parts of a target direct light in much the same way as a target spot. In the Directional Parameters rollout, you'll find the similar parameters for the target direct light. Although the spotlight and the directional light don't seem to be very different, the way they light is strikingly different, as you can see in Figure 14.6. The spotlight rays cast an entirely different hotspot and shadow than the directional light, despite having the same values for those parameters.

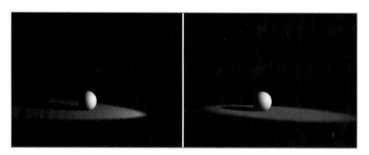

FIGURE 14.6 A target spot (left) and a target direct spot (right)

Free Spot or Free Direct Light

A *free spotlight* or *free direct light* is virtually identical to a target spot, except that this light has no Target object. You can move and rotate the free spot however you want, relying on rotation instead of a target to aim it in any direction, as shown in Figure 14.7.

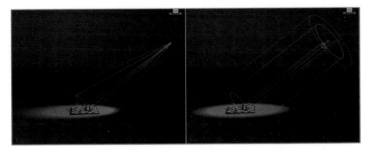

FIGURE 14.7 Free spot (left) and free direct (right) lights

To create a free spot or direct light, choose Free Spot or Direct and in the Create panel, select Lights. Click in a viewport. Then move and rotate the free spot however you want. Another difference between a free spot or direct light and a target spot or direct light is that whereas the length of the target spotlight is controlled by its target, a free spot or direct light instead has, in the General Parameters rollout, a parameter called Targ. Dist. The default is 240 units.

Adjusting the length of a spot or direct light will not matter when the light is rendered; however, seeing a longer light in the viewports can help you line up the light with objects in the scene.

Spot and direct (including target spot and direct) are great for key lighting because they are very easy to control and give a fantastic sense of direction.

Omni Light

The 3ds Max *omni light* is a point light that emanates light from a single point in all directions around it. Figure 14.8 shows an omni light. Unlike the spot and directional lights, the omni light does not have a special rollout, and its General Parameters rollout is much simpler.

Omni lights are not as good for simulating sunlight as directional lights are. In Figure 14.9, the omni light in the image on the left creates different shadow and lighting directions for all the objects in the scene, and the directional light in the image on the right creates a uniform direction for the light and shadow, as would the sun here on Earth.

FIGURE 14.8 An omni light is a single-point-source light.

FIGURE 14.9 Omni light (left) and directional light (right)

Try to avoid casting shadows with omni lights because they will use a lot more memory than a spotlight when casting shadows.

Omni lights are good for fill lights as well as for simulating certain practical light sources.

Lighting a Still Life in the Interior Space

Now that you have an overview of how lights work in a 3ds Max scene, let's put them to good use and light the room from Chapter 10, "Introduction to Materials: Interiors and Furniture," and create the three-point system. Set your current project to the Arch Model project you copied to your hard drive from this book's web page, www.sybex.com/go/3dsmax2013essentials. Open ArchModel_light_start.max from the Scenes folder of the Arch Model project. This file is a version of the room built and materials added in earlier chapters. Models and more materials have been added to beef up the file. We will start with a still life scene set up in the dining room.

1. Go to the Create panel and select the Lights icon () to bring up the selection of lights you can create. Click the Photometric drop-down menu and choose Standard, as shown in Figure 14.10.

FIGURE 14.10
Choose Standard from the Lights drop-down menu.

2. Select the target spot and go to the Front viewport. Click and drag from the ceiling above the dining room table to the floor below the table. The click will create the light and the mouse drag places the target.

3. In the Top viewport, select the light and the target by dragging a selection box around both. Move so they are over the dining room table in the Top viewport. The light's position should resemble Figure 14.11. The objects in the scene, except for the target spotlight, are frozen. To do this, select the objects you want frozen and right-click to access the Quad menu and then choose Freeze Selected from the menu.

4. Select just the Light object and name the light **Key Light**. In the Intensity/Color/Attenuation rollout, set the Multiplier to **1.2**. The Multiplier acts as a dimmer switch for the key light. This light will have shadows and give the scene its main source of light and direction.

   You want to take advantage of the Nitros display driver that is available; it is turned on by default. This driver gives the most information in the Camera viewport about lights, cameras, and shadows without the need of rendering.

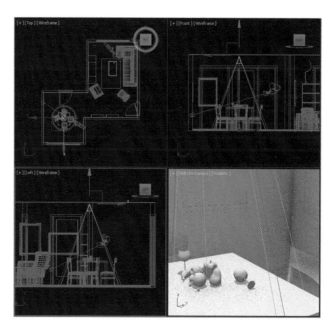

FIGURE 14.11 The spotlight's position in the room

5. In the Still Life Camera viewport, click on the Shading Viewport Label menu. This brings up the menu. Choose Realistic from the list. You can also use the keyboard shortcut Shift+F3.

6. Click again on the Shading Viewport Label menu, go down to Lighting and Shadows, and choose Illuminate with Scene Lights, as shown in Figure 14.12. Now the Still Life camera can be used to judge the lights and shadows for this scene. Keep in mind that rendering a viewport is always the most accurate way of testing lights and shadows.

FIGURE 14.12 The Shading Viewport Label menu with drop-down menu

7. Select the key light by clicking on the cone-shaped light in the view-port. Go to the Modify panel and select the Spotlight Parameters roll-out. Set the Hotspot/Beam to 40 and the Falloff/Field to 80.

8. As you can see in the Camera viewport the light spread out farther toward the walls; now render by clicking on the Render Scene button in the main toolbar (▦), as shown in Figure 14.13. You can see from the two side-by-side images that the Realistic viewport setting is fairly accurate. However, reflections and transparencies that are seen in renders are not shown in the viewport.

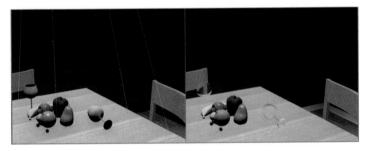

FIGURE 14.13 The Still Life viewport set to Realistic showing new Hotspot/Beam and Falloff/Fields settings (left); the rendered scene (right)

A few things need to be added to the rendered scene to make it look more realistic. First the scene needs shadows. Second, the area outside of the light is too dark; it looks too moody and mysterious. You need to add a fill light and back light to complete the lighting in the following steps:

1. In the Key Light parameters, the light should still be selected. In the General Parameters ➢ Shadows area, check the On box. In the Camera viewport a low-resolution version of the shadows appears but a render of the scene will show it more accurately. Render the scene, as shown in Figure 14.14.

2. In the Shadow Map Params rollout, change the Size to 2048. This parameter adds more pixels to the shadow, which makes it more defined and less diffused. Change the Sample Range to 2.0; this parameter adds softness to the edge of the shadow. The default is 4.0, so lowering the number makes the edge sharper.

   In the viewport, the shadow already looks better; but in the render because the glasses are transparent the shadow looks a bit weird—too dark and solid for a shadow for a transparent glass.

FIGURE 14.14 It looks good, but the scene shadows are too soft.

3. In the Create panel, select Lights➤ Omni. In the Top viewport click to create the omni light in the lower-right corner of the dining room; and then in the Front viewport move the omni light up so it is just below the ceiling of the dining room. Change the name to **Fill Light**.

4. Select Omni Light and in the Intensity/Color/Attenuation rollout, change the Multiplier to 0.2. You are using the omni light to fill in the dark corners of the scene.

   The omni is just a fill light in this scene that is used to simulate the indirect light you see in the real world. You don't want any shadows or specular highlights from this light to make sure the render looks as if there is only one light in the room. By default, shadows are always off, but you must turn off specular highlights manually.

5. With the omni light selected, go to the Modify panel and, under the Advanced Effects rollout, uncheck Specular.

6. Render again (press F9), and you'll see the render looks better, but the still life's shadow is still dark, as shown in Figure 14.15. The shadow darkness looks much better but is still too dark. To fix the darkness of the shadow, you will adjust the density of the shadow.

7. Select the Key Light, go to the Modify panel, and in the Shadow Parameters rollout, change the Object Shadows Dens parameter to 0.8.

8. You can press F9 for another render or press the teapot icon in the main toolbar, and you will see that the shadow looks much better, as shown in Figure 14.16.

FIGURE 14.15 Interior room with key light and omni light

FIGURE 14.16 Shadow with Density set to 0.8

This looks good but the light is too even overall. The omni light needs to have what is called *decay* or attenuation applied. This means light over distance loses its intensity or energy. Standard lights don't do this by default; it has to be simulated within the parameters. For the room scene, you will be using attenuation.

1. Select the Fill Omni light. In the Intensity/Color/Attenuation rollout, click on the Far Attenuation check boxes for Use and Show, as shown in Figure 14.17.

   When Use is checked in Far Attenuation, two circles appear that can be best seen in the Top viewport, as shown in Figure 14.18. The Start value defines the decay of the hottest part of the light. The end value defines the distance when the light drops off to zero.

2. Set the Start value to **12′0** and the End value to **16′0**. This gives some variation to the fill light, as shown in Figure 14.19.

FIGURE 14.17
Check the Use and Show
boxes for Far Attenuation.

Far Attenuation   Start

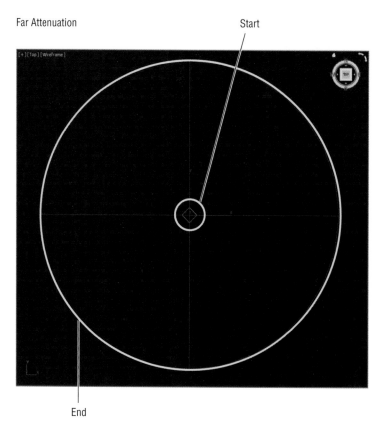

End

FIGURE 14.18   Far Attenuation set on the fill light as viewed from the Top viewport

FIGURE 14.19 A still life rendered with Attenuation

Using shadows intelligently is important in lighting your scenes. Without the shadows in the scene, the still life would float and have no contact with its environment.

You can create the following types of shadows using the 3ds Max program:

- ▶ Advanced raytraced

- ▶ mental ray shadow map

- ▶ Area shadows

- ▶ Shadow map

- ▶ Raytraced shadows

Each type of shadow has its benefits and its drawbacks. The two most frequently used types are shadow maps (which you've already seen) and raytraced shadows.

Selecting a Shadow Type

To get shadows to respond to transparencies, you will need to use raytraced shadows instead of shadow maps.

Shadow Maps

The shadow map is often the fastest way to cast a shadow. However, shadow map shadows do not show the color cast through transparent or translucent objects.

When you are close to a shadow, in order to avoid jagged edges around the shadow, use the Size parameter to make the resolution higher for the cast shadow.

The following parameters are useful for creating shadow maps:

Bias The shadow is moved, according to the value set, closer to or farther away from the object casting the shadow.

Size Detailed shadows will need detailed shadow maps. Increase the Size value, and the 3ds Max geometry will increase the number of subdivisions for the map, which, in turn, increases the detail of the shadow cast. Figure 14.20 compares using a low Shadow Map Size setting to using one four times larger. Notice how the shadows on the left (Size = 1024) are somewhat mushy and less noticeable, and the shadows on the right (Size = 4096) are crisp and clean. Setting the Shadow Map Size too high, though, will increase the render time for little to no effect. A size around 2048 is good for most cases. Scenes like this chessboard that have a large scale to them will require higher size values, such as the 4096 that was used. The rule of thumb is to use the lowest size value that will get you the best result for your scene.

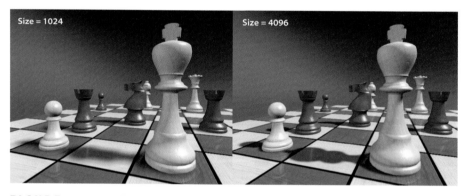

FIGURE 14.20 The Shadow Map Size setting affects the shadow detail.

Sample Range This option creates and controls the softness of the edge of shadow-mapped shadows. The higher the value is, the softer the edges of the shadow will be.

Raytraced Shadows

Raytracing involves tracing a ray of light from every light source in all directions and tracing the reflection to the camera lens. You can create more accurate shadows with raytracing than with other methods, at the cost of longer render times. Raytraced shadows are realistic for transparent and translucent objects. Figure 14.21 shows the still life rendered with a plane casting a shadow over it. The plane has a logo mapped to its opacity map, so it has alternating transparent and opaque areas defining the solid and transparent parts of the logo. On the left side of the image in Figure 14.21, the light is casting shadow map shadows; and on the right, the light is casting raytraced shadows.

FIGURE 14.21   Raytraced shadows react to transparencies, and shadow maps do not.

Use raytraced shadows when you need highly accurate shadows or when shadow map resolutions are just not high enough to get you the crisp edges you need. You can also use raytraced shadows to cast shadows from wireframe rendered objects.

The Ray Traced Shadow Params rollout controls the shadow. The Ray Bias parameter is the same as the Shadow Map Bias parameter in that it controls how far from the casting object the shadow is cast.

Atmospheres and Effects

Atmospheric effects with lights, such as fog or volume lights, are created using the Atmospheres & Effects rollout in the Modify panel for the selected light.

Using this rollout, you can assign and manage atmospheric effects and other rendering effects that are associated with lights.

Creating a Volumetric Light

Let's create a fog light now:

1. Open the ArchModel_LightEnviro_start.max scene file in the ArchModel Scenes folder on the book's web page. Go to the Create panel, select Lights, and in the drop-down window select Standard and then select the Target Direct light. Go to the Left viewport and click from the left outside of the room and drag toward the living room window to set the light's position. Then in the Top viewport, click on the line that connects the light and its target, which will select both easily. Then move the light so it is aligned with the living room window, as shown in Figure 14.22. Name the light **Sunlight**.

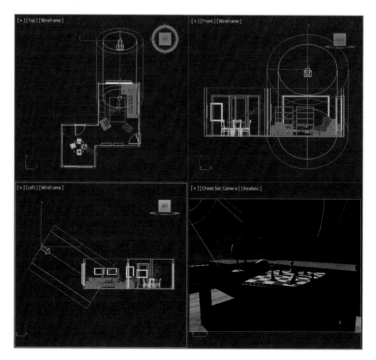

FIGURE 14.22 The light's position shown in all the viewports

2. Select the main Light object and go to the Modify panel. In the Intensity/Color/Attenuation rollout, change the Multiplier to **1.2**.

3. In the Directional Parameters rollout, change the Hotspot/Beam to 5′0″ and the Falloff/Field to 6′11″.

Looking at the Camera viewport, you will see the light coming in through the window, but it is very dark everywhere else, as shown in Figure 14.23. More lights need to be added.

FIGURE 14.23 Interior room with the direct light in place as the sun

4. In the Create panel, select Lights ➢ Omni. Place the light in a position near the Sunlight's position. Name the light **Fill Light_1**.

5. With the omni light selected, go to the Modify panel; and in the Intensity/Color/Attenuation rollout, change the Multiplier to 0.5.

6. In the Advanced Effects rollout, uncheck the Specular check box. This keeps the light on but does not show any specular highlights in the scene.

Adding Shadows

Now you need some shadows in the scene:

1. Select the Sunlight light, and from the Modify panel, open the General Parameters rollout; in the Shadows section, check the box to enable shadows. Select Shadow Map from the drop-down menu. Doing so turns on Shadow Map Shadows for this light.

2. Go to the Shadow Map Params rollout and set the size to 2048 and change the Sample Range to 2.0; this will add some sharpness to the shadow's edge and make it more like a daylight shadow. If you perform a render, you won't see any shadows.

   This is because the window is blocking the light. The Window Glass object has a material that has its Opacity value turned down to 0. However, shadow map shadows don't recognize transparency in materials. To solve this problem, you need to exclude the Window Glass object from the light. When the window was created, the glass was attached to the overall Window object. It will take a few extra steps to access the glass and make it a separate object.

3. Select the FixedWindow001 object; and in the Graphite Modeling Tool ribbon, select Poly: Edit ➢ Edit Polygon ➢ Convert to Poly.

4. Enter the Element mode (▣) and click on the glass; it should become shaded in red. In the Geometry (All) tab, select Detach; and in the type-in next to Detach As, change the name from Object001 to Window Glass.

Excluding an Object from a Light

1. Select the Sunlight light, and go to the Modify panel. In the General Parameters rollout, just below Shadows, is the Exclude button. Click the Exclude button to open the Exclude/Include window shown in Figure 14.24.

2. Click on the Glass object and click the right arrows in the middle of the window, as shown in Figure 14.24, to add the Glass object to the other side, excluding the object from receiving light and casting shadows. Click OK.

3. Render your scene to take a look. Now you can see shadows. You didn't exclude the whole window with its frame because the inside frame is a nice detail to cast shadows.

4. Select the Fill Light. You need to set Attenuation on the light to vary the fill light and make it look more realistic. In the Intensity/Color/Attenuation rollout, in the Far Attenuation section, check the Use and set the Start to 13′0 and set the End to 33′0.

The final results are still not there. The shaded areas facing the camera are still too dark. On a bright sunny day, the light coming through that big window would bounce light all over the room. Another fill light should do the trick.

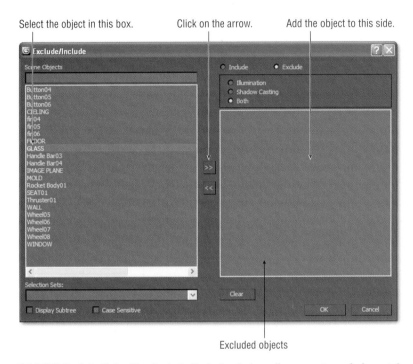

FIGURE 14.24   The Exclude/Include window allows you to exclude certain objects from being lit by the light in the scene.

5. In the Create panel, select Lights ➢ Omni, and place the light behind the Chess Set camera. Move the camera so it is just below the ceiling, as shown in Figure 14.26. Name the light **Fill Light_2**.

6. With the omni light selected, go to the Modify panel; and in the Intensity/Color/Attenuation rollout, change the Multiplier to 0.3.

7. In the Advanced Effects rollout, uncheck the Specular check box.

8. In the Intensity/Color/Attenuation rollout, in the Far Attenuation section, check the Use and set the Start to 4′0 and set the End to 15′0. The final results are shown in Figure 14.27.

Key Light

Fill Light_1

Fill Light_2

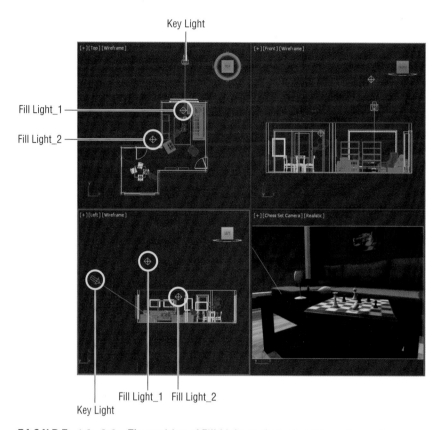

Fill Light_1   Fill Light_2

Key Light

FIGURE 14.26   The position of Fill Light_2 shown in all four viewports

FIGURE 14.27   The final results of the newly added fill light

Adding a Volumetric Effect

The whole point of this exercise is to add volume to the light. This will give the scene some much needed atmosphere. You need to switch to another camera. Select the camera view and press the C key on your keyboard, which will bring up a dialog box to choose from different cameras in the scene.

1. Go to the Atmospheres & Effects rollout for the light. Select Add from the rollout to open the Add Atmosphere and Effect window, select Volume Light, and click OK to add the effect to the light. Volume Light will be added to the rollout.

2. Render the scene. You should see a render similar to Figure 14.28.

FIGURE 14.28   Ooo! Volume light!

To adjust the volume light, go back to the Atmospheres & Effects rollout and select the Volume Light entry and click the Setup button. This will bring up the Environment and Effects dialog box. Scroll down to the Volume Light Parameters section to access the settings for the volume light, shown in Figure 14.29.

3. In the Volume section, change the Density to .25. This lessens the intensity of the volume and makes it more realistic. Also, change the Max Light % to 10.0. Render, as shown in Figure 14.30.

FIGURE 14.29 The Environment and Effects window displays the Volume Light parameters.

FIGURE 14.30 The final results of the volume light in the interior room

You can use `ArchModel_LightEnviro_End.max` in the `Scenes` folder of the Lighting Scene Files project from the book's web page to see the results of this work and to adjust as you wish.

Volume Light Parameters

The default parameters for a volume light will give you some nice volume in the light for most scenes, right off the bat. If you want to adjust the volume settings, you can edit the following parameters:

Exponential The density of the volume light will increase exponentially with distance. By default (Exponential is off), density will increase linearly with distance. You will want to enable Exponential only when you need to render transparent objects in volume fog.

Density This value sets the fog's density. The denser the fog is, the more light will reflect off the fog inside the volume. The most realistic fogs can be rendered with about 2 to 6 percent density value.

Most of the parameters are for troubleshooting volume problems in your scene if it is not rendering very well. Sometimes you just don't know what that problem is and you have to experiment with switches and buttons. The Noise settings are another cool feature to add some randomness to your volume:

Noise On This toggles the noise on and off. Render times will increase slightly with noise enabled for the volume.

Amount This is the amount of noise that is applied to the fog. A value of 0 creates no noise. If the amount is set to 1, the fog renders with pure noise.

Size, Uniformity, and Phase These settings determine the look of the noise and let you set a noise type (Regular, Fractal, or Turbulence).

Adding atmosphere to a scene can heighten the sense of realism and mood. Creating a little bit of a volume for some lights can go a long way to improve the look of your renders. However, adding volume to lights can also slow your renders, so use it with care.

Light Lister

If several lights are in your scene and you need to adjust all of them, selecting each light and making one adjustment at a time can become tedious. This is where 3ds Max Light Lister comes in handy. Accessed through the main menu bar by choosing Tools ➢ Light Lister, this floating palette gives you control over all of your scene lights, as shown in Figure 14.31.

FIGURE 14.31 The Light Lister window

You can choose to view or edit all the lights in your scene or just the ones that are selected. When you adjust the values for any parameter in the Light Lister window, the changes are reflected in the appropriate place in the Modify panel for that changed light.

THE ESSENTIALS AND BEYOND

This chapter reviewed key concepts in CG lighting, including three-point lighting. You learned about the various types of lights that the 3ds Max program has to offer, from default lights to target spots, and how to use them. You explored the common light parameters to gauge how best to control the lights in your scene before moving on to creating various types of shadows. You ran through a set of short exercises in which you created a volumetric light for a fog effect, and you finished with a tour of the Light Lister window.

ADDITIONAL EXERCISES

▶ Try lighting the Interior scene to evoke different moods: somber, jubilant, scary, and so forth.

▶ Add a new camera to the scene and light again to see the various problems that arise.

▶ Change the lighting for a night scene.

CHAPTER 15

3ds Max Rendering

Rendering is the last step in creating your CG work, but it is the first step to consider when you start to build a scene. During rendering, the computer calculates the scene's surface properties, lighting, shadows, and object movement, and then saves a sequence of images. To get to the point where the computer takes over, you'll need to set up your camera and render settings so that you'll get exactly what you need from your scene.

This chapter will show you how to render your scene using the 3ds Max® Scanline Renderer and how to create reflections and refractions using raytracing.

Topics in this chapter include the following:

▶ **Rendering setup**

▶ **Cameras**

▶ **Safe frame**

▶ **Raytraced reflections and refractions**

▶ **Rendering the rocket**

Rendering Setup

Your render settings and the final decisions you make about your 3ds Max scene ultimately determine how your work will look. If you create models and textures with the final image in mind and gear the lighting toward elegantly showing off the scene, the final touches will be relatively easy to set up.

The Render Setup dialog box is where you define your 3ds Max render output. You can open this dialog box by clicking the Render Setup icon (▣) in the main toolbar, by selecting Rendering ➤ Render Setup, or by pressing F10. You've already seen how to render (▣) a frame in your scene to check your work. The settings in the Render Setup dialog box are used even when the Render button is invoked, so it's important to understand how this dialog box works. Figure 15.1 shows the Common tab in the Render Setup dialog box.

FIGURE 15.1   The Common tab
in the Render Setup dialog box

Common Tab

The Render Setup dialog box is divided into five tabs; each tab has settings grouped by function. The Common tab stores the settings for the overall needs of the render—for example, image size, frame range to render, and type of renderer to use. Some of the most necessary render settings are described here.

Time Output   In this section, you can set the frame range of your render output by selecting one of the following options:

>   **Single Frame**   Renders the current frame only
>
>   **Active Time Segment**   Renders the current range of frames
>
>   **Range**   Renders the frames specified

Output Size   The image size of your render, which is set in the Output Size section, will depend on your output format—that is, how you want to show your render.

> **Resolution**   By default, the dialog box is set to render images at a resolution of 640×480 pixels, defined by the Width and Height parameters, respectively.
>
> **Image Aspect Ratio**   Changing the Image Aspect value will adjust the size of your image along the Height parameter to correspond with the existing Width parameter. For example, regular television is 1.33:1 (simply called 1.33) and a high-definition (HD) television is a widescreen with a ratio of 1.78:1 (simply called 1.78). The resolution of your output will define the screen ratio.
>
> In the Output Size section of the Render Setup dialog box, there is a drop-down menu for choosing presets from different film and video resolutions. The image quality and resolution of a render affect how long a render will take. In addition to turning down the resolution for a test render, you can use a lower-quality render or turn off certain effects, such as atmospherics.

Options   The Options section lets you access several global toggles. You can toggle the rendering of specific elements in your scene. For example, if you are using atmospherics (volume light) or effects (lens flare) and don't want them to render, you can clear the appropriate boxes.

Render Output   Use the Render Output section to indicate that the file should be saved. The image format can be selected to be a single image file or sequence of image files (such as Targa or TIFF files) that form a sequence, or it can be a movie file such as a QuickTime.

Choosing a Filename

To specify a location and file type for the render, click the Files button to open the Render Output File dialog box shown in Figure 15.2. Select the folder to which you want to render, and set the filename. You can set the file type using the Save As Type drop-down menu.

Rendered Frame Window

When you click the Render button in the Render Setup dialog box, the Rendered Frame window opens, as shown in Figure 15.3.

> Name your rendered images according to the scene's filename. This way, you can always know from which scene file a rendered image was produced.
>
>

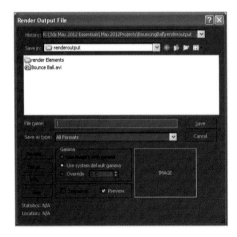

FIGURE 15.2 The Render Output File
dialog box defines how the render saves to disk.

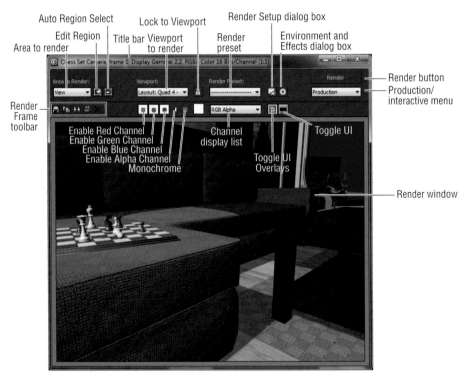

FIGURE 15.3 The Rendered Frame window

The Rendered Frame window shows you how the frames look as the renderer processes through the sequence of frames. A collection of quick-access buttons on the frame is also available in the Render Setup dialog box.

Render Processing

When you click the Render button in the Render Setup dialog box, the Rendering dialog box shown in Figure 15.4 appears. This dialog box shows the parameters being used, and it displays a progress bar indicating the render's progress. You can pause or cancel the render by clicking the appropriate button.

FIGURE 15.4 The Rendering dialog box shows you everything you want to know about your current render.

Assign Renderer

Five types of renderers are available in the 3ds Max 2013 program by default (without any additional plug-ins installed), as shown in Figure 15.5. The Scanline Renderer is the default renderer, and mental ray rendering is covered in Chapter 16, "mental ray and HDRI." To access the Choose Renderer dialog box, click the ellipsis button to the right of Production (■).

FIGURE 15.5 The Choose
Renderer dialog box

Rendering the Bouncing Ball

Seeing is believing, but doing is understanding. In this exercise, you will render the Bouncing Ball animation from Chapter 5, "Animating a Bouncing Ball," to get a feel for rendering an animation using the 3ds Max program. Just follow these steps:

1. Set your Project folder to the Bouncing Ball project that you down-loaded to your hard drive from the companion web page at www .sybex.com/go/3dsmax2013essentials. Open the Animation_ Ball_02.max file in the Scenes folder. Let's render a movie to see the animation.

2. Open the Render Setup dialog box. In the Time Output section, select Active Time Segment: 0 to 100.

3. In the Output Size section, select the 320 X 240 preset button and leave Image/Pixel Aspect as is.

4. Leave the Options group at the default, and skip down to the Render Output section. Click the Files button to open a Render Output File dialog box. Navigate to where you want to save the output file, pref-erably into the RenderOutput folder in your Bouncing Ball project. Name the file **Bounce Ball**, and click the drop-down menu next to Save As Type to choose MOV QuickTime File (*.mov) for your render file type. Normally, you would render to a sequence of images rather than a movie file like this; however, for short renders and to check animation, a QuickTime file works out fine.

Apple's QuickTime movie file format gives you a multitude of options for compression and quality. The quality settings for the QuickTime file are not the same as the render quality settings.

5. After you select MOV QuickTime File and click the Save button, the Compression Settings dialog box, shown in Figure 15.6, opens. Set the parameters for the QuickTime file as indicated:

> Compression Type: Photo–JPEG
>
> Frames Per Second: 30
>
> Compressor Depth: Color
>
> Quality: High

Click OK.

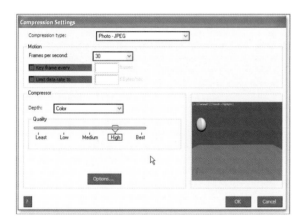

FIGURE 15.6 QuickTime compression settings affect the quality of the rendered QuickTime video file.

6. Skip down to the bottom of the Render Setup dialog box, and verify that Production is selected. Select the viewport you want to render in the View drop-down menu. You need to render Camera01.

7. Click Render.

After the render is complete, navigate to your render location (by default, it is set to the RenderOutput folder for the Bouncing Ball project). Double-click the QuickTime file to see your movie, and enjoy a latte.

By default, the 3ds Max program renders your files to the RenderOutput folder in the current project directory.

Cameras

3ds Max cameras, as shown in the Perspective viewport in Figure 15.7, capture and output all the fun in your scene. In theory, 3ds Max cameras work as much like real cameras as possible.

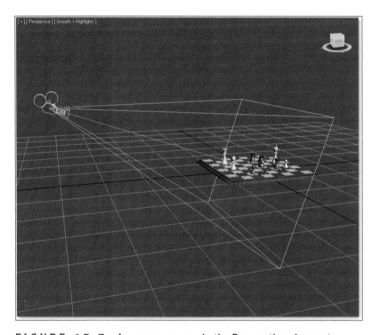

FIGURE 15.7 A camera as seen in the Perspective viewport

The *camera* creates a perspective through which you can see and render your scene. You can have as many cameras in the scene as you want. You can use the Perspective viewport to move around your scene as you work, leaving the render camera alone.

Creating a Camera

There are two types of 3ds Max cameras: target and free. A *target camera*, much like a target spotlight, has a Target node that allows it to look at a spot defined by where the target is placed (or animated). A target camera is easier to aim than a free camera because once you position the Target object at the center of interest, the camera will always aim there.

On the other hand, *free cameras* have only one node, so they must be rotated to aim at the subject, much like a free spotlight. If your scene requires the camera to follow an action, you will be better off with a target camera.

You can create a camera by clicking the Cameras icon (▣) in the Create panel and selecting either of the two camera types. To create a free camera, click in a viewport to place it. To create a target camera, click in a viewport to lay down the Camera node, and then drag to pull out and place the Target node.

Using Cameras

A camera's main feature is the *lens,* which sets the *focal length* in millimeters and also sets the *field of view* (FOV), which determines how wide an area the camera sees, in degrees. By default, a 3ds Max camera lens is 43.456mm long with an FOV of 45 degrees. To change a lens, you can change the Lens or FOV parameters, or you can pick from the stock lenses available for a camera in its Modify panel parameters, as shown in Figure 15.8.

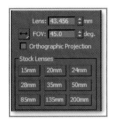

FIGURE 15.8 Stock lenses make it easy to pick the right lens for a scene.

The most interactive way to adjust a camera is to use the Viewport navigation tools. The Camera viewport must be selected for the Viewport camera tools to be available to you in the lower-right corner of the UI. You can move the camera or change the lens or FOV. You can also change a camera by selecting the Camera object and moving and rotating it just as you would any other object.

Talk Is Cheap!

The best way to explain how to use a camera is to create one, as in the following steps:

1. Set your project to the Rendering Scene Files project you have downloaded to your hard drive from this book's web page. Open the ArchModel_Render_Start.max scene file in the Arch Model Files folder downloaded from the web page. This is the scene from the lighting chapter, but without a camera. Creating a camera is the same as creating a light. It's easier to create a camera

in the Top viewport, so you can easily orient it in reference to your scene objects.

2. In the Create panel, click the Cameras icon. Select the target camera and go to the Top viewport. Click from the window and drag toward the gap between the coffee table and the couch. The first click creates the Camera object. The mouse drag and release sets the location of the target, just like creating a target light.

3. The camera was created along the ground plane. You need to move the entire camera up using the Front viewport. Select both the camera and target to move them as a unit by clicking on the line that connects the camera and target in the viewport. Use the Move tool to relocate the camera higher in the scene. The position of the camera and the way it looks in the Camera viewport is shown in Figure 15.9.

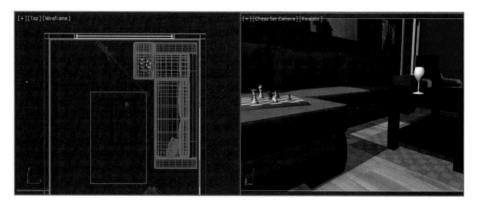

FIGURE   15.9   The position of the camera in the Top viewport and the Camera viewport

Zooming a lens (changing the Lens parameter) is not the same as a dolly in or dolly out. The field of view changes when you zoom, and it stays constant when you dolly. They will yield different framings.

▶

4. To see the Camera viewport, select a viewport and press the C key. This changes the viewport to whatever camera is currently selected. If there are multiple cameras in your scene and none are selected, when you press C, you will get a dialog box that gives a list of the cameras from which you can choose.

5. Now render the scene (press F9 or click the Teapot icon in the main toolbar) through the camera you just created and positioned. Find a good framing for the chessboard and set your camera.

When the camera is set up, take some time to move it around and see the changes in the viewport. Moving a camera from side to side is known as a *truck*. Moving a camera in and out is called a *dolly*. Rotating a camera is called a *roll*. Also change the Lens and FOV settings to see the results.

Animating a Camera

Camera animation is done in the same way as animating any object. You can animate the camera or the target or both. You can also animate camera parameters such as Lens or FOV.

1. In the scene you just worked in, select the camera.

2. Move the Time slider to frame 30.

3. Press the N key to activate Auto Key, or click its icon.

4. In the Top viewport, use the Move tool to move the camera farther away from the still life; watch the Camera viewport to be sure you don't go outside the room.

5. Look in the Camera viewport and then scrub through the animation; the camera should just move away from the chess set toward the window, as shown in Figure 15.10

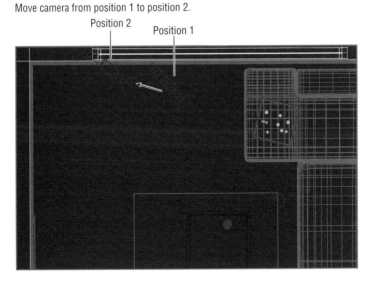

FIGURE 15.10   Move the camera in Top viewport.

Clipping Planes

In a huge scene, you can exclude or *clip* the geometry that is beyond a certain distance by using *clipping planes*. This helps minimize the amount of geometry that needs to be calculated. Each camera has a clipping plane for distance (far range), as shown in Figure 15.11 (right image), and foreground (near range), as shown in Figure 15.11 (left image), respectively. The near clipping plane clips geometry within the distance designated from the camera lens.

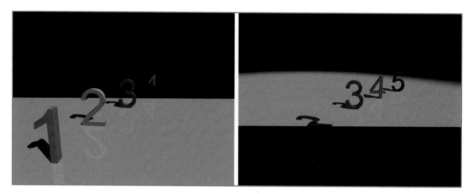

FIGURE 15.11   A near clipping plane cuts off the extents directly in front of a camera (left). A far clipping plane cuts off the distant extents of a scene (right).

If you find that a model or scene you have imported looks odd or is cut off, check to make sure your clipping planes are adjusted to fit the extent of the scene, especially with imported models.

To enable clipping planes, click the Clip Manually check box and set the distances needed. Once you turn on manual clipping planes, the camera displays the near and far extents in the viewports with a red plane marker.

Safe Frame

To help make sure the action of your scene is contained within a safe area on standard-definition TV screens, you can enable the Safe Frame view. In the Camera viewport, right-click on the General Viewport Label menu (⊞) and choose Configure Viewport from the bottom of the menu. In the dialog box, choose the Safe Frames tab; this panel contains settings for frame types, as shown in Figure 15.12. The default shows only the Live Area; if you want to see the others, you must check the boxes in the Safe Frame panel. The keyboard shortcut to toggle Safe frame is Shift+F.

The Live Area is the extent of what will be rendered. The Action Safe area is the boundary where you should be assured that the action in the scene will display on most if not all TV screens. The Title Safe boundary is where you can feel comfortable rendering text in your frame. Finally, the User Safe setting is for setting custom frames, as shown in Figure 15.13.

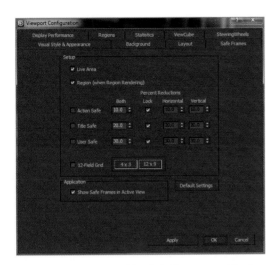

FIGURE 15.12 The Safe Frame panel in the Configure Viewports dialog box

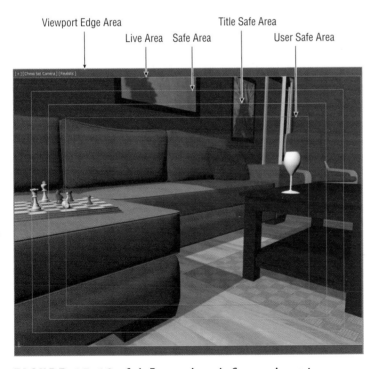

FIGURE 15.13 Safe Frames shown in Camera viewport

Raytraced Reflections and Refractions

As you saw in Chapter 10, "Introduction to Materials: Interiors and Furniture," you can apply an image map to a material's Reflection parameter to add a fake reflection to the object. To get a true reflection of the other objects in the scene, you will need to use the raytracing methodology. There are essentially two ways to create raytraced reflections in a scene: by using a raytrace map or by using a Raytrace material.

In many cases, the raytrace map looks great and saves tons of rendering time as opposed to using the Raytrace material. Keep in mind, though, the amount of control you will have with a raytrace map is significantly less than with the Raytrace material.

Raytrace Material

In the following steps, you will learn how to use the Raytrace material to create reflections in a scene with a fruit still-life arrangement.

1. Open the Slate Material Editor and select a sample slot. In the Material/Map browser, select Material ➤ Standard and drag Raytrace into the View Area. Double-click on the node title area to load the parameters into the Parameter Editor. Change the Material to **Coffee Table Dark Wood**.

2. The parameters to create reflections are available through the Raytrace Basic Parameters rollout. Leave most of these parameters at their default values, but change the Reflect color swatch from black to white. This sets the reflection of the material all the way to the maximum reflectivity.

3. In the Material/Map browser, choose Maps ➤ Standard and drag a bitmap to the Diffuse input socket of the Raytrace material. This will bring up the Select Bitmap Image File; the folder should show the Images folder of the Arch Model scene file. Choose **Dark Wood_ Grain** and Open.

4. Apply the Coffee Table Dark Wood raytrace material to the coffee table in the scene. Render the Camera viewport. The coffee table is very reflective; it looks like a mirror, as shown in Figure 15.14.

5. Go back to the Raytrace Basic parameters and select the color swatch next to Reflect and change the Reflect color to R: 20, G: 20, B: 20, which is a darker gray and will lessen the reflections even more. This will lessen the reflection amount, but it still looks too reflective.

FIGURE 15.14   The Raytrace material with reflections set to the maximum

6. In the Specular Highlight area, change the Specular Level to 30 and Glossiness to 30. This will change how clear the reflection appears.

7. Go to the Raytracer Controls; and in the Falloff End Distance, check the box next to Reflect and change the value to 50. This parameter will fade the reflection over distance, which is more accurate, as shown in Figure 15.15.

FIGURE 15.15   More accurate reflections are added to the coffee table.

Raytrace Mapping

You can apply raytracing only to a specific map; you can't apply it to the entire material. In this case, you will assign a raytrace map to the Reflection map channel of a material to get truer reflections in the scene and at a faster render time than when using the material as you just did. Follow these steps:

1. In the Material Editor and in the Material/Map browser, select Material and drag a Standard Material to the View Area. Load the parameter into the Parameter Editor and change the name to **Hardwood Floors**.

2. In the Material/Map browser, choose Maps and drag a raytrace map into the Reflection input socket.

3. In the Material/Map browser, choose Maps and drag a bitmap into the Diffuse input socket. From the Explore dialog box, choose the **Hardwood_Honey** from the Images folder.

4. In the Maps rollout, change the Reflection Amount to 50.

5. Apply the new Hardwood Floor material to the floor model in the scene by dragging from the output socket to the Floor model in the Camera viewport. In the Material Editor toolbar, select the Show Map in Viewport button (▦).

6. So you can get the full force of the new Hardwood Floors material, hide the rug. Select the Rug object in the scene and then right-click over it; and from the Quad menu choose Hide Selected.

7. Render the Camera viewport; the floors look good but too reflective and a falloff needs to be added.

8. Double-click on the Raytrace Map node to load the parameters into the editor. In the Attenuation rollout, change the Falloff Type to **Linear**. Then change the Range End to **25**. The results are shown in Figure 15.16. Unhide the rug.

Take a look at both the images created with reflections using the Raytrace material, and those created using the Standard material with the raytrace map applied to reflection. They look almost the same. However, you will notice slightly better detail in the reflections created with the Raytrace material, but with longer render times.

FIGURE 15.16   The reflection map with falloff

Refractions Using the Raytrace Material

Creating raytraced refractions in glass can be accomplished using the same two workflows as raytraced for reflections. The Raytrace material renders better, but it takes longer than using a raytrace map for the refraction map in a material.

Keep in mind that render times are much slower with refractions—so don't freak out. Now you will create refractions using the Raytrace material:

1. In the same scene, change the Chess Set Camera viewport to Perspective, do this by selecting the Camera viewport and pressing P on the keyboard. Select the wineglass in scene and then press Z on your keyboard; this will frame the wineglass in the Perspective viewport. Use Ctrl+C, which is a shortcut, to create a camera from a Perspective viewport. Name the camera **WineGlass Camera**.

2. In the Material Editor, drag a Raytrace material from the Material/ Map browser into the Active View Area. Name it **WineGlass**. Apply the material to the wineglass.

3. Go to the Raytrace Basic Parameters rollout, and change the color swatch for Transparency from black to white. (Black is opaque and white is fully transparent.)

4. Uncheck the box next to Reflect and change that spinner to **10**. This sets a slight reflection for the material.

5. Take a look at the Index Of Refr parameter. This value sets the index of refraction (IOR) value that determines how much the material should refract its background. The value is already set to 1.55. Leave it at that value.

6. Go to the Extended Parameters rollout, as shown in Figure 15.17. The Reflections section of the parameters is at the bottom. Select Additive and change Gain to 0.7. This gives a bit of reflective brightness for the clear wineglass.

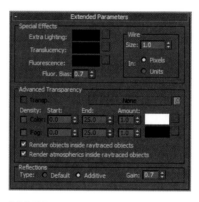

FIGURE 15.17 The Extended Parameters rollout for the Raytrace material

The render shows the Raytrace material on the wineglass refracting and reflecting, but you may notice the jagged edges or artifacts around the reflected objects. What you're seeing is aliasing in the reflections. Clone this rendered image by pressing the Clone Rendered Frame Window icon (⊞), which is found in the Rendered Frame Window toolbar. This allows you to compare the before and after shots of the SuperSampling. SuperSampling is an extra pass of anti-aliasing. By default, the 3ds Max program applies a single SuperSample pass over all the materials in the scene.

7. Go to the SuperSampling rollout and uncheck Use Global Setting. Check Enable Local SuperSampler and keep it set to Adaptive Halton. Leave the parameters at their default, as shown in Figure 15.18. In Figure 15.19 it shows the before and after of the SuperSampling added.

FIGURE 15.18 The
SuperSampling rollout

8. In the Specular Highlights group, change the Specular Level to 98
and Glossiness to **90**.

FIGURE 15.19 The wineglass without SuperSampling (left); the SuperSampling
applied (right)

You will notice a very nice wineglass render. Change the Index Of Refr
parameter on the material to 8.0, and you will see a much greater refraction, as
shown in Figure 15.20. That may work better for a nice heavy bottle, but it is
too much for the glass. An Index Of Refr parameter between 1.5 and 2.5 works
pretty well for the wineglass, particularly at the bottom of the glass where it
rounds down to meet the stem.

FIGURE 15.20 A much more pronounced refraction is rendered with an IOR of 8.0.

Refractions Using Raytrace Mapping

Just as you did with the reflections, you will now use a raytrace map on the Refraction parameter for the Wineglass material. In the following steps, you will create another refraction material for the wineglass:

1. In the Material Editor, drag a Standard material from the Material/ Map browser into the View Area. Name it **New WineGlass**. Apply the material to the WineGlass.

2. Drag the raytrace map from the Material/Map browser into the Refraction input slot.

3. Drag the raytrace map from the Material/Map browser into the Reflection input slot. Be warned that this setting will take a long time to render the image. If you have a slower computer or perhaps are in a rush, uncheck the Reflection Map box in the Maps rollout of the reflection.

4. Go to the Maps rollout and change the Reflection amount to 6. This will reduce the amount of reflection.

5. Go to the SuperSampling rollout and uncheck Use Global Settings. Check Enable Local SuperSampler and keep it as Max 2.5 Star.

6. In the Specular Highlights group, change Specular Level to 98 and Glossiness to 90.

7. Apply the material to the Wineglass object in the scene and render as shown in Figure 15.21. Save the scene if you want to keep it.

FIGURE 15.21 Use the raytrace map on the Refraction parameter to create refraction in the wineglass.

You can control the IOR through the material's parameters in the Extended Parameters rollout, in the Advanced Transparency section, shown in Figure 15.22. Set the IOR to different numbers to see how the render compares to the Raytrace material renders.

FIGURE 15.22 The Advanced Transparency section in the Extended Parameters rollout

The raytracing reflections and refractions slow down the render quite a bit. You can leave out the reflections if you'd like, but that will reduce the believability of the wineglass.

Rendering the Interior and Furniture

Let's take a quick look at rendering the short 30-frame sequence of the scene you did earlier in the chapter. You will essentially take the interior scene laid out in the previous chapter (with the atmospheric fog light through the window you set up). You'll need to tweak a few of the scene settings, such as setting the furniture and the interior materials to have raytraced reflections for maximum impact. Let's go!

Adding Raytraced Reflections

In Chapter 10, you used a reflect/refract map to add the reflections to some of the furniture. It is a way to add reflections but is not as accurate as the raytrace map. The raytrace map calculates reflections as they work in the real world, reflecting the object's environment. Of course, in order for raytraced reflections to work, there has to be something around the object to reflect. To demonstrate this, you are going to add raytracing to the furniture and the room. The materials created for the scene from Chapter 10 and some that were added for this exercise are in the Material Editor. You need to go into any of those materials and switch out the reflect/refract maps with raytrace maps.

1. In the Material Editor, at the bottom left of the View Area is an icon of a pair of binoculars. This is a search feature. Click on it and a type-in area appears. Type **Light Wood for Chess** in the type-in area; the material will be zoomed in on in the view area, as shown in Figure 15.23. Select and delete the reflect/refract map that is plugged into the Reflection input node.

2. In the Material/Map browser, select Maps ➤ Standard, drag a raytrace map into the Active View area, and then drag from the output socket of the raytrace map into the input socket of the Light Wood for Chess material, as shown in Figure 15.24.

3. Double-click on the title of the Light Wood for Chess material to load the parameters into the editor. In the Maps rollout, change the Amount value for Reflection to 20.

4. Render a frame, and you should see some reflections of the room. If you want the rocket to have a higher amount of reflection, go back to the Maps rollout and make the Reflection value higher than 20.

It will frame the material in the Active view.

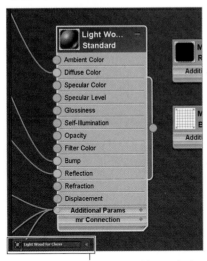

Type in material name in the
Zoom to Results tool.

FIGURE 15.23 Frame the material
using the Search for Nodes feature in the
Slate Material Editor.

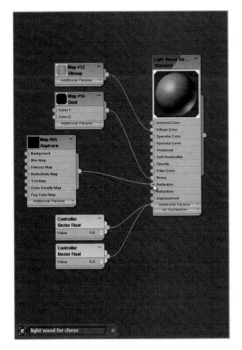

FIGURE 15.24 Plug the raytrace map
into the Light Wood for Chess material.

5. Go through the materials in the Material Editor for the remaining materials to add raytrace to their reflections as well. If there is a reflect/refract map, delete it and follow the previous steps to replace it with a raytrace map. The materials you will need to edit are

▶ Dark Wood for Chess

▶ Chess Board

▶ Window

Outputting the Render

You need to render out the entire 30 frames of the camera move. As you saw with the Bouncing Ball render earlier in the chapter, rendering out a sequence of images is done through the Common tab of the Render Setup dialog box. In the Time Output section, click to select Range and change it to read 0 to 30, as shown in Figure 15.25.

FIGURE 15.25 The Time Output section setup for a range from 0 to 30

The resolution of the render is set in Output Size. The default resolution is 640×480. If your computer isn't a powerful one, drop the size to half the default size of 320×240 and it will cost you one-fourth of the higher resolution's time to render.

Go to the Render Output section of the Render Setup dialog box and click Files to open the Render Output File dialog box. Typically, animations are rendered out as a sequence of images, but for simplicity's sake, you will render it out to an AVI.

In the Render Output File dialog box, select the Files button; and in the Explore window, choose where you want to store the rendered file and pick a name for the movie (Room_Raytrace.avi, for example). Then, in the Save As Type drop-down menu, choose AVI file (.avi) and click Save. The Compression Settings dialog box will appear. Again, it is generally preferable to render to a sequence of images rather than a movie file; however, in this case, an AVI movie file will be best.

In the Compression Settings dialog box, select MJPEG Compressor for the compression type, and set the Quality slider to 100. This Quality setting applies only to the compression of the AVI file and not to the render itself. Click OK to return to the Render Output File dialog box, and click Save to return to the Render Setup dialog box.

Save your scene file, and you are ready to render! Just click Render in the Render Setup dialog box, and go outside to play catch with your kids or hassle your spouse or sibling into a needless argument for a little while. Then run back inside and play the QuickTime file saved in the location you chose earlier. Then take a huge magnet and stick your monitor to your fridge door. Voilà! You are now ready to enter the world of rendering with mental ray.

THE ESSENTIALS AND BEYOND

Rendering is the way you get to show your finished scene to the world, or whoever will stop and look. Nothing is more fulfilling than seeing your creation come to life, and that's what rendering is all about. In this chapter, you learned how to set up and render your scenes out to files. In addition, you took a tour of raytracing and cameras.

Rendering may be the last step of the process, but you should travel the entire journey with rendering in mind, from design to models to animation to lighting.

ADDITIONAL EXERCISES

- ▶ Try rendering different resolutions and qualities for your scene, and make note of the times each frame took so you can better evaluate which settings work best versus time involved in processing the render.
- ▶ Create multiple cameras of different areas of your scene. Play around with lenses and FOV. Animate the cameras and render.
- ▶ Explore the Raytrace materials and maps by adding them to objects in the scene.

mental ray and HDRI

This chapter will show you how to render your scene using Autodesk® 3ds Max® software's Scanline Renderer and how to create reflections and refractions using raytracing. In addition, this chapter will introduce you to the popular mental ray Renderer and HDRI lighting workflow.

Topics in this chapter include the following:

▶ **mental ray Renderer**

▶ **Final Gather with mental ray**

▶ **HDRI**

mental ray Renderer

mental ray is a popular general-purpose renderer that has fantastic capabilities. One of mental ray's strengths is its ability to generate physically accurate lighting simulations based on *indirect lighting* principles. *Indirect lighting* is when light bounces from one object in a scene onto another object. In addition, incandescence or self-illumination from one object can light other objects in the scene. *Direct light,* such as from an omni light, is not necessarily required. Another thing to consider is that mental ray's reflections and refractions take on very real qualities when set up and lighted well.

Enabling the mental ray Renderer

To enable mental ray, in the main menu, choose Rendering ➢ Render Setup to open the Render Setup dialog box. On the Common tab, scroll down to the Assign Renderer rollout, and then click the ellipsis button for the Production entry shown in Figure 16.1. This opens the Choose Renderer dialog box shown in Figure 16.2.

FIGURE 16.1 The Assign Renderer rollout

FIGURE 16.2 Select mental ray Renderer in the Choose Renderer dialog box.

In the Choose Renderer dialog box, highlight mental ray Renderer and then click OK. Once the mental ray Renderer is assigned, you can make it the default renderer by clicking the Save As Defaults button on the Assign Renderer rollout. Now the Render Setup dialog box opens with the mental ray controls in tabs.

mental ray Sampling Quality

Once the mental ray Renderer is enabled, click the Renderer tab in the Render Setup dialog box. The following is a brief explanation of the render settings most useful for you in your work.

Under the Sampling Quality rollout, shown in Figure 16.3, are the settings that let you control the overall image quality of your renders.

FIGURE 16.3 The Renderer tab shows mental ray's common settings.

The Minimum and Maximum Samples Per Pixel values specify the number of times mental ray samples a pixel to determine how best to anti-alias the result to avoid jagged lines. Spatial Contrast values for Red, Green, Blue, and Alpha determine the exact sample level within that range. The lower the values set for Spatial Contrast, the higher the sample rate, leading to a smoother render at a higher render time.

The image shown in Figure 16.4 was rendered with a Minimum Samples Per Pixel value of 1/16 and a Maximum Samples Per Pixel value of 1, using a Spatial Contrast setting of 0.1 for all four RGBA values. With the Minimum Samples Per Pixel value at 4, the Maximum Samples Per Pixel value at 16, and the Spatial Contrast value at 0.04 for RGBA, the render becomes much cleaner, with an acceptable increase in render times, as shown in Figure 16.5.

FIGURE 16.4 A jagged render

FIGURE 16.5 A clean render

Final Gather with mental ray

A popular feature in mental ray is *indirect illumination*—the simulation of bounced light (explained in the next section). In the tabs at the top of the Render Setup dialog box, click the Indirect Illumination tab. There are three rollouts, the first of which we will explore further:

▶ Final Gather

▶ Caustic And Global Illumination (GI)

▶ Reuse (FG And GI Disk Caching)

Final Gather

Final Gather is a method of mental ray rendering for estimating global illumination (GI). In short, *global illumination* is a way of calculating indirect lighting. This way, objects do not need to be in the direct path of a light (such as a spotlight) to be lit in the scene. In short, mental ray accomplishes this by casting points throughout a scene. These light points are allowed to bounce from object to object, contributing light as they go, effectively simulating how real light photons work in the physical world.

This type of rendering can introduce artifacts or noise in the render. Finding the right settings to balance a clean render and acceptable render times is an art form all its own and is rather difficult to master. Figure 16.6 shows the Final Gather rollout. Some of Final Gather's options, including how to deal with quality and noise, are explained next.

FIGURE 16.6 The Final Gather rollout in the Indirect Illumination section of the Render Setup dialog box

Basic Group

These are the most important parameters in the Basic section of the Final Gather rollout; they set the accuracy and precision of the light bounces, thereby controlling noise.

FG Precision Presets Slider   Sets the accuracy level of the Final Gather simulation by adjusting settings for the renderer such as Point Density, Rays Per Point, and Interpolation. Use this slider first in setting how good your render's lighting looks. In Figure 16.7 (left image), three spheres are rendered with a Draft setting for Final Gather, while Figure 16.7 (right image) is set to High. Notice the right image is a cleaner render, and it also shows more of the background and the spheres than does the Draft quality in the left image. This slider will adjust the settings for several of the values covered in the following list.

Initial FG Point Density   This multiplier is one of the settings adjusted by the FG Precision Presets slider, but it can also be set manually. This value sets the quantity and density of FG *points* that are cast into the scene. The higher the density of these points, the more accurate the bounced light appears, at a cost of render time.

Rays Per FG Point   This value is controlled by the Precision slider but can also be manually set. The higher the number of rays used to compute the indirect illumination in a scene, the less noise and the more accuracy you gain, but at the cost of longer render times.

Interpolate Over Num. FG Points   Interpolation is controlled by the FG Precision Presets slider as well as manual input. This value is useful for getting rid of noise in your renders for smoother results. Increasing the interpolation will increase render times, but not as much as increasing the Point Density or Rays values.

Diffuse Bounces   The number of bounces governs how many times a ray of light can bounce and affect objects in a scene before stopping calculation. If you set the bounces higher, the light simulation will be more accurate, but the render times will be costly. A Diffuse Bounces setting of 1 or 5 is adequate for many applications. Figure 16.8 shows the same render of the spheres as Figure 16.7, but with a Diffuse Bounces value of 5. This render is brighter and also shows color bleed from the purple spheres onto the gray floor.

FIGURE 16.7   A Draft setting produces a test render of the spheres (left). A High setting produces a better-quality render of the spheres (right).

FIGURE 16.8 More diffuse bounces mean more bounced light.

Advanced Group

The Advanced group of settings gives you access to additional ways of controlling the quality of your Final Gather renders. Some are described next in brief. You should experiment with different settings as you gain more experience with Final Gather to see what settings work best for your scenes.

Noise Filtering (Speckle Reduction)   This value essentially averages the brightness of the light rays in the scene to give you smoother Final Gather results. The higher the filtering, the dimmer your Final Gather simulation, and the longer your render times will be. However, the noise in your lighting will diminish.

Draft Mode (No Precalculations)   This setting allows you turn off a good number of calculations that mental ray completes prior to rendering the scene. Enabling this setting results in a faster render for preview and draft purposes.

Max. Reflections   This value controls how many times a light ray can be reflected in the scene. A value of 0 turns off reflections entirely. The higher this value, the more times you can see a reflection. For example, a value of 2 allows you to see a reflection of a reflection.

Max. Refractions   Similar to Max. Reflections, this value sets the number of times a light ray can be refracted through a surface. A value of 0 turns off all refraction.

The mental ray Rendered Frame Window

When you render a frame using the 3ds Max program, the Rendered Frame window opens, displaying the image you just rendered. When you render with mental ray, an additional Control panel is displayed under the Rendered Frame window, as shown in Figure 16.9.

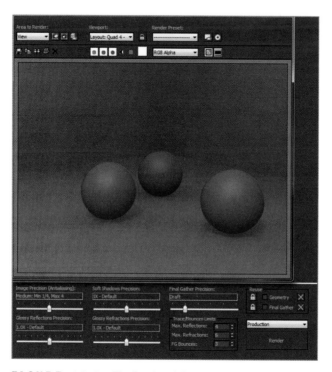

FIGURE 16.9 The Rendered Frame window now shows several mental ray controls.

This Control panel gives you access to many of the most useful settings in the Render Settings dialog box so you can adjust render settings easily and quickly.

mental ray Materials

For the most part, mental ray treats regular 3ds Max maps and materials the same way the Default Scanline Renderer does. However, a set of mental ray–specific materials exists to take further advantage of mental ray's power.

The mental ray Arch & Design material works great for most hard surfaces, such as metal, wood, glass, and ceramic. It is especially useful for surfaces that are glossy and reflective, such as metal and ceramic.

To showcase these materials, let's retexture a few of the features from the room from Chapter 10, "Introduction to Materials: Interiors and Furniture."

1. Set your project to the Arch Model project that you downloaded from the web page. Open the ArchModel_mentalray_start.max file from the Scenes folder of the mental ray Scene Files project on the book's web page. This file has mental ray already assigned as the renderer. The scene has the room, and the furniture textured. There are no lights in the scene; but because mental ray is the assigned renderer, it utilizes the default lights to generate a lighted scene, as shown rendered in Figure 16.10. mental ray renders the materials from the previous chapter. Some look the same, but others don't look so good—the coffee table in particular. Start with it.

FIGURE 16.10 The Interior file rendered with mental ray

2. Open the Slate Material Editor; at the top of the View Area. You will see a tab called View 1; it holds all the materials you built in the previous chapters for the room. To keep the materials separate and organized, create another tab for the mental ray materials. To create a new tab, right-click in the blank area next to the tabs, as shown in Figure 16.11, and create a new View Area. Name it **mental ray**.

FIGURE 16.11 Create a new View Area.

3. Drag an Arch & Design material to the new View Area from the mental ray material section of the Material/Map browser.

4. Double-click on the title of the node; this will display the Arch & Design material in the Material Parameter Editor. Name the material **Dark Wood Coffee Table**.

5. Drag a bitmap from the Maps rollout into the input socket of the Arch & Design material. This will bring up an Explore window; choose the Dark Wood_Grain.tif. Leave all the other parameters at the default.

   By default, Arch & Design materials have reflection enabled. The area below the Diffuse group in the Parameter section of the Slate is the Reflection group of parameters. Reflections for this material are calculated using the Reflectivity and Glossiness values. The higher the Reflectivity value is, the clearer the reflections are. The Glossiness value controls the blurriness of the reflections from sharp (a value of 1) to completely blurred (a value of 0). When you blur your reflections, the blurrier they are and the noisier they will be in the render. You can use the Glossy Samples value to increase the quality of the blurred reflections once you set Glossiness to anything less than 1.

6. Drag a wire from the material's output socket to the Coffee Table in the viewport, as shown in Figure 16.12.

   Render the Camera viewport to see the new material on the coffee table. The Coffee Table Material is too reflective.

FIGURE 16.12   The Coffee Table material applied to the object in the scene

7. In the Reflection group, change the Reflectivity to 0.4 and the Glossiness to 0.4. When it renders, there is a lot of graininess in the reflection.

8. Change the Glossy Samples to 40; this will shoot more "rays" into the glossiness and change the graininess.

9. Check the box next to Fast (Interpolate); this will help to speed up the render and works best when the reflections are on a flat surface. Render the camera to see the results, as shown in Figure 16.13.

FIGURE 16.13 The new Coffee Table material using the Arch & Design material

Multi/Sub-Object Materials and Arch & Design

By using the Multi/Sub-Object material and dragging the individually created materials to the selected polygons, you can use the same technique for the window that you used in Chapter 10. The difference now is you will use the Arch & Design material instead. The window is divided into two materials: shiny white for the frame and a shiny transparent material for the glass.

1. In the Slate Material Editor, you'll create a shiny white material. Drag an Arch & Design material to the mental ray View Area. Change the Diffuse color to R: 0.8, G: 0.0, B: 0.0 and rename it **White Window Frame.**

2. Based on what you know about reflections from the previous steps, the default reflections are too high, especially for the frame on the window. In the Reflections group, change the Reflectivity to 0.4 and the Glossiness to 0.4.

3. Select the window and enter Element mode (Graphite Modeling Tools ➤ Polygon Modeling) 🔲. Select all the polygons for the window frame. In the Material Editor toolbar, select the Assign Material to Selection 🔧.

4. Back in the Material Editor, drag an Arch & Design material to the mental ray View Area. In the Refraction group, change the Transparency to 1.0. In the toolbar, select the Show Background in Preview icon (▓). This will place a checker pattern behind the sample sphere to make the transparency easier to edit. Double-click on the sphere icon on the Material node. This will enlarge the sample sphere, making it easier to edit.

5. Render the Camera01 viewport. If it isn't loaded into a viewport, just select a viewport and press the C key. This will change the viewport to a camera. If there are multiple cameras in the scene, a Camera List dialog box will appear, allowing you to choose a specific camera to apply to the viewport. You can see that the window and frame look very similar to the Standard materials, but the coffee table looks significantly better. When using mental ray, Arch & Design materials are superior. Sometimes the look of a particular object can change depending on the camera angle and lighting. Let's keep an eye on the window to see if the look maintains the realism you are after.

Arch & Design Templates

Arch & Design materials have a special feature: templates. *Templates* provide access to already-created materials and parameters for different types of materials such as wood, glass, and metal. These templates can also be used as a starting point for material creation. For the wine glasses in the scene, you will use a template material.

1. In the Material Editor, drag an Arch & Design material into the View Area. Double-click on the title of the Material node to load the parameter in the Parameter Editor. Name the material **Wine Glass**.

2. At the top of the parameters is the Templates rollout, shown in Figure 16.14. Click on the Select A Template down arrow; from the drop-down menu under Transparent Materials, select Glass (Solid Geometry).

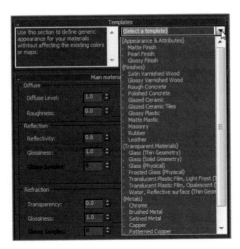

FIGURE 16.14 The Template rollout
in the Arch & Design material showing the
Materials drop-down menu

3. Apply the material to the Wine Glass objects in the scene. Render the
scene. The wineglasses look good, but there is a blue tint to the glass
that is unappealing.

4. Back in the Material Editor, in the Refraction group, click on the
color swatch next to Color. Change the RGB values to R: 1.0, G: 1.0,
B: 1.0. For future reference, this is a way to create color-tinted glass.
Render the scene. This time the glasses look stunning! The final
results are shown in Figure 16.15.

FIGURE 16.15 The final results of adding the Arch &
Design materials to the scene

The Arch & Design material type is an elaborate construct of mental ray shaders, and with proper lighting it can make any render look special. If you open the `ArchModel_mentalray_end.max` file, you will see several materials examples beyond what you created in the previous exercise.

3ds Max Photometric Lights in mental ray Renderings

Many of the parameters for photometric lights are the same as or very similar to the standard lights you looked at in Chapter 14, "Introduction to Lighting: Interior Lighting." Here, you see the parameters that are specific to photometric lights. Photometric lights simulate real lighting by using physically based energy values and color temperatures.

1. Either continue with the file you are working with or open the `ArchModel_mentalray_light.max` file from the Scenes folder of the mental ray Scene Files project from the book's web page.

2. In the Menu Bar, choose Create ➤ Lights ➤ Photometric Lights ➤ Target Light to create a photometric target light.

3. When you click on the photometric target light, you will get a pop-up recommending that you use the mr (mental ray) Photographic Exposure Control. Click OK.

4. In the Left viewport, click to create the light from ceiling and then drag down to the floor. Make sure the light stays within the room.

5. Switch to the Top viewport and move the light and its target so it is above the coffee table. The easiest way to make sure you select both the light and target is to select the blue string that runs between the two and then just use the Move tool. Once the light is in the scene, change the viewport rendering type to Realistic.

6. With the light still selected, go to the Modify panel. The first rollout under the modifier stack is Templates.
   This rollout gives you access to several light type presets to save you time in creating a light. Feel free to play around with the different presets and render the room frame a few times to see the differences before continuing with the exercise and the next step.

7. In the Select A Template drop-down menu, select Recessed 75W Lamp (Web).

   A photometric light with a "web" distribution essentially defines the light's behavior and the light it casts. Lighting manufacturers provide web files that model the kinds of lights they make, so using these distribution patterns as templates will give you a lot of options in simulating real-world lights, such as this 75-watt recessed lamp. Figure 16.16 shows the distribution pattern for this light as shown in the Command panel.

FIGURE 16.16 The Distribution (Photometric Web) rollout

8. You need to take care of some basic stuff now, so with the light still selected, open the General Parameters rollout and check the Targeted box. You originally created a targeted light but when you used the template, it took away the target. Having a target on a light makes it easier to edit the light's position. Checking this box turns the target back on for the light.

9. Click the Shadows On box to turn it on. From the drop-down menu, choose Ray Traced Shadows.

10. Make the Camera001 viewport active and on the Menu Bar, choose Rendering ➢ Exposure Control and click the Render Preview button, as shown in Figure 16.17. The preview may show as either very bright or very dark at first. If so, the preview function will work perfectly once you render a frame for the first time.

FIGURE 16.17 Exposure Control and mr Photographic Exposure Control rollout in the Environment And Effects dialog box

> Exposure controls adjust output levels and the range of colors of a rendering. These controls are similar to real-world film exposure settings on a physical camera.

11. Under the mr Photographic Exposure Control rollout, select Exposure Value (EV), if it isn't already selected. Set some different values for the EV and see what happens in the Render Preview dialog box. The higher the EV number, the darker the scene will be. Set the EV value to 5 or so and render, as shown in Figure 16.18. You can continue to work with the EV value to experiment with the luminance level. When you're finished experimenting, be sure to set the EV back to 5 and close the Environment And Effects dialog box.

Photometric Light Parameters

Now let's look in the Command panel at the photometric light's Intensity/Color/Attenuation rollout for the 75W light, as shown in Figure 16.19.

FIGURE 16.18 The room so far

FIGURE 16.19
Photometric light's Intensity/
Color/Attenuation rollout in the
Command panel

The Color group of parameters controls the color temperature of the light, which you can set either with a color value or in Kelvin degrees, just as with real-world photographic lights. In the drop-down menu, there are different color/temp settings. The default is D65 Illuminant (Reference White).

The Intensity group of parameters controls the strength or brightness of the lights measured in lm, cd, or lx at:

lm (lumen)   This value is the overall output power of the light. A 100-watt general purpose lightbulb measures about 1750 lm.

cd (candela)   This value shows the maximum luminous intensity of the light. A 100-watt general-purpose lightbulb measures about 139 cd.

lx at (lux)   This value shows the amount of luminance created by the light shining on a surface at a certain distance.

The parameters in the Dimming section are also used to control the intensity of the light. When the Resulting Intensity box is checked, the value specifies a multiplier that dims the existing intensity of the light and takes over control of the intensity. Picking up from the last step in the previous exercise, let's start to experiment with these values in the following steps:

1. With the 75W light still selected, go to the Modify panel and, in the Color group under the Intensity/Color/Attenuation rollout, click the button next to Kelvin and change the value to **4500**. This will give the light a bit more warmth by adding more yellow/red.

2. In the Dimming group, uncheck the box next to the 100% spinner under Resulting Intensity to enable the Intensity parameter.

3. In the Intensity group, select cd and set the cd amount to **4000**. This will brighten things up a bit.

4. Render the scene, as shown in Figure 16.20.

   The scene still looks a bit dark and the shadows are very dark; they look like black holes. You will use Final Gather to brighten up the overall render. So far, you have used Final Gather's default settings. The one thing you need is for the rays that are generated by the light to bounce. The more bounces the light makes, the more luminance there is in the room—but more bounces slow down the render. For the best and most efficient results, try to balance the bounces with exposure control and the intensity of the light.

FIGURE 16.20   The room render with color and intensity changes

5. When you are rendering with mental ray, the mini Final Gather panel in the Rendered Frame window is available for quick changes. Most of these controls also have a home in the Render Setup dialog box, and changing the value in one dialog box updates the corresponding value in the other. In the mini panel below the Rendered Frame window, as shown in Figure 16.21, change FG Bounces to 7. Render and compare the resulting render shown in Figure 16.20 to Figure 16.22. Figure 16.22 is the final room.

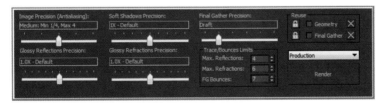

FIGURE 16.21   This mini panel gives you access to Final Gather controls to adjust your render easily.

FIGURE 16.22   The final mental ray render of the room's interior lighting

3ds Max Daylight System in mental ray Renderings

The Sunlight and Daylight systems simulate sunlight by following the geographically correct angle and movement of the sun over the earth. You can choose location, date, time, and compass orientation to set the orientation of the sun and its lighting conditions. You can also animate the date and time to achieve very cool time-lapse looks and shadow studies. In essence, this type of light works really well with mental ray and Final Gather. In this exercise, you will use it in the most basic way, using all of its defaults:

1. Open the `ArchModel_mentalray_final.max` file from the `Scenes` folder of the mental ray Scene Files project on the book's web page. This is the file you ended with after applying the Arch & Design textures earlier in the chapter.

2. In the Menu Bar, choose Create ➢ Lights ➢ Daylight System.
   A Daylight System Creation warning will come up, as shown in Figure 16.23, asking if you want to change the exposure controls to suit the Daylight system. Click Yes.

3. In a Top viewport, click and drag at the center of the scene. This will create a compass that is attached to the Daylight system. Make it the size of the room.

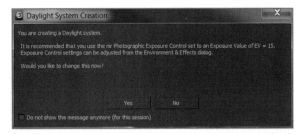

FIGURE 16.23 The Daylight System Creation warning

4. When you release the mouse button, move the mouse so the light is placed outside the walls of the room. The Daylight system is supposed to simulate the sun and sky, so it needs to be outside the room.

5. With the light still selected, open the Modify panel and in the Daylight Parameters rollout, change the drop-down menus under both the Sunlight and Skylight parameters to mr Sun and mr Sky, respectively. When you change the Skylight parameter, a mental ray warning will appear asking if you want to place an mr Physical Sky environment map in your scene. Click Yes, as shown in Figure 16.24.

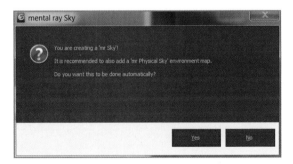

FIGURE 16.24 Add the mr Physical Sky environment map into the scene.

6. Also in Daylight Parameters, under Position, select Manual. This will allow you to use the Move tool to move the light to where you want it. The default position represents noon. The lower the light is to the horizon in your scene, the more it will simulate darker skies at sunset. Leave the light in the default position.

7. Select the Chess Set Camera viewport and render. As you can see, it is too dark. You are trying to simulate a sunny day, and beyond the direct light coming through the window, it's pretty dark, as shown in Figure 16.25.

FIGURE 16.25 Rendering with the Daylight system is too dark.

A good tool to use in this situation is mr Sky Portal. It gives you an efficient way of using a scene's existing sky lighting within interior scenes that do not require costly Final Gather or GI, resulting in very long render times. A portal acts just like a mental ray area light. This light gets its brightness and color from the environment already in your scene.

8. In the Menu Bar, choose Create ➢ Lights ➢ Photometric Lights ➢ mr Sky Portal.

9. In the Front viewport, drag an mr Sky Portal so it fits the window size in the wall. Then in a Top viewport, move the mr Sky Portal back so it is aligned with the opening of the window inside the room, as shown in Figure 16.26. Make sure the arrow is pointing into the room. Render the Camera viewport again. That helps but it is not enough; it is still too dark, so it's time to play with exposure controls.

10. In the Menu Bar, choose Rendering ➢ Exposure Control. Click Render Preview.

11. In the mr Photographic Exposure Control rollout, change Exposure Value (EV) from 15 (the default) to 11, as shown in Figure 16.27. You should see the rendered preview change to show the update. Render the Camera viewport again to see the difference. It looks good but is still a bit dark, so it's time to add Final Gather bounces.

mr Sky Portal
The arrow should point in toward the room.

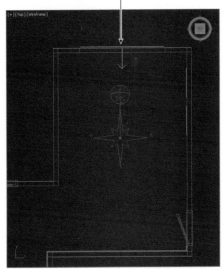

FIGURE 16.26 Move the mr Sky Portal to the window in the wall in the Top viewport.

FIGURE 16.27 The mr Photographic Exposure Control rollout

12. In the Rendered Frame Window mini mental ray controls, change FG Bounces to **5**. Render the image again; it should look like Figure 16.28.

FIGURE 16.28   Render with Final Gather Bounces set to 5.

That's it! If you want to play around some more, try moving the light for a more dramatic shadow on the floor. Moving the light can have a dramatic effect on the luminance levels too, so be prepared to edit FG Bounces and Exposure Controls. The last render is shown in Figure 16.29.

FIGURE 16.29   The final render

HDRI

The high-dynamic-range image (HDRI) is used in CG to create more realistic scenes than the more simplistic lighting models used.

An HDRI is created when several photos at varying exposures are taken of the same subject, ranging from very dark (underexposure) to highlight only the brightest parts of the scene, to very bright (overexposure) to capture the absolute darkest parts of the scene. When these images (typically five or seven images) are compiled into an HDR image, you get a fantastic range of bright to dark for that one subject or environment.

mental ray can create an environment map in your scene to which you assign an image, usually an HDRI. That environment map uses the brightness of its image to cast light in your scene.

The best type of image to capture for an HDRI is sometimes called a *light probe*. This is a series of pictures of an environment, such as the living room, using a fish-eye camera lens taken at 90-degree angles on a tripod to capture a full 360-degree panorama. These photos are then stitched together using an image editor like PTgui to create one large panorama showing almost a full 360 degrees of the environment.

Figure 16.31 shows the range of photos from underexposed (dark) to overexposed (bright) that were used to compile this sample HDRI.

FIGURE 16.30 The top row of images shows a series of images taken with a fish-eye lens. The bottom image has those images stitched together creating a panoramic of the living room.

FIGURE 16.31   The five exposures that make up a
sample HDRI of a living room

In the next exercise, you will use an HDRI that was taken of the real living room used as reference for the scene. See Figure 16.32.

FIGURE 16.32 An HDR image

Open the ArchModel_HDRI_start.max file from the Scenes folder of the Arch Model Scene Files project on the book's web page.

1. When the scene is open, in the Menu Bar, choose Create ➢ Lights ➢ Standard Lights ➢ Skylight. Click anywhere in your scene to create the skylight.

2. Next, load the HDRI file into the environment. Choose Rendering ➢ Environment. In the Common Parameters rollout in the Environment tab, click the None button under Environment Map. This will bring up the Material/Map browser.

3. Choose Bitmap from the Standard Maps rollout. In the Explore window, navigate to SceneAssets\Images folder in the Arch Model project, and select the LivingRoomPanoramic.hdr image file. The HDRI Load Settings dialog box appears; click OK, as shown in Figure 16.33.

4. The mapping of the HDRI that is loaded in the environment needs to be edited. With the Environment And Effects dialog box still open, open the Slate Material Editor and place the windows side by side. Drag the Environment Map button in the Environment tab to the View Area of the Slate Material Editor. This will open an Instance (Copy) dialog box. Click Instance and then OK to load the HDRI map into the Material Editor. Double-click on the HDRI Map node to load the parameters. In the Coordinates rollout, select Environ and change the Mapping drop-down menu to Spherical Environment, as shown in Figure 16.34.

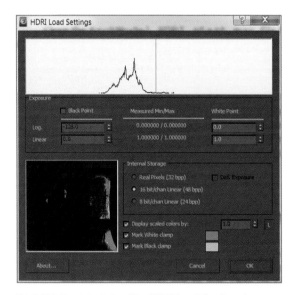

FIGURE 16.33   The HDRI Load Settings box

FIGURE 16.34   The Mapping parameter set to Spherical Environment

5. Select the skylight and in the parameters, under Sky Color, select Use Scene Environment. This will tell the light to refer to the HDRI loaded into the environment for the lighting.

6. Render the Camera viewport, as shown in Figure 16.35. As you can see, the reflective surfaces look good overall, but the scene appears fairly dull. It certainly doesn't look like it is daytime, as shown in Figure 16.35.

7. The HDRI has created an even light overall but is too dark. Select the Skylight and turn the Multiplier to 8.0. Render the camera again to see the difference, shown in Figure 16.36.

FIGURE 16.35 The chess set scene showing an example of just the HDRI applied to the skylight.

FIGURE 16.36 The scene rendered with the Multiplier set to 8.0 on the skylight, which brings up the indirect light.

This improves the look but it is still too dark. The goal for this scene is to create a daylight environment, as if the sun were coming in through the window on the camera's left. It needs more light—specifically, sunlight! The skylight's job is to create the indirect illumination. Now, for the sun. With the Daylight system, the scene had both direct and indirect illumination, but the Daylight system doesn't work with HDRI, so you need another way to create sunlight for this scene. For the sun, you can use almost any light that can be directed. For this exercise, use the mr Area Spot. These lights work well with mental ray and have parameters very similar to any standard lights. Shadows are turned on and set to Raytraced by default.

8. In the Menu Bar, select Create ➢ Lights ➢ Standard Lights ➢ mr Area Spot. To create the light in the viewport, start in the Top viewport and drag from outside the window toward the coffee table; then switch to the Left viewport and move the light up, as shown in Figure 16.37.

9. In the Intensity/Color/Attenuation rollout, change the Multiplier to **1.6**.

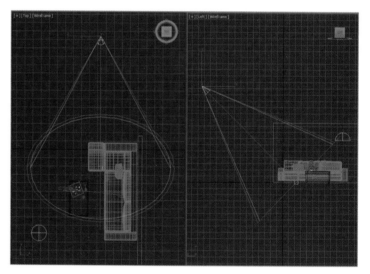

FIGURE 16.37   Place the mr Area spotlight.

10. Select the mr Area Spot and in the Spotlight parameters, change the shape of the cone to Rectangle, as shown in Figure 16.38, and then move the target on the light so that the edge of the light is partially on the chess set. This will create an indoor look in a scene that has no walls, ceiling, or floors. Experiment with the light's location until you get a look similar to the render in Figure 16.39.

FIGURE 16.38
Change the light cone shape
to Rectangle in the Spotlight
Parameters rollout of the mr
Area Spotlight.

FIGURE 16.39 The final chess set render

With the still life example, as shown in Figure 16.39, the HDRI environment map created an overall fill light for the scene, but also acted as a great reflection environment. Adding the extra mr Area Spotlight allowed you to create a sunlight for a key light that gave the scene highlights as well as defined directional shadows. HDRI environment maps are very good ways to insert complex lighting scenarios, but are often augmented with standard or photometric lights to bring out the subject of the scene.

The Essentials and Beyond

In this chapter, you learned the basics of rendering with mental ray in the 3ds Max 2012 program. You saw the quality settings and how they could help you with better renders. Finding the right balance of settings for a clean render is an art all to itself. You also started lighting with Final Gather and then learned how HDRI can be useful for lighting.

Additional Exercises

▶ Create new objects for the scene to which chrome and glass materials can be applied, and then play with rendering the scene to make these objects look photo-real.

▶ Experiment with different Final Gather settings to get the best look for the least render time in the chess set example.

▶ Try creating an outdoor scene and use the Daylight System to light.

▶ Light the outdoor scene using HDRI techniques. The HDR image used for this exercise won't work well for that outside scene, but you can search online for copyright-free downloadable HDRI images. They may not be free, but making a small investment in a few images would benefit your experience. There are many websites that offer inexpensive packages of themed HDRIs.

INDEX

Note to the Reader: Throughout this index **boldfaced** page numbers indicate primary discussions of a topic. *Italicized* page numbers indicate illustrations.